Management Training
and
Corporate Strategy

How to Improve Competitive Performance

Other Books by D. E. Hussey and published by Pergamon

Corporate Planning: Theory and Practice

Introducing Corporate Planning

Corporate Planning: The Human Factor (with M. Langhan)

The Realities of Planning (with Prof. B. Taylor)

Pergamon Titles of Related Interest

BLOOR, I. G.
Reference Guide to Management Techniques and Activities

EIMICKE, V. W.
Managing Human Resources: Documenting the Personnel Function

NEBSS Super Series (Pergamon Open Learning)

Related Journals

Long Range Planning

Omega

Management Training
and
Corporate Strategy

How to Improve Competitive Performance

by

DAVID E. HUSSEY
Harbridge Consulting Group Ltd
London, U.K.

PERGAMON PRESS
OXFORD · NEW YORK · BEIJING · FRANKFURT
SÃO PAULO · SYDNEY · TOKYO · TORONTO

U.K.	Pergamon Press, Headington Hill Hall, Oxford OX3 0BW, England
U.S.A.	Pergamon Press, Maxwell House, Fairview Park, Elmsford, New York 10523, U.S.A.
PEOPLE'S REPUBLIC OF CHINA	Pergamon Press, Room 4037, Qianmen Hotel, Beijing, People's Republic of China
FEDERAL REPUBLIC OF GERMANY	Pergamon Press, Hammerweg 6, D-6242 Kronberg, Federal Republic of Germany
BRAZIL	Pergamon Editora, Rua Eça de Queiros, 346, CEP 04011, Paraiso, São Paulo, Brazil
AUSTRALIA	Pergamon Press Australia, P.O. Box 544, Potts Point, N.S.W. 2011, Australia
JAPAN	Pergamon Press, 8th Floor, Matsuoka Central Building, 1-7-1 Nishishinjuku, Shinjuku-ku, Tokyo 160, Japan
CANADA	Pergamon Press Canada, Suite No. 271, 253 College Street, Toronto, Ontario, Canada M5T 1R5

Copyright © 1988 David E. Hussey

All Rights Reserved. No part of this publication may be reproduced, stored in a retrieval system or transmitted in any form or by any mean: electronic, electrostatic, magnetic tape, mechanical, photocopying, recording or otherwise, without permission in writing from the publishers.

First edition 1988

Library of Congress Cataloging in Publication Data
Hussey, D. E. (David E.)
Management training and corporate strategy.
1. Management – Study and teaching – Great Britain.
2. Executives – Training of – Great Britain. I. Title
HD30.42.67H87 1987   658.4'07124   87-22075

British Library Cataloguing in Publication Data
Hussey, D. E.
Management training and corporate strategy how to improve competitive performance.
1. Executives – Training of
I. Title
658.4'07124   HF5549.5.T7

ISBN 0-08-034036-9 Hardcover
ISBN 0-08-034035-0 Flexicover

*Printed in Great Britain by
Richard Clay Ltd, Bungay, Suffolk*

THIS BOOK owes much to my friends and colleagues at Harbridge Consulting Group Ltd. The research base was created by colleagues. Many ideas have emerged from our joint work so that "ownership" is often uncertain, and the stimulating environment has made it possible for ideas to be discussed and developed.

It also owes something to our many clients where the concepts have been put into practice. My thanks extend to all clients, and particularly those who have provided case studies for the book. While acknowledging the very great help from these sources, I have to retain personal responsibility for the book and the particular applications and interpretations suggested. Any errors are mine.

Contents

	INTRODUCTION	ix
1	The cult of the amateur	1
2	Management and strategy: lessons from success and failure	9
3	Education	25
4	Management and the educational institutions	35
5	Management training in British industry	58
6	Strategy, people and change	71
7	Management training as a competitive weapon	86
8	The tailored course	96
9	Coopers and Lybrand: choosing an outside supplier	110
10	British Petroleum's business management programme: management education for future growth	115
11	L'Oreal: implementing a corporate strategy	125
12	Otis Elevator Co. Ltd: implementing change	133
13	Distance learning	142

14	Evaluation	164
15	IPM and ABCD	175
16	Recent changes in the USA	182
17	Towards a solution	188
	APPENDIX: *The Harbridge House research into management training and education*	197

Introduction

I came to write this book from a dawning realisation that British business as a whole was neglecting one of the most powerful tools to achieve competitive success: management training and education. Not only were they failing to use training for this purpose, but a great deal of the resources devoted to management training were wasted, while at the same time the activity as a whole is under-resourced.

This realisation built incrementally from a number of stimuli. Much of my business life has been spent in tasks associated with business planning: several years planning industrial development in a third world country, followed by nearly 12 as a planner in industry, and 11 in consultancy. In this last (and current) activity I split my professional work between strategy consulting and management training and education.

During my time in consultancy I have come to realise that many British companies have failed to achieve their full potential, because they have failed to get the most from their strategic planning. Among the common faults is a failure to plan for competitive success in the world as it really is. Too many companies view their strategic horizons from some deep pit, and have a restricted view of the options open to them and the competitive threats they face. Even when a strategy is sound, it is often not implemented. Some of the assignments I have handled demonstrated that both problems can be solved by a combination of planning knowledge and management training.

In 1982 we took a decision at Harbridge Consulting Group to begin a programme of research to find out what was going on in management education and training in the UK. At that time comparatively little research was undertaken in the areas that interested us. Our motives were partly that we wanted to improve our own marketing information for our own strategies, partly that we wished to add to our ability to give more help to our clients, and partly that we felt that the making available of such information fitted with our corporate image. All researches have led to published reports, although we have much more information from the studies than we have included in the reports.

This body of research, which is described in the book, gave a factual platform to many of my ideas and concepts. The approaches which we used to combine training and consultancy were clearly unknown to the majority of companies, but worse than this was the clear evidence that too many companies neglected training, and so gained little from it.

Government interest in training began to take a new form with funding provided to a number of organisations (alas, not to us) to research the training area, and some significant reports were published in 1985–1986, with others in the pipeline. Those that were published before the book was written have been drawn on. None of the additional findings contradict our own research, although of course, they broaden the research base and add more insight.

What I had at this stage was a view that much was wrong with planning in the UK, a certain knowledge that much was wrong with training, some views of how to combine these two issues, some case evidence that these views worked, and an awareness that there were more facets to the problem that I had first thought.

This book is the result. It does not take a "do-gooder" view of management training and education, but seeks to show how this can be an economically viable activity. However, it goes deeper than this and begins with the issue of achieving competitive success. Put simply, the theme of the book is that management training and education is a powerful tool (a) to help a company properly define what it is trying to achieve and how it will do it, and (b) to ensure that it does it. The book turns most traditional thinking about management education and training on its head, and so will not be well received in all quarters.

It is not written to appeal to those with vested interests in defending the *status quo*, but it is for those who are interested in restoring the competitive strength to British business. My view is that this is something that can be achieved, and is the responsibility of managers much more than it is of government. I have tried to show how to do it.

Horsham, West Sussex
January 1987

1
The Cult of the Amateur

The UK is not the only country that has been suffering a long-term decline in its international position. A number of recent articles[1] have drawn attention to a similar trend in the USA Lodge,[2] in his book *The American Disease*, defines a situation that superficially seems very similar to that in the UK. The promotional survey on the dust jacket uses key words such as "failing industries, stubborn unemployment, lagging economic growth, stagnant productivity, overseas competition, focus on short term economic gain".

If the USA suffers from a disease, the UK is even more ill. On most economic indicators the USA is consistently better than the UK, even if the trends in the two countries have some similarity. The symptoms of the English disease have been recorded in many comparative economic studies, of which those mentioned are examples. The Hudson Institute Europe,[3] in its study of the future of the UK, drew attention to the length of time during which the UK's economic growth rate had lagged behind most other industrial countries. Annual average growth between 1949 and 1963 was at the rate of 2.6 per cent. Over the 18 years up to 1973 it averaged 2.8 per cent; France, Italy and Spain grew at more than twice this rate, and most other competitor nations did better. (It is scant comfort to point to the fact that US growth rates were also low: they were higher than those in the UK.)

Long Range Planning,[4] in its British Planning Data Book, among other things reviewed the performance of the UK compared to its OECD competitors up to 1980. It drew attention to the fact that over the previous 25 years the UK had fallen from being second only to the USA among OECD members in 1950, to "become one of the least prosperous countries of the OECD". By 1980 only Italy among the more industrialised OECD members had a lower average per capita income. Western Germany's was 74 per cent higher and France 50 per cent.

A more popularly presented study was carried out by *Which?*,[5] with the headlines "Still ahead of Italy but watch out for Taiwan". It also pointed out that in 1883 the UK had the largest economy in the world and sat at the top of the "first division". By 1983 it was heading fast towards the third division.[6]

Most of the published studies indicate that, as might be expected, a poor record in overall economic performance has been matched by poor records

2 Management Training and Corporate Strategy

on other economic indicators, such as trends in productivity increases, the declining share of world trade, and the lower (and steadily declining) net rates of return on capital in manufacturing. Only in research and development expense as a percentage of GDP, does the UK appear to be better than, or equal to, most competitor nations. yet all is not as it seems for half of UK research and development expenditure is reputed to be on defence with few commercial benefits, which means that its ranking on commercial expenditure plummets. In any case we are left with the frequently stated observation that the failure of the UK in innovation is not in the brilliance of its new inventions but in the failure of British management to turn them to commercial reality. Overseas countries seem to be able to make industries from the brilliance of British scientists and technologists.

It is a common human tendency to blame outside events as the cause of poor economic performance. Apologists for the UK can certainly find many crises which have triggered economic problems. Yet it is difficult to think of crises which somehow affected only the UK among all its competitors. The Hudson Institute Europe[3] report (page 7) argued that the cause was quite different from the normal explanations. "We hold that Britain's fundamental troubles come from within the society, and from certain economic, social and institutional forces which are fundamentally British: aspects of British culture and an inheritance of a particularly British historical experience."

The complexity of the issue makes it difficult to separate cause and effect, and indeed these become intertwined. Similarly, we cannot be certain that all the "right" causes have been identified, or how an all-sweeping fundamental change could be made to UK culture and society. As the suggested causes are studied it becomes apparent that the opportunity to bring about some considerable improvement lies in the hands of management. It is my belief that appropriate action, by those who manage the productive resources of the country, will trigger changes to the other factors. The main purpose of the analysis in this and the next chapter is to point the way to actions that management should take. Thereafter the concentration is on one theme which can do much to influence the competitive success of business.

Which?[5] suggested eight reasons for the failure of the UK, and these have a ring of truth about them, which comes across even louder from the more detailed studies of others. The *Which?* reasons are paraphrased below:

1. *Complacency.* Because we were the first country to industrialise we became complacent in the belief that "British was best". It was assumed that people would always buy British. Scant regard was given to marketing.
2. *Low status of manufacturing industry.* Because of the low status of manufacturing industry the brightest graduates find academia, the city, the professions or government more attractive. British management tends

to be much less well educated than in other advanced countries.
3. *Low status of engineers.* Engineers do not progress as well in British industry as they do in other countries. The comparatively low status discourages some people from becoming engineers, particularly as it is reflected in lower pay.
4. *The cult of the amateur.* There has been a historical preference for Oxbridge arts graduates as the "best" training for industry and the civil service. Although trends are changing somewhat, there is still prejudice in favour of such a background.
5. *Delusions of grandeur.* Research and development has concentrated on prestige government-funded projects, often with little chance of commercial payoff. Concorde is an example. This and heavy defence research and development has drawn scarce technologists away from manufacturing industry.
6. *Government.* The "stop-go" policies of successive governments have created an unstable economic background for business.
7. *Trade unions.* Unions have historically pressed their short-term interests at the expense of the long-term, counting an immediate improvement in pay more important than the future of the industry.
8. *Management.* Managers have been unwilling to learn from others, and are unadventurous. As with the unions, so management too tends to focus on short-term gain at the expense of the long-term.

How far can these assessments by *Which?* be justified from other studies? The rest of this chapter will focus on studies concerned with the general social, cultural and historical background. The following chapter will examine other evidence which looks particularly at the failings of management; failings which might be considered a consequence of the broader issues which shaped managers' views.

Wiener[7] provides a comprehensive analysis of the "decline of the industrial spirit". He states "In England, the symbols of Machine and Garden, Workshop and Shire, were in more direct opposition." These symbols embodied a tension that had become implanted deep within middle- and upper-class culture over at least the previous century. Much of the peculiar character of English domestic history over this period was the result of a nation, or at least an elite, at war with itself. "This inner tension in modern British culture is something of a puzzle. Why did hostility to industrial advance persist and even strengthen in the world's first industrial society? Why did such hostility so often take the form of rural myth making?" (page 7).

He argues that the UK's transition to an industrial state was a peaceful evolution rather than a revolution or upheaval. Because it grew from within it accommodated to the norms of the existing political and cultural leadership. In other countries industrialisation came from without, challenging existing patterns and forging a new society. The gain of the evolution was a political and social stability: the cost was to contain capitalism under a variant of the old aristocratic leadership, whose value system held industrial activity to be inferior.

From the earlier period of industrial development those that succeeded and made money would aspire to live like gentlemen. The influence of a virtually homogeneous public school system, and the ancient universities of Oxford and Cambridge, the attractiveness of a leisured life and the emotive appeal of ideals such as honour and service to one's country, led by the end of the Victorian age to a homogeneous and cohesive elite, "sharing a common education and a common outlook and a common set of values". Unfortunately these values put a "cultivated style, the pursuits of leisure, and political service" in place of the desire for economic growth and material gain. The process of disassociation from the taint of industry was continued with the growth of the new professions in the nineteenth century, who through their professional associations put themselves above the economic rules of the market place. "As the nineteenth century drew to a close, a culture took root in the rapidly growing upper-middle and professional classes – the heirs of the old landed elite – that put the ideals of economic growth and material progress in their place..." (page 40).

Wiener expresses the polarisation of views as the pastures green compared to the dark satanic mills, and notes the common desire, which still continues in the UK, for the possession of a country house not for economic production but for leisure. "The pastoral dream remained very much alive in post-World War II England. It continued encapsulated within the ancient universities" (page 77). "Village values could be perceived as an alternative to the worship of efficiency, the domination by machinery, the materialism that seemed part and parcel of industrial society" (page 79).

Until recent years the universities provided a way out of industry rather than a way into it. The sons of industrialists might attend Oxford or Cambridge, but their aspirations would rarely be to follow in their fathers' footsteps. "Technological education made slow headway. Manufacturers aspiring to the status of full-fledged gentlemen recognised that engineering was not a suitable career for such a goal. Consequently they did not seek it for their sons . . . Thus engineering was left to the sons of the skilled working class" (page 132).

There was a rise in the number of graduates entering industry during the interwar years, largely caused by lack of demand in the preferred occupations of the professions and the civil service.

Wiener notes two reinforcing ideals that found their way into management increasingly in the twentieth century as the larger businesses filled their top ranks with men who fitted the gentlemanly mould, and who have been termed the "educated amateurs". This brought out another ideal, that of the practical man.

The "practical" man was the defensive ideal of those who had not received an elite education, and who responded (not necessarily with logical consistency) by disparaging the value of education or formal training for their work – while at the same time aspiring to the ranks of gentlemen. The "cult of the practical man" was thus not what it might once have been – an alternative ideal – but a transitional ideology, for managers not yet become gentlemen . . . . The twin cults of the educated amateur and the practical man strengthened resistance to science-based innovation. Both parties had a built-in distrust of any theoretically grounded knowledge (page 139).

He goes on to argue that the gentlemanly ideal has created a legacy of status among occupations and functions. Bankers deprecated industrial managers. Managers held salesmen and technicians in low esteem. Selling was repugnant in many ways. Production has had less status than sales, and in contrast to the UK's country competitors has been low-paid and offering little opportunity for promotion to higher management.

For the moment I should like to leave Wiener's analysis and turn to the less well-documented but nevertheless insightful view of the Hudson Institute Europe report. Some points are very similar. They, too, argue that the Britain of the 1970s* is a legacy of the Victorian era. "Many of the country's problems are Victorian problems, or stem from attempts to operate Victorian solutions in a society that exists in a late twentieth-century world. In a nutshell, Victorian Britain attempted to come to terms with a crude industrialisation: the Britain of the 1970s has refused to look beyond it" (page 110).

The Hudson Institute report stated: "We would argue that Britain's present economic difficulties and social difficulties derive ultimately from a kind of archaism of the society and national psychology: a habit of conciliation is social and personal relations for its own sake, a lack of aggression, a deference to what exists, a repeated and characteristic flight into pre-industrial, indeed pre-capitalist, fantasies. A suspicion of efficiency as somehow 'common', a dislike for labour itself . . . ." (page113). These comments were written during a time of industrial strife and unrest, and the more recent years have seen a little less compromise on the part of British managers, together with the more aggressive pursuit of improvement in productivity and competitiveness. Despite this modest change, many of the comments still seem to be relevant.

A further factor identified in the Hudson Institute study is an indifference to Europe which often appears to turn to animosity.

I remember listening to an after-dinner speech by Professor Ed. Stillman about some of the data quoted in the report on the quality of life in the UK. Birth and death statistics were quoted to demonstrate that the UK was lagging behind other European countries on longevity. My guest, who was also my managing director at the time, posed the question (or perhaps statement would be a better word) that Professor Stillman had quoted birth rates and

---

*There is every reason to believe that this also applies to the Britain of the 1980s.

6 Management Training and Corporate Strategy

death rates, but surely the quality of life was the bit in the middle? In a way this illustrates a neat intellectual way of avoiding a serious point. I often wonder whether the issue of setting quality of life in preference to economic growth would have been treated more seriously 10 years later in 1985, when high unemployment rates were ensuring that whatever quality of life is, too many people did not have the incomes to enjoy it.

Some of Wiener's views of the way education has contributed to the development of British culture have been summarised above. He has much more to say on this subject, and will be referenced again in a later chapter when we look at the trends in business education in the UK. The Hudson Institute Report[3] also refers to education and argued that "Britain today educates too few people and for the wrong subjects" (page 85).

So far, through the careful work of others, the argument has been made that the UK's relative economic decline is a consequence in part of its cultural heritage. There is no escape from the need to build competitive advantage and strive for economic growth. The Hudson Institute report argues:

Britain is a country of 56 million people living on a crowded and poor island, in no sense self-sufficient in food or raw materials and, as we have seen, decreasingly self-sufficent even in manufactured goods. There is no possibility of supporting Britain's population except through the mechanism of modern industrial society: the option of retreat into a rural, stable-state society or zero-growth economy are sentimentalities. The result of such an effort would be widespread economic distress, and if the process were carried far enough, actual physical distress and finally hunger (page 60).

Events have moved since 1974, when this statement was published, and from the crisis situation of 1976 the economy has shown many signs of improvement, except for unemployment. Productivity has increased. Unfortunately so has that of the UK's national competitors, so that the UK's relative position has shown little improvement. Indeed despite all the efforts, a 1983 study of international industrial competitiveness[8] showed that the UK slipped from 14th place the previous year to 15th out of 22 OECD countries. The study, by the European Management Foundation, examined nearly 300 criteria for competitiveness and surveyed the views of about 1000 leading business executives. Only the natural resource sector, mainly oil, kept the UK in its position. On dynamism of the economy it ranked 18th.

While the comparative failure of the UK is related to its cultural heritage, so too is much of the success of Japan dependent on its culture and society. There have been many recent accounts of the Japanese way of doing things, all of which would be of no more than passing interest to the UK were it not for the fact that some Japanese firms have been able to make their method work in the UK environment. This supports my contention that management is in a position to initiate many of the changes needed to restore the competitive advantage of their firms. To achieve this they may need to feel their way through the mists of the cultural heritage, and to question their own perceptions and values.

While Japanese management methods may be transferable, the reasons why they have so successfully evolved in Japan has much to do with culture. Considerable insight is provided by Christopher.[9] Among his propositions is the belief that Japan is a more homogeneous country in terms of race and culture than any other major nation. Direct personal confrontation is disliked, and society and business will almost invariably choose to operate by consensus. There is a strong sense of responsibility to the various groups to which they belong, which feeds the drive for efficiency. The primary commitment is to the well-being of the tribe, instead of to religion or ideology, which makes it easier for the country to accept change. Behind these propositions lies a complex culture which no outsider will ever fully understand.

In contrast to the success of the Japanese we have the recent focus on the decline of the USA. It is highly unlikely that the special relationship between the UK and the USA has led to a "disease" with origins in the UK's cultural heritage. Indeed all the evidence points otherwise, although some of the manifestations of the "American disease" may resemble those of the British. Lodge,[2] in his study of the US situation, suggests that it too is a psychological ailment. There are many symptoms. Complacency had allowed US industry to grow inefficient and careless. Adversarial trades union/management relations have contributed to the decline of certain industries. As in the UK, successive governments have had a record of incoherent and shortsighted policies. Management has been trained or conditioned to take shortsighted views, with quarterly results gaining precedence over the longer-term plans. The perception of work interdependence is only just beginning to dawn in an economy previously large enough to practise isolationist policies.

Lodge sees the American disease in these terms. "These three characteristics of our unwanted transition – the creedal passion to stay with the old, the inefficient and illegitimate transition to the new, and our confusion about the bases of authority – begin to define the disease which affects America. It is a disease about which little is known, and for which there is as yet no remedy. It is in the realm of collective psychology."

Part of his argument about the causes of the American disease relate to a failure to recognise that the USA is now no longer economically independent of the outside world, and that like other countries it is now dependent on the "real world". This real world has forced changes that America has often refused to notice, or when it has noticed has refused to accept. Managers have an adherence to an outdated ideology, or system of values, which does not suit the new conditions. However, the ideology has to change because the system is no longer played according to American rules.

The differences in the British and American diseases, if the analyses of this chapter are correct, are quite profound. Both, however, have one thing in common: the cultural value systems of each are inappropriate for the globally competitive world in which we now operate. However, Chapter 16 shows that in the USA managers have taken action to change. The same cannot be claimed for more than a handful of British firms.

What can we make of all this? Certainly the stereotype of educated amateur and practical man fit many who operate in the UK. We do not divide into these two groups only, and if we did there would be little point in writing this book. Fortunately there are people who might be termed educated managers.

It is not necessary to be the "amateur" or the "practical" to be a prisoner of the cultural heritage, and one argument I will develop later is of the "perceptual boundaries" within companies, which bring a collective misunderstanding of the strategic situation and contribute to the taking of inappropriate decisions.

There is also much in our culture that is good, provided we can become aggressive competitors despite inhibiting ideals. I confess to a deep love of the countryside, a personal desire to prevent areas of beauty from being swallowed up in an industrial sprawl and an admiration of ideals of honour and service. If others share these or similar feelings, does it mean that we have no hope? My belief is that we can improve our world competitive rating without giving up every principle and ideal. The arguments in the book try to show how this can be done through developing different ways of seeing business situations, and more dedicated approaches to training managers.

References

1. (a) *Business Week*; (b) Abernathy & Hayes
2. G. C. Lodge (1984): *The American Disease*, Knopf
3. Hudson Institute Europe (1974): *The United Kingdom in 1980*, Associated Business Programmes
4. Taylor *et al*. British Planning Data Book, *Long Range Planning*, special issue, October 1982.
5. *Which?* (1983): British Industry, *Which?* October 1983
6. *UK Competitiveness*, NEDC (85) 25 (Revised), 16 April 1985
7. M. J. Wiener (1983): *English Culture and the Decline of the Industrial Spirit 1850-1980*, Cambridge University Press
8. Reported in the *Guardian*, January 1984
9. R. C. Christopher (1984): *The Japanese Mind*, Penguin

2

Management and Strategy: Lessons from Success and Failure

Strategic failings

One contributory factor to the relative decline of the UK has been continued strategic failure by British business in general. Undoubtedly the cultural heritage has contributed to this situation, but I believe that it is possible to improve without having to undergo a social revolution. What is needed is a managerial revolution, leading to different ways of thinking.

Whole industries have declined and disappeared, and although in some cases this has been because of a "natural" change in economic advantage, in others it has been because foreign competion has had a superior strategy to the British firms. There is no natural reason why Japan should have been able to destroy the British motor cycle industry, or become world leaders in the car industry: superior strategic thinking features highly as a reason.

My intention is firstly to review the evidence of strategic failings, stressing that the average picture is not true for all managers, to postulate that one cause of these failings is the perceptual boundary within which many managers operate – in some cases this is almost a nationwide blockage – and to describe briefly how a different approach to strategic thinking can change the patterns of perception and enable better decisions to be made. This will take us to a review of the failure of corporate planning to improve decision-making in many companies. However, one cannot expect an improvement simply by knowing where to do better. There has to be the will to do better, and those concerned have to know what to do. This avenue of thought takes us into management education and training, as the only viable way through which the managerial revolution can occur.

The published research on which this chapter is based studies the postwar period and draws most heavily on an analysis by Channon[1] and on the *Report of the Commission of Enquiry into the Engineering Profession* ("Finniston Report").[2] Although some years separate these two studies, and Channon was not referred in the Finniston report, there is a remarkable compatibility of their findings about British management. Other research is quoted to give additional insight into specific areas.

Channon's research identified four major trends in the environment of British firms in the 25 years to 1970.

1. After the war the major industrial problems were those of reconstruction and the relief of shortages. "In a few short years, Britain was transformed to an economy of relative abundance, and its problems changed to those of growth in a competitive market place" (page 219). Not only did national prosperity increase dramatically (although at a slower rate than many other industrial nations), but there were many new trends in the market (e.g. convenience foods). An economy of shortages provides a sellers' market and shelters the inefficient: a sudden change to a competitive environment and a buyers' market leaves them exposed and under threat.
2. Until just after the war the UK had operated in a relatively protected economy. Domestic production had been protected by cartels and restrictive practices: exports had been largely dependent on the "imperial preference" protected position of the Empire. "There was little rationalisation of production: small inefficient units could survive and prosper (page 219). The postwar period brought a rapid increase in international competition, at a time when the Empire, and its protected markets, was dissolving. Restrictive practices, which protected the inefficient firm and held back the efficient, could not be tolerated in the face of international competition: a steady stream of legislation began to remove them. (e.g. Monopolies Commission 1948: Restrictive Trade Practices Act 1956: Resale Price Maintenance 1964).
3. Social conditions changed dramatically, altering the pattern of supply and demand. Government policies aimed to re-distribute wealth, and to manage the economy to achieve full employment. "Consumer aspirations rose with growing affluence, and government undertook to fulfil these aspirations by seeking economic growth; it also sought to remove the spectre of unemployment, and thus became an increasingly important consumer of production" (page 277).
4. Rapid changes in technology brought new products and processes, and an increase in the scale of development costs in industries such as aircraft and computers. Patterns of competitive advantage changed: new industries emerged; many old industries had to be transformed; many traditional industries came under increasing threat over this period.

In addition to these four major trends identified by Channon there were a number of other significant areas of change emerging over this period, and many more have emerged subsequently. For example:

- Social changes, already mentioned, included better educational opportunities, which also affected aspirations.

- The trade union movement was a very powerful force. The 1970s were characterised by a marked growth in white-collar unions, although in the late 1970s there was a decline in the numbers of trade unionists.
- Governments, with their commitments to full employment and redistribution of wealth, applied a series of stop-go" economic policies; a point mentioned in Chapter 1.
- International competition was intensified when the UK joined the EEC in the mid-1970s, and when Taiwan and South Korea joined Japan in attacking the markets in the old industrialised countries.
- Inflation became a major problem from 1973. Although a world phenomenon inflation was consistently higher in the UK than in many of its international competitors. Although in the early 1980s inflation has returned to tolerable levels, it is worth mentioning that what we now find acceptable was a trigger point for government action in the late 1960s.

Channon's study covered the two decades ending in 1970. What he found was that the strategic responses to the changes he had observed were not always adequate. The following analysis is drawn from his findings and other studies.

(a) Consolidation and diversification

One major response to the trends was the adoption of diversification strategies. Channon's research showed that only 24 per cent of the top 100 companies were diversified in 1950, compared with 60 per cent by 1970. Although some companies had institutionalised the search for new products and markets, Channon found that many had not done so, and in 1970 many firms had only recently diversified. Many companies were not organised to generate new opportunities. Much diversification was by opportunistic acquistion rather than planned strategy.

Other industries, "notably aircraft, automobiles, ship-building, cables, brewing, newspapers, steel and computers", sought to reduce competitive pressures by amalgamation. "This concentration was often achieved by the largest and strongest concerns acquiring the weakest, frequently with encouragement from government. The result of these actions was to build a series of highly concentrated industries, often increasingly buttressed against outside competition by high entry barriers or government protection". (Channon[1] page 277) Channon noted that, the lack of growth and profitability in many of these firms, although giving an entry barrier against competition, restricted the further development of those firms.   Channon noted the failure of many British acquisitions. Few British companies attempted to rationalise their acquisitions. "Frequently, acquired concerns were allowed to continue along much as before without real influence from the parent. The acquisition was in name only, not in managerial action" (page 240).

Similar conclusions on the failure of acquistions were drawn from a survey by Kitching.[3] Nearly half of British mergers were unsuccessful. (Very similar failure patterns were found in Europe as a whole and in the USA.)

Buckner[4] found that in 200 companies he studied over the period 1960-1970 over half of diversification moves were failures, and that the failure rate was higher when diversification was by acquisition rather than internal development. The dry statistics can best be brought to life by an example of British acquisition behaviour. The extracts are from *Management Today*.[5]

the industry (motor cycles) emerged after the second war in a dominant world position. BSA at that time employed 25,000 (it was bigger than GKN) on activities including steel, machine tools, Daimler cars, and of course guns and bikes. Triumph had prospered under Sangster's shrewd eye.

Sangster sold Ariel to BSA in 1945 and Triumph six years later. He went on to the BSA board, where he clashed head-on with the chairman, Sir Bernard Docker. "I either had to fight him or get out, so we pushed him out and I became chairman."

In spite of its size at that time, BSA was not very profitable, and its management controls and internal organisation were weak, to say the least. BSA, Triumph and Ariel were run completely separately, so that there was no hope of rationalised production at that stage. Personal animosities between BSA and Triumph were remarkably strong . . . . Edward Turner was nominally in charge of all the group motor cycle interests, but in practice he stayed at Meriden and left the BSA management much to its own devices.

(b) The divisionalised structure

Channon[1] noted the adoption of the multi-divisional structure by an increasing number of companies over the two decades he studies. Eight per cent of the top 100 companies had this structure in 1950, compared to 70 per cent in 1970. No fewer than 32 of the largest 100 used outside consultants: 22 employed McKinsey.

The multi-divisional structure gives a greater orientation to market needs and permits the more efficient use of resources. It allows the organisation to apply a "portfolio" approach to the development of its strategies. According to Channon, "the adoption of the new structure helped to develop the new general management skills which had been lacking in British enterprises" (page 220).

Channon found that despite widespread adoption of many of the features of the US pattern of multi-divisional management, many "traditional techniques" were used in place of parts of the US system.

There was little use of performance-related rewards or sanctions, except through the indirect link of promotional prospects. The divisional general managers were participating in the formation of central policy in a way that made monitoring and performance measurement difficult. The general officers of many corporations had not yet divorced themselves from the operations of the divisions in order to concentrate on their entrepreneurial role of strategic decision-making. In some corporations transformation to a formal divisional system was incomplete, with parts of the business still run as a holding company, or specific functions, especially marketing, still centrally managed. Finally, there was little generation of internal competition between divisions, to allow the enterprise to allocate it resources as a small, but highly effective, capital market (page 240).

(c) Marketing

Channon observed that British industry had many deficiencies in its marketing and strategic thinking. "In Britain there has been a tendency for management to produce products with advanced engineering or design for its own sake, rather than to cater for market needs and/or products which would show an adequate return or investment" (page 34). British concerns were production or quality oriented, without due regard to the needs of the market place.

The same lament is given substance in the *Management Today*[5] article on the motor cycle industry.

In the event, BSA had no option but to concentrate on the bigger machines which were selling so well in the US. But even here, marketing let it down. The full implications of the change in market had not sunk in, and the BSA and Triumph designers gave scant attention to the new demand for luxury – smooth engines and riding characteristics, trouble-free performance, clean and oil-free running, et. The old traditional image of the hairy motor-cyclist who liked kick-starting his machine and doing all his own maintenance persisted right through; and it was assumed he would always recognise the long-life qualities of the slower-revving British machines compared to their Japanese counterparts.

The report on the motor cycle industry prepared for HMG by the Boston Consulting Group[6] in 1975 stated:

The loss of market share by the British motor cycle industry over the last fifteen years resulted from a concern for short term profitability. During the 1960's in any model in which the industry was confronted with Japanese competition, the British manufacturers found it difficult to make profits at a competitive price. Their response was essentially to withdraw from the smaller bikes in which the Japanese were competing so effectively. This led to a situation in which by the late 1960's the British industry was predominately active only in large bikes where the Japanese were not yet represented.

When the Japanese attacked this segment in the 1970s further withdrawal was impossible without ceasing production: "now, response in the superbike segment took the form of a failure to introduce new models".

A decade after the period researched by Channon, the Finniston[6] report (page 18) stated:

Sectoral studies, from shipbuilding to electronic components, have cited opportunities missed and markets lost due to non-price factors. These range from failure of British producers to innovate or to match changed requirements, through specific shortcomings in the design or performance of products, to a general reputation of British goods for inferior quality, late delivery and unreliability in service (e.g. the provision of spares).

The report quotes a British Institute of Marketing survey which found that marketing was perceived as synonymous with selling in most companies, "and that many managements did not stand back from their day-to-day activities to relate the directions that the technology of their products and the market demand for them were taking" (page 39).

(d) Innovation

By and large British companies have failed to innovate; a failing which may in part relate to the lack of attention to marketing. The Finniston Report (page 26) drew attention to the relative backwardness of the UK in commercial innovation, and ascribed the losses of world market shares to this fact.

Sharp[7] sees a European-wide "management gap" in the commercialisation and use of new technology, which means that it has fallen, or will fall, behind the USA and Japan in the new technological industries. The industries studied were computer-aided design, advanced machine tools, telecommunications, videotex, biotechnology and offshore supplies. She remarks that Europe is more risk-averse than Japan or the USA. This is an echo of an observation in the Finniston Report (page 26) which noted the fact that major corporate decisions are made predominantly by non-technical senior managements in the UK. Lack of technical knowledge is seen as a factor which reduces taking chances on engineering projects.

Corporate planning: success or failure?

Most companies which have followed the corporate planning path have been seeking better strategic decisions through improved analysis, more concern about the future, more effective coordination of different functions and activities and wider management involvement in the planning process. Many saw involvement as one of the keys to success, in that it could unlock more brain-power to think of solutions, would bring into the process both those at the coal face and those in the ivory tower, and motivate so that plans were implemented.

The classic planning process has postulated a blend of top-down and bottom-up thinking that in theory enables the final plan to be a rational amalgam of all viewpoints, argued out in a constructive manner.

Additional emphasis has been given because of the increasing recognition that business has to manage itself in relation to the changing environment. Corporate planning offered a means to do this. It is interesting that most research into why companies introduced corporate planning showed that in most cases it was a response to a changed situation or crisis conditions. These findings have been noted in Japan, Europe and the USA, and it would seem fairly safe to extend them to the world.[8]

It was not long before people began to question whether corporate planning, which had become very popular during the 1960s, actually contributed to profits. At first the replies were on the lines of "it must be good because so many people do it", or citing the rather rare situations where obvious benefit had occurred within seconds of the arrival of the corporate planner.

However, human ingenuity soon found a way of measuring the impact of planning, and a series of studies were carried out in the USA proving that planning did pay. Most were based on some form of matched-pairs analysis, for example comparing company performance of each "planner" before and after introducing planning and with the performance of its "non-planning" pair. The general conclusion was that individual companies could do well without planning, but on average those that planned did better than those which did not. The Bowman study[9] analysed company reports and deduced from these that companies which talked about objectives, plans and new product policies were successful, while others in the same business which blamed government or the weather were unsuccessful. This particular study is fun to read, but seems to me to prove that managers have a propensity to take personal credit for things that go right, but to avoid taking personal blame for things that go wrong.

Generally, the case has been made – at least in the USA – that corporate planning is beneficial and does improve the economic results of those companies that practise it. It is not really surprising that corporate planning should be a good thing, although some surprise does creep in when one considers the departures that have been made in implementation from the original theoretical concepts, a point to which I shall return.

It seems to me that the research proves beyond doubt that corporate planning *can* be beneficial, but does not prove that it *will* always be beneficial in every case. Firstly, if it is applied badly it is unlikely to succeed. Secondly, there must be degrees of success and not all organisations allow corporate planning to run to its full potential: my impression in the UK is that many top managers do not set high enough an expectation from their planning work and therefore have a satisfaction level that is too low.

Perhaps the most important point is that strategic decisions have to be made whether or not the company plans, and these decisions can be good or bad. All managers are prisoners within the boundaries of their own perception, and although corporate planning is supposed to move these boundaries it does not always do so. It is thus possible for a company to achieve better results because of the coordination and motivational impact of its planning process and yet still to be following the wrong strategic path. My argument is that this has certainly happened in the UK, and that in many companies planning has failed to change these perceptual boundaries, through failings of managers and planners. The real test will be whether British managers have failed in the strategic sense.

Can corporate planning be better?

While one group of researchers were proving the economic value of corporate planning, others had observed that some organisations appeared to be better at it than others. This led to numerous sound studies[10]* of the factors that contribute to the successful or unsuccessful implementation of planning systems.

The sad thing is that managements still fall into pitfalls that were identified over a decade ago. Modern research frequently underlines the conclusions of the older work. Common management "faults" include treating planning as something different from the management process, lack of understanding of planning, failure to involve the right people in the process, abdication of planning responsibility by top management, failure to obtain the necessary information for planning, failure by top management to back the process, political issues around the power structure, and the calibre of the people involved.

From observation of many UK planning processes I would say that the most common fault is that they are bottom-up systems with little top-down influence. I call this the church collection approach, where every contribution to the plan is dropped in the plate (sometimes generously but often grudgingly) by those down the line, accepted gratefully by the corporate planner who adds it all up and thinks he has a strategic plan.

Deficiences of planning in the UK can be examined from a large-scale survey of the Society for Long Range Planning.[11] For example, of companies that employ members of the Society:

- less than half practise manpower planning;
- only a quarter have contingency plans;
- as many as 30 per cent do *not* formally forecast events outside the organisation;
- nearly 67 per cent do *not* plan diversification;
- 80 per cent give *no* attention to divestment;
- a considerable number have no formal mechanisms for proposing and selecting objectives, or setting and reviewing objectives.

It is not difficult to define a few important points if planning is to have any chance at all of really contributing. The following extract comes from one of my earlier articles.[12]

*References are a sample: there are numerous other useful studies.

> **The 10 major traps in corporate planning**
> 1. Top management's assumption that it can delegate the planning function to a planner.
> 2. Top management becomes so engrossed in current problems that it spends insufficient time on long-range planning, and the process becomes discredited among other managers and staff.
> 3. Failure to develop company goals suitable as a basis for formulating long-range plans.
> 4. Failure to obtain the necessary involvement in the planning process of major line personnel.
> 5. Failure to use the plan as standards for measuring managerial performance.
> 6. Failure to create a climate in the company which is congenial and not resistant to planning.
> 7. Assuming that corporate comprehensive planning is something separate from the entire management process.
> 8. Injecting so much formality into the system that it lacks flexibility, looseness and simplicity, and restrains creativity.
> 9. Failure of top management to review with departmental and divisional heads the long-range plans which they have developed.
> 10. Top management's consistently rejecting the formal planning mechanism by making intuitive decisions which conflict with formal plans.
>
> (Adapted from a study of 215 companies by George Steiner: published as *Pitfalls in Comprehensive Long Range Planning*, Planning Executives Institute, 1972.)

There are some fundamental principles which are inportant for effective corporate planning. First, *management must have the will to make plans work*. No outsider can create this, although he may be able to help management understand the actions that must be taken and their implications. Second, *contrary to normal architectural practice, building must start from the top down*. The foundations must be in the boardroom. But building must go through the organisation. This usually means retraining middle and senior managers in ways of thinking and in using methods which improve their individual planning skills. It is not enough for top managers to issue enthusiastic edicts unless they first ensure that those receiving the edicts are qualified to respond.

Third, *the emphasis of the planning process must be on strategy*. A common approach is for goals and assumptions to go down the organisation and detailed plans to go up. My colleagues' experience has been that in most organisations this is not a good mechanism for identifying and dealing with the strategic issues. What we find appropriate is a strategic review concept, which ensures that the right type of analysis is carried out; that there is participative and objective discussion between the corporate top management and heads of business units; and that strategic issues are identified from both corporate and divisional perspectives. In this way, it is possible for corporate plans to be thought about at the "input" stage, normally plans are only reviewed by top management at the "output" stage when opinions have hardened and a great deal of work has been invested in pulling the plans together. Only after full discussion and decision processing of the strategic review do we recommend that clients proceed to the detailed tasks of preparing long-term plans. This in turn links with other management processes, such as the annual budget.

Fourth, *the breath of life must be put into the process by the company*. No ready-made blueprint for corporate planning can be handed on a plate to an organisation. Where outside help is used, it is important to use it in a "process" rather than a "task" mode. The process role means that the consultant works to help the company effect change through its own personnel: he gives help, guidance, advice and training on a continuing basis, but leaves the organisation's own personnel to take the necessary actions and implement them. Few reports are produced, since the consultant's work only produces paper when it gets into the internal documents and decisions. Task-consulting, on the other hand, consists of the preparation of a report with recommendations, which the company then has to adopt and implement: it is the right mode for some problems, but not for the development of a corporate planning process.

Fifth, *if the planning process allows for the involvement of lower level managers, this must be genuine involvement*. While every organisation has to decide on the appropriate involvement for its own situation, implementation must be more than lip-service. Middle management involvement may well be shallow and not very creative if the manager's 'plan' is merely an indication of how he will meet an objective set by his boss. It may be much more creative if involvement allows some share in determining the objective, and even more so if the middle manager is allowed to contribute some thought to the wider problems and opportunities faced by the division or business unit in which he works. Philips of Eindhoven, starting in one of its product divisions, produced an organisational development approach to strategy which allows genuine middle management participation in planning the strategy of that division. The approach is not limited to a statement of intent, but is a process which ensures that full involvement does take place, and that those concerned are put into a situation where they can contribute.

Finally, *planning must give attention to objective analysis and human behavior*. Good planning must be well rooted in objective analysis. But this is only one part of the equation. Human organisations are not logical machines, and to be effective plans need more than a sound analytical base. The process must also give weight to human behavioural issues, such as motivation, power structures, fear, creativity, and the like. The way planning is approached for a particular organisation must achieve the correct balance between the two. Processes which consist solely of cold analysis will lead to plans that do not get implemented: those which are all participation and no analysis lead to misdirected plans which quite probably will be implemented, to the detriment of the organisation.

Evolution of planning thought

Corporate planning has not been a static topic. The modern emphasis is on the management of strategy, and this is healthy. Recent research by Gluck, Kaufman and Walleck[13] has postulated four phases in the evolution of strategic planning:

1. Basic financial planning, seeking better operational control, aiming to meet budgets.
2. Forecast-based planning, seeking more effective planning for growth and trying to *predict* the future.
3. Externally oriented planning, seeking increased responsiveness to markets and competition, trying to think strategically.
4. Strategic management, seeking to manage all resources to create competitive advantage and trying to "create the future".

My own work in corporate planning and management education has convinced me that one of the main roles of the planning process must be to challenge the perceptual boundaries within which top management makes its strategic decisions. Many of the modern techniques of strategic analysis which I use are of value because, by ordering information in a different way, they enable new patterns to be seen and different perceptions to be formed.

Perceptual boundaries

From the foregoing analysis it is possible to see how perceptual boundaries will affect strategic decision-making. The managers of the motor cycle companies made many product decisions that would have been quite logical if their perceptual boundary had been correct. Their decisions were made in the firm belief that their motor cycles were the best, their engineering talent was superior, and that the world would always want a British motor cycle. Production decisions were made within the parameters of the situation as they saw it – factories in the UK which would export their surplus production. They were ignorant of the global strategy of companies like Honda, and of the differences in productivity. At one plant Honda produced 350 motor cycles per man-year: Britain's best plant produced 18.

It is a natural and human trait to simplify the world by shutting out certain possibilities.

Most people have a built-in tendency to stabilise the world around them. In an effort to cope with the enormous amount of information bombarding us and the infinite number of problems, great and small, which require immediate solution, we have developed a mental system that tries to deal with them in ways which require less time and energy: that is by habit and exclusion. When looking for novelty, this natural conservation of industry can be a positive hindrance (Whitfield).[14]

Most of us recognise that the world-as-we-see-it is not necessarily the same world-as-it-really-is. Our answer depends on what we heard, not what was really said. The consumer buys what he likes best, not what is best. Whether we feel hot or cold depends on us, not on the thermometer. The same job may look like a good job to one of us and a sloppy job to another (Leavitt).[15]

Unless we are very careful the perceptual boundaries may be passed from one manager to another, without challenge, just as generations of medieval European men made all their decisions in the knowledge that the world was flat. In the UK we have a strong preference for "industry experience" as the way to learn how to be a manager, which brings the risk of passing on the bad things as well as the good. Only 20 per cent of British managers have degrees or professional qualifications;[16] although degrees and strategic expertise are by no means synonymous, one might expect the graduate to be more trained to challenge the established order. Recent research by our organisation[17] showed that a majority of the largest UK companies will not recruit British MBAs, denying themselves the chance of having concepts applied from the bottom up, to challenge the established boundaries.

Corporate planning has been translated by too many organisations into an empty paper chase, which consumes management time, but which has next to no impact on real decisions and actions.

Many leading managers have no real standard with which to compare their own performance. They therefore believe that they are doing things well, although in fact their performance in corporate planning may be inadequate . . . . few directions will admit to knowing little about corporate planning, since part of their job is strategy. Yet few have taken steps to learn about the subject . . . . most executives believe that the knowledge of corporate planning that they have picked up by exposure to the practical issues of management is adequate. It is not (Hussey).[12]

Towards strategic management

I know of enough situations in the UK where the corporate planning process has been effective to know that things do not have to be as bad as they are. In all these cases there is a strong central strategic role, and no assumption that the corporate strategy will evolve from simply consolidating the plans of the sub-units. The chief executive is heavily involved, and there is an intelligent use of modern approaches to strategic analysis, which provide a continuing challenge to the perceptual boundaries in those firms.

Some companies are known to have made very valuable use of portfolio analysis techniques. I have been able to help challenge the perceptual boundaries within a number of companies, from small to very large, teaching them to use the appropriate techniques, and tying this to a process of planning which blends the analytical with the behavioural.

That boundaries have changed has been obvious from the subsequent strategic decisions. One approach I use is called *industry structure analysis*, and it is designed to foster a full understanding of competitive forces and the relative power and influence on economic results of the industry, its suppliers and its buyers. So often I have started using this technique with managements who are convinced that they have a leadership position in a UK market which is just beginning to come under unfair price competition from Japan. Often they end up by realising that they are really trading in a world market, have virtually no market position, are thinking in production rather than market terms about their products, and have to take some very different decisions if they are going to survive in the long term. The change in thinking is often from "I have a UK plant, use 70 per cent of capacity for my main market and export the rest", to "I see a world market. How can I obtain a significant share in the face of tough competition?" For many British industries the insular thinking is the path to doom. The alternative is difficult, may require some clever segmentation analysis, but offers some hope of survival. It postulates a manufacturing strategy united to corporate objectives and does not necessarily tie down thinking to the existing UK plant. We have found it sensible to develop a battery of techniques, which can be linked together. Figure 2.1 illustrates the concept.

Thus industry structure analysis may be used to understand a business unit,

Management and Strategy: Lessons from Success and Failure

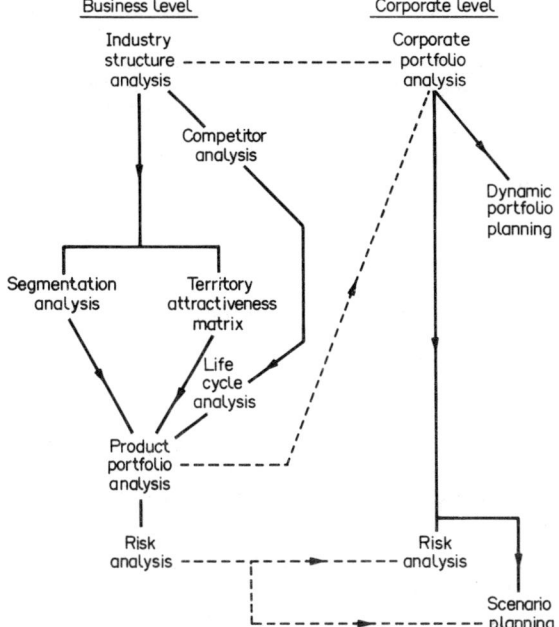

FIGURE 2.1. Integration of planning techniques.

to enable that unit to make better strategic decisions, and as a source of information that contributes to corporate-level portfolio analysis. Portfolio analysis may be used at corporate level to compare stratetic business units, and at unit level to compare products.

My industry structure analysis approach was stimulated by work by Professor Mike Porter of Harvard. His book, *Competitive Strategy*,[18] has been a management best-seller, reprinted 10 times during the first two years after publication. My contribution has been the development of checklists, questionnaires and conceptual models which make the approach an even more workable and helpful tool.

My firm's approach to portfolio analysis is based on some original work by Shell, although we have developed the concept and devised methods of application that suit a variety of industries. It is a sophisticated tool, and can be used dynamically as well as for its original purpose of comparing the relative strategic positioning of different businesses. With some clients we have been able to test out from historical data the validity of general conclusions that might be drawn from the matrix. Businesses in the poor end of the spectrum have indeed lost cash over time; those in a cash generator box have contributed cash, even though they may not have been run as tightly as we should have recommended.

The management requirements for different positionings within the matrix are different, and the personnel management implications of this are

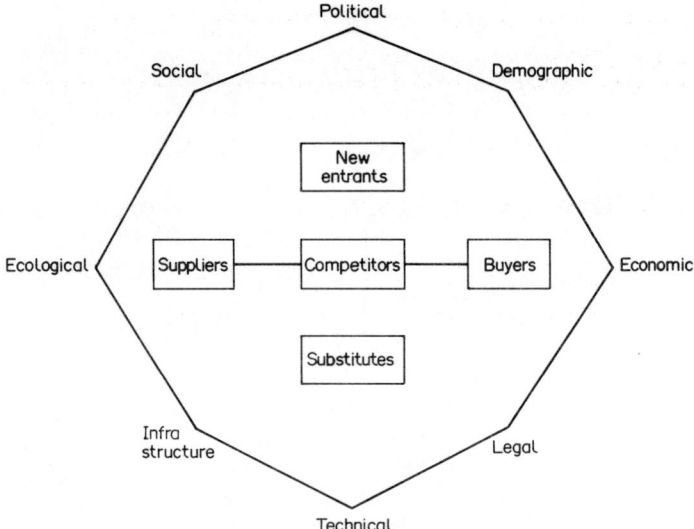
FIGURE 2.2. Basic elements affecting industry profitability

important. There are many other techniques listed in the outline diagram, including some very simple approaches to strengths and weakness analysis.

Harbridge House has two unique offerings in the area of relating the organisation to the business enviroment. One assesses an organisation's responsiveness to change: the other looks at environmental risk and can be used to produce a three-dimensional portfolio analysis, with the portfolio on one plane and risk on another. One of our clients has his portfolio modelled in a Perspex block.

It is one of our disappointments that few clients have wanted to proceed beyond portfolio analysis. British firms, I believe, lose out by not relating to risk analysis their planning systems to the outside world in an adequate way. We see this again in our educational work where the courses we run for one client on understanding the environment are less popular among managers – until they have attended – than the other ten courses we run for that client.

I am concerned at this, since research has shown that it is a concern about external events which often causes a company to begin a process of planning. Yet I am not surprised, as it is very difficult for any group of people to handle very large and disparate pieces of information. It may be that our techniques do not refine the problem of the environment in a manageable way, whereas industry structure and portfolio analysis do get to the essentials very effectively. The answer may lie in more work on scenario planning.

I know from our experience that sensible and selective use of modern analytical techniques can shift those perceptual boundaries, provided the behavioural issues are identified and dealt with. I know that these techniques can fit very well into a participative process of planning, provided it is

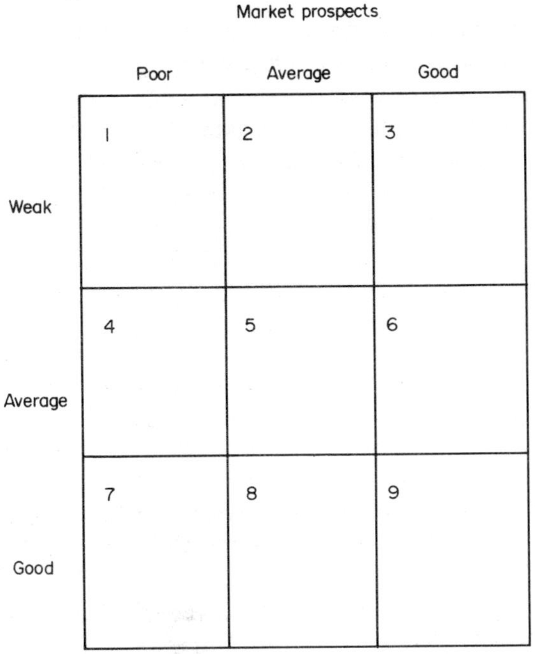

Market prospects

	Poor	Average	Good
Weak	1	2	3
Average	4	5	6
Good	7	8	9

FIGURE 2.3. Directional policy matrix

recognised that the corporate strategy of a complex group cannot be led from the bottom.

In the final event it must be management which uses the techniques, and one of the essential skills of the corporate planner or consultant is to help them do this. I do not believe in doing the analyses for a client: my role is to help make the technique work, and this means behaviourally and analytically. My philosophy is to have no secret techniques that only I can apply. All my approaches, including worksheets, checklists, scoring rules and questionnaires, are written into a handbook which is made available to clients.

We must never forget that corporate planning stands or falls on the twin pillars of the analytical and the behavioural. The real ability to change the perceptual boundaries of a strategic problem, or even to recognise that they exist, must come from managers themself, if better strategies are to result. Yet I also know that had British industry in general used some of these approaches in the 1960s, it would be in a much healthier situation. My fear is that many British firms will continue making logical actions within a wrongly perceived arena, until they disappear.

All the evidence suggests that I am justified in my fears. Most of the research into strategic failings, either implicitly or explicitly, blames lack of management leadership and skills as major contributors to the situation.

My hope is based on the certain knowledge that British management may be misguided, but is not stupid. We may have reached a certain position from cultural and social reasons, but given the right motivation we have the ability to do something about it.

It is *what* to do about it which will increasingly become the focus of this book.

References

1. D. F. Channon (1973): *The Strategy and Structure of British Enterprise,* Macmillan
2. HMSO (1980): *Report of the Committee of Enquiry into the Engineering Profession*
3. J. Kitchling (1974): *Management Today,* November
4. H. Buckner (1974): *Seeking new sources of earnings. In* The Corporate Planners' Yearbook 1974–75 (D. E. Hussey, ed.), Pergamon
5. T. Lester (1974): How the British bikes crashed, *Management Today,* November
6. HMSO (1975): *Strategy Alternatives for the British Motor Cycle Industry*
7. M. Sharp (ed.) (1985): *Europe and the New Technologies,* Frances Pinter
8. (a) K. A. Ringbakk (1969): Organised Planning in major US companies, *Long Range Planning,* December
   (b) B. W. Denning and M. E. Lehr (1971/1972): Extent and nature of corporate long range planning in the UK, 1 and 2, *Journal of Managment Studies,* May and February
   (c) B. Taylor and P. Irving (1971): Organised planning in major UK companies, *Long Range Planning,* June
   (d) T. Kono (1976): Long range planning – Japan – USA – a comparative study, *Long Range Planning,* October.
9. (a) S. S. Thune and R. J. House (1970): Where long range planning pays off: findings of a survey of formal, informal planners, *Business Horizons,* August
   (b) R. F. Vancil (1970): The accuracy of long range planning, *Harvard Business Review,* September/October
   (c) H. I. Ansof *et al.* (1970): Does planning pay? The effect of planning on success of acquisition in American firms, *Long Range Planning,* Vol. 3, No. 2
   (d) Z. A. Malik and D. W. Karger (1975): Does long range planning improve company performance?, *Management Review,* September
   (e) E. H. Bowman (1976): Strategy and the weather, *Sloan Management Review,* Vol. 17, No. 2
   (f) D. M. Herold (1972): Long range planning and organisational performance, *Academy of Management Journal,* March
10. (a) K. A. Ringback (1971): Why planning fails, *European Business,* Spring
    (b) P. M. Grinyer and D. Norburn (1974): Strategic planning in 21 UK companies, *Long Range Planning,* August
    (c) G. A. Steiner and H. Schollhammer (1975): Pitfalls in multi-national, *Long Range Planning,* April
    (d) J. Martin (1979): Business planning: The gap between theory and practice, *Long Range Planning,* December
11. P. Knowlson (1974): *Organisation and Membership Survey,* Society for Long Range Planning.
12. D. E. Hussey (1978): How to plan success, *Management Today,* November
13. F. W. Gluck, S. P. Kaufman and A. S. Walleck (1980): Strategic management for competitive advantage, *Harvard Business Review,* July–August
14. P. R. Whitfield (1975): *Creativity in Industry,* Pelican
15. H. J. Leavitt (1978): *Managerial Psychology,* 4th edition, University of Chicago Press
16. Office of Populations Censuses and Surveys (1983): *Labour Force Survey 1981,* HMSO
17. K. Ascher (1983): *Management Training in Major UK Organisations,* Harbridge House
18. M. E. Porter (1980): *Competitive Strategy,* Free Press

3

Education

The education system

Almost all of the commentators on the "British disease" who have been referenced in the preceding chapters put some of the blame for the decline of British competitiveness on education. The educational system is probably a result of the cultural heritage, rather than a cause of it, but in the view of some reinforces those elements of our heritage which are most disadvantageous to commercial and industrial success. Other observers see faults in what is actually taught rather than in the system itself.

This chapter will review this evidence. Next it will examine the contention that British management suffers from being less well educated than that of major competitor countries. It will conclude by looking at the extent of business education in the UK.

The text of this chapter might well be this quotation taken from the Plowden report on education.[1]

Comparisons with other countries – all of them more recently industrialised than Britain but all now at a similar stage of economic development – suggest that we have not done enough to provide the educational background necessary to support an economy which needs fewer and fewer unskilled workers and increasing numbers of skilled and adaptable people.

Hudson Institute Europe[2] saw education in the UK as a major asset that had been wasted.

The Finniston Report[3] described the misleading tendency to regard engineering as a subordinate branch of science:

This view of engineering science as an offshoot or application of science is held to have underlain many of the current criticisms of engineering formation in Britain today; in particular, engineering courses constructed on the basis of teaching *first* the underlying scientific analysis and theory and *then* the potential application of it, build into engineering formation a dichotomy between "theory" and "practice". This dichotomy does not arise in courses built upon the philosophy of "Technik" which places everything taught in the context of economic purpose. Theoretical training is from early on linked to its potential usefulness within the overall theme of an engineering system, be it mechanical, electrical or process. The final years of "German model" and French engineering courses are then concentrated upon specialised projects designed to focus and bring together what has been learnt about various aspects of a particular system. The debate which has continually dogged engineering teachers over the appropriate balance in engineering formation between theory and practice is a non issue within the continental mode of engineering teaching.

The report (page 91) reached the conclusion that the "quality and balance" of engineers, at the point when they emerged as fully fledged engineers, was inferior in the UK to that in its major country competitors. A sad finding, considering the world-beating achievements of the Victorian engineers.

Sharp[4] concluded that the UK's well-publicised ability to excel in science but fail in commercial exploitation of innovation must be blamed partly on the "elitist" education system, which treats the arts and pure sciences as superior to applied science.

The Finniston report makes comments on the quality of mathematics and science teaching in schools, and the lack of links between schools and industry. It stresses the lack of "demand-pull" to attract good candidates into industry, because advancement prospects for engineers are often poor, and many employers "have often taken the attitude that few engineers are properly equipped to take on broader management responsibilities and have employed them instead as providers of technical services". (ref. 3, page 61).

It is the creation of attitudes of this type which is the root of the criticisms of many observers of the British education system. Weiner[5] sees the dominance of the public school and Oxbridge route to leadership positions as one of the factors that has preserved the cultural values which have inhibited industrial progress. Even the new universities, he argues (pages 132-54) have followed the Oxford and Cambridge tradition, devoting most of their resources to the arts and social sciences, and forging few links with industry. University education provides a way to escape from life, rather than a preparation for it. Traditional values, he maintains, also hamper the development of the polytechnics. Those polytechnics which had been upgraded to full universities soon fitted in to the existing pattern, turning their backs on their technical college tradition.

Given this state of affairs it is not surprising that those who can afford it see the best route for their children as a public school education, with Oxford or Cambridge as the preferred universities. In some families this may also be a matter of tradition, but even without a background belief in the superiority of this educational route it is possible to develop a completely pragmatic argument that it provides the best economic prospects for the child. Although some argue against the public school system on political grounds, as creating unequal opportunities, the cultural argument would appear to be that it is not their existence which is the problem, but the way in which they help maintain a self-perpetuating system of values which are not necessarily the best values for the economic development of the UK.

The Hudson Institute[2] (pages 82-91) saw the educational system as a major cause of the decline of the UK. "Britain today educates too few people, and for the wrong subjects".

The reinforcement of the "ideal of genteel governance" led, in the view of the Hudson Institute, to a strange separation of pure learning from the practical application of knowledge.

While traditional British educational practice provided a formidable defence of the classical and humane studies and of scholarship as a civilising force, this essential task was accomplished by making a humane education and prerogative of a social class. A drastic line was drawn on an irrelevant criterion between education and scholarship on the one hand and the practical employment of human knowledge in the affairs of society on the other. Pure science was admitted to the great universities: technology and engineering were consigned to schools whose social inferiority was unmistakable. In short, a legitimate intellectual distinction that set off an elite from the rest. This did violence to the mind: scholarship, to say nothing of wisdom, is not class-restricted. But it also had pernicious effects upon the society and economy of the country. Those who actually applied knowledge in the ordinary life of the country were made to feel the inferiority of their role.

My own view is that American writers tend to exaggerate class differences in the UK. However, I do accept that some who hold leadership positions in industry are there by right of privilege, rather than ability. Channon[6] drew attention to studies that showed a disproportionate public school and Oxbridge education among company directors, and a lower level of educational attainment in the population in general than is the case in most other industrialised nations. We have already seen how the training given to engineers in the UK is regarded as inferior to that in other countries.

Educational level of British management

Given this background it is not surprising that British management as a whole is less well educated than that of other industrial nations. This is not only about absolute numbers who have received higher education, but also what they have been trained in. There is an argument that, for many jobs in industry, the exact nature of the degree taken is not important. After all, education is a broadening process, related to the quality of life as well as material knowledge, whatever the basic discipline. This argument has considerable appeal (although we do not use it when seeking accountants, engineers or various other specialists where a vocational element to their courses is considered essential). My view is that life would be the poorer if people did not study non-vocational subjects, but that what is next needed is either a higher degree in management, or (and probably, as well) a training scheme within the firm whereby the new entrant is taught the skills of management. As we shall see, neither happens to the extent needed, and in any case the graduate is a minority member of the ranks of British management.

Official statistics[7] show that only about 8 per cent of British managers have a university degree, and a further 7 per cent have the examinations of a profesional body as their highest qualification. Only 2 per cent have any form of management qualification in their educational background.

It is possible to study management. In the USA over 60,000 MBA degrees are awarded through more than 600 business schools annually, and although the nature of the training given has recently come under some criticism (see Chapter 1), the number of graduates is considerably greater than the annual output of Europe. Melcher and Sneider[8] estimate that Europe produces 2500 MBAs every year, plus another 3000 who earn an equivalent of an MBA. This compared with 1000 MBSs or equivalent 10 years ago.

The UK produces an impressive proportion of the European total. Ascher,[9] in the Harbridge House report on MBAs, estimates that a total of 1500 postgraduate degrees in business are awarded annually. However about 25 per cent of these are overseas students, which reduces the number available to the UK employment market to approximately 1100 per annum. Thus it would take about 54 years for the UK to produce the same number of MBAs as the USA produces in one year.

Much of the information used in this and other chapters of this book is drawn from original Harbridge House surveys with which I was associated. Because extensive use is made of these, they will only be given as general references. The reports provide much of the factual basis of this book; quotations from them are generally used without further acknowledgement. Further details of the Harbridge House research are provided in the Appendix.

The MBA is a postgraduate degree, and some 80 per cent of those taking it have a first degree: some business schools make this a requirement for entry. Most of the rest will hold a professional qualification. It is different from the normal pattern of postgraduate degree in that it is rarely related to the subject of the first degree. Thus it is not continuation of a discipline to a higher academic level, but a completely new course of study. Many business schools prefer students to have some work experience. The typical business school student in the UK might enter his course at age 26 with 3 years' work experience, and graduate at 27 or 28 (depending on whether 1-year or 2-year course). However the "typical" student conceals a wide range of deviations, with students ages varying between 21 and 47 years, and work experience from zero to extensive. We found the average of 3 years' work experience quoted by one business school to be highly misleading, as 45 per cent of its intake had never worked.

More will be said about the MBA, but before exploring its history further, we should not forget the other management qualifications offered by universities and colleges.

It is estimated that some 3500 first degree-level graduates entered employment in the UK in 1984 with what might loosely be termed business-related degrees. (This compared with a total of 54,932 new graduates who entered UK employment in that year.) Of the 3500, just under half took degrees in management science or accountancy, leaving about 1900 whose degrees are classified in the statistics as Business, Commerce and Management Studies.

Education

FIGURE 3.1. First degree students entering home employment, 1983-84

	Polytechnic	University	College of further education	Total
Management science	338[a]	—	—	338
Business, committee, management studies	1069[b]	859	—	1928
Accountancy, banking insurance	508[c]	698	—	1206
	1915	1557	—	3472

[a] 37% sandwich students
[b] 99% sandwich students
[c] 16% sandwich students
Source: AGCAS: *University Statistical Record.*

It is perhaps illustrative of the traditional academic approach that the polytechnics produce more than half of the graduates in these subjects, although only a quarter of total graduates earn their degrees from this source.

Many of the polytechnic courses include a mandatory spell of work experience, so that it is possible to recruit a first-level business studies graduate with more work experience than the MBA who has gone from, say, an economics degree into an MBA course.

Education statistics[14] suggest that the polytechnics also produce some 1500 successful students annually with the diploma in management studies. Figure 3.2 shows that 30 per cent of the first degree graduates take up employment in industry, 27 per cent in commerce, and 3 per cent in the public services or education. However, those obtaining employment amounted to some 49 per cent of all graduates. What happens to the majority is shown in Figure 3.3.

Some secondary schools give attention to management studies, but this is a minority activity. The BBC has produced a schools radio programme, *"Business Matters"*, to provide a basic understanding of business and management for secondary school pupils.

Undergraduate business education courses have been available in the UK for some 65 years, but postgraduate courses are of fairly recent origin. The Robbins Report[11] noted that the absence of such courses was a weakness in management education. This led to the Franks Report[12] in 1963, which recommended the establishment of two "centres of excellence" for business education which would offer courses leading to a postgraduate degree in management. In 1965 the London and Manchester Business Schools were established, sponsored jointly by industry and the University Grants Committee.

Development has not been at the rate expected. The Franks Report envisaged 2000 MBAs per year by the late 1970s; only 75 per cent of this figure is being achieved in the mid-1980s. One may also query the wisdom of moving from a few "centres of excellence" to the 40 establishments that

FIGURE 3.2. First degree graduates, UK, permanent employment, 1984/5

	UK employment total	Public service	Education	Manu-facturing	Building and civil engineering	Public utility	Total industry	Account-ancy	Banking/ insurance, Finance	Other Commerce	Total Commerce	Private practice	Other + unknown	Total graduates
First degrees														
Polytechnics	14,056	2,572	1,363	3,416	1,119	509	5,044	724	483	2,439	3,646	76	1,355	29,469
University	35,309	8,716	2,032	8,808	1,076	1,303	11,187	3,789	2,309	4,426	10,524	778	2,072	72,046
College of higher education	5,567	689	2,698	393	51	103	547	79	142	667	888	20	725	10,950
Total	54,932	11,977	6,093	12,617	2,246	1,915	16,778	4,592	2,934	7,532	15,058	874	4,152	112,465
Percentage	100	21.803	11.092	22.968	4.0887	3.4861	30.543	8.3594	5.3411	13.711	27.412	1.5911		8

Source: AGCS.
Note difference in time between Figures 3.1 and 3.2.

112,465 Graduates

49.0% Perm UK employment

Other employment 5.0%

13.0% Unknown

Proceeding to further education 19.0%

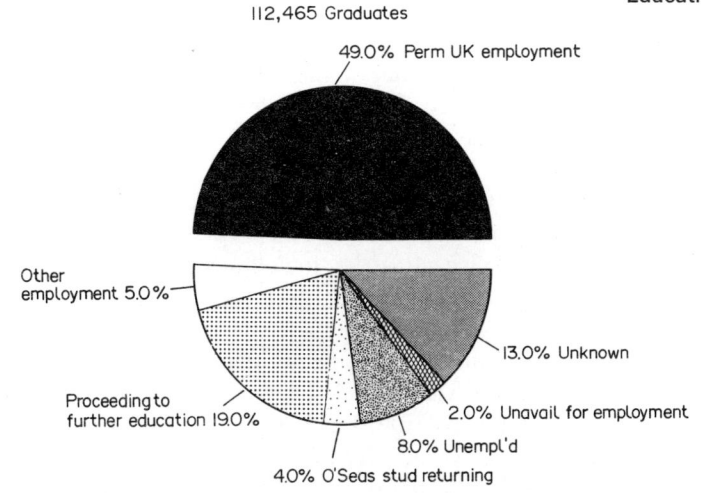

2.0% Unavail for employment

8.0% Unempl'd

4.0% O'Seas stud returning

FIGURE 3.3. First degrees: destinations, 1984/5 (source: ACGAS)

currently offer postgraduate qualifications in management in the UK today. This limited supply of MBAs is one reason why they are not found more widely in manufacturing in the UK.

British business schools were originally intended to follow the American pattern of an intensive 2-year MBA course. Only London and Manchester adhere to this, and the remainder have adopted the European pattern of a programme condensed into a 10- or 12-month period.

Part-time MBA options are now offered by a number of business schools. The latest variant of these is a distance learning option developed by Warwick and a correspondence course firm, Wolsey Hall.

The MBA degree is by no means a standard product, and the nature, structure and quality of the programmes varies widely between the business schools. The 60,000-plus US MBAs are by no means a homogeneous product either, and there is possibly a greater difference between the top and the bottom schools than there is in the UK.

The existence of a postgraduate qualification in management that could be taken at virtually any age might have been expected to lead to significant company sponsorship of students, particularly between the ages of 30 and 35. Sponsorship is a minority activity, with many companies never entertaining the idea. We found that the proportion of sponsored students ranged between 5 and 25 per cent, with one exception: 85 per cent of students at Henley are sponsored. However we are talking about small numbers (Henley had 35 MBA students at the time of our research), and overall there are probably no more than 100–150 sponsored British students in the UK, plus a few more at Pan-European (e.g. INSEAD) and US business schools.

There are criticisms that can be fairly made of the MBA degree, and these will be returned to in the next chapter. For a variety of reasons British manufacturing industry shows little interest in the qualification. The two reasons for this appear to be ignorance or apathy by industry, and the market forces which mean that MBAs from those schools with the highest reputation can earn high salaries outside of manufacturing (and find it easy to obtain jobs).

Roughly a third of all MBA students join consulting or finance firms. (This proportion rises to over 50 per cent in certain business schools). About 60 per cent of MBAs move into service industries, including finance and consulting. This means that, of the 1200 new graduates each year, only 480 are available for the whole of manufacturing industry.

Because the supply is limited, with heavy demand led by US-owned consultancy and financial service firms, salary expectations of the MBA graduates from those schools with the best reputations are high. Top students, recruited from London, Manchester or Cranfield, may obtain starting salaries of £30,000 (1983 data), and often be given a "golden hello" to pay for their past tuition costs. The majority of MBA students from the more prestigious business schools are likely to obtain starting salaries of £15,000 to £20,000 p.a. Figures are markedly lower for students from schools such as Bradford and Aston. Nevertheless the high expectations, which are realised by a significant number of MBA graduates, mean that starting salaries required for a person of perhaps 1 or 2 years' experience are often greater than those paid to experienced and senior managers within the company (and interestingly to an MBA with many years postgraduation experience). There are many senior managers in British industry who do not earn £30,000 per year. Were there a greater supply of MBAs, forces of demand and supply would operate and salary levels would tend to lower.

As things are, many British firms are most unlikely to recruit someone with an MBA. Our research included a sample of 50 of the larger companies. We certainly found a proportion of dedicated MBA recruiters. These companies (and the sample by its very nature was biased towards recruiters of MBAs), revealed the following pattern (percentages):

Active recruiters (milk round)	24
Recruit via school biography volumes	4
No particular policy MBAs	52
Will not recruit MBs	20

We found a strong bias to US-owned multinational firms among the active recruiters. What the figures suggest is that some 70 per cent of the largest UK firms are either indifferent to the MBA as a relevant qualification, or are positively against it. In 1970 a NEDO report[13] drew attention to the persistent belief of many in British industry that their management systems and processes were unique. The belief that management can only be learned from experience is shared by both the "educated amateur" and the "practical"

TABLE 3.1. *Reasons for and against recruitment of MBAs*

Reasons for not recruiting (28 firms)	Reasons for recruiting (16 firms)
Prefer school-leavers to graduates	MBA motivation and ambition
Interested in individual, not degree	Understanding of business principles
MBA unsuited to company culture	High potential and ability
No requirements for MBA expertise	Can cope under pressure
Prefer sponsorship	Good on finance
Good in-house training sufficient	Ability to integrate concepts
Bad experience of MBA	Level of maturity

Source: Harbridge House, *Masters of Business?*

man stereotypes distinguished in Chapter 1. We were not surprised to find, in 1983, some very strong prejudices against the recruitment of newly qualified MBAs.

A few companies, including a high proportion of US-owned firms, felt that most MBAs can cope better under pressure, are more mature, and are more competent than other graduates or potential applicants. Fast movers, such as top MBAs, were seen as ideal for these firms.

Another school of thought, represented by many traditional manufacturing and service firms, believe that first degree students are just as good and cheaper. (A few are biased against any graduates.) They feel that, regardless of salary levels, MBAs are unsuited for their companies.

Fast movers have "rocked the boat" in the past, and this is seen as a thing to be avoided.

Company culture plays a key role in determining whether to recruit MBAs. When a company with a hostile culture has recruited an MBA in the past, the predictable failure of the experiment has reinforced the prejudices. An ambitious MBA will rarely remain in a company which is slow-moving, old-fashioned, and scornful of the methods he has learned.

Salary demands of MBAs can cause problems, and some companies feel that, regardless of worth, paying high salaries to a few employees will alienate others.

A more detailed exploration will be made of the business schools and the MBA in the next chapter. For the present it is sufficient to observe that the relatively small number of business graduates, the market forces, and the hostility of much of British industry means that the MBA is not having the impact on management which might have been expected at the time of the Franks Report.

One would expect that, if the educational system does not provide the appropriate training for management, companies themselves would redress the balance through their own internal training programmes. That this is a false hope will be revealed in the next chapter. One reason why it is a false hope is that the educational system tends to reinforce the cultural heritage, and the overwhelming belief that experience is the only way to learn.

Learning by experience is essential. However, it is noteworthy that passing on the same lessons of experience ("this is the way we do things here") is a direct cause of the distorted perceptions of the strategic issues described in the previous chapter. This ignorance of strategic choice which pervades whole organisations is mirrored in functional knowledge. The Finniston report[3] (page 38) references a study by the Engineering Industry Training Board, which found that new techniques were often not used in companies, not because they were inappropriate, but because senior management was ignorant of them.

The sad fact is that British management in general is less well educated than that of its country competitors, and as we will see, for the most part will receive little or no training of any kind during a career of service. Cultural forces mean that many are scornful of the idea of training. This is the content of a subsequent chapter, and only after we have looked at the overall picture can we begin to focus in on the activities of some of the firms who do not fit the norm, and who by practical demonstration offer us some hope that the adverse patterns can be changed.

References

1. HMSO (1967): *A Report of the Central Advisory Council for Education (England)*, Vol. 1, ("Plowden Report")
2. Hudson Institute Europe (1974): *The United Kingdom in 1980*, Associated Business Press, page 82
3. HMSO (1980): *Report of the Committee of Enquiry into the Engineering Profession*, page 90
4. M. Sharp (ed.) (1985): *Europe and the New Technologies*, Frances Pinter, page 286.
5. M. J. Weiner (1981): *English Culture and the Decline of the Industrial Spirit*, Cambridge University Press
6. D. F. Cannon (1973): *The Strategy and Structure of British Enterprise*, Macmillan, page 44
7. T. Glynn Jones (1986): *A New Look at a Multi Nationals' Training Needs*, paper presented at the 1986 World Congress on Management Development.
8. R. A. Melcher and A. R. Schneider (1985): Europe's business schools are earning higher markets, *Business Week*, 16 September
9, K. A. Ascher (1983): *Masters of Business? The MBA and British Industry*, Harbridge House Europe
10. Government Statistical Service (1985): *Educational Statistics for the UK*, Table 34, page 40, note 4
11. HMSO (1962): (Robbins report)
12. HMSO (1963): (Franks Report)
13. HMSO (1970): *Management Education in the 1970s'* National Economic Development Office, page 7.

4
Management and the Educational Institutions

In Chapter 3 we looked at the general pattern of education in the UK, with the emphasis on higher education and particularly that offered by the business schools. There are many criticisms of the entire British educational system. Clare,[1] for example, argues convincingly that the 40 per cent of least able children are streamed for failure in today's schools, and on leaving are barely numerate or literate. He contrasts the UK experience with schools in Germany, where the least academically gifted are offered a vocational curriculum which fits them for the world of work, and through the enhanced motivation, also gains impressive academic results. Industry frequently criticises British schools for turning out pupils who are unprepared for work.

Cultural pressures have, as we have seen, led to a bias in our university system to "pure" as distinct from "applied" subjects, and polytechnics are still seen as second rate by many, partly because they *do* get their hands dirty on practical issues.

If we accept the lack of higher education among the UK's managers as serious, the most significant criticism of the system must be that insufficient graduates are getting into management. There may be many reasons for this, which include:

- insufficient opportunities for school-leavers to obtain higher education;
- lack of attractiveness of a management career in industry to many of those that do obtain degrees;
- lack of interest by many employers in recruiting graduates;
- "wrong" subjects offered at centres of higher education.

Insufficient opportunities for school-leavers to obtain higher education

Education Statistics for the UK[2] shows that 12 per cent of the population aged between 19 and 20 were able to undertake full-time or sandwich courses at a higher education establishment in the UK. Not all undertook degree

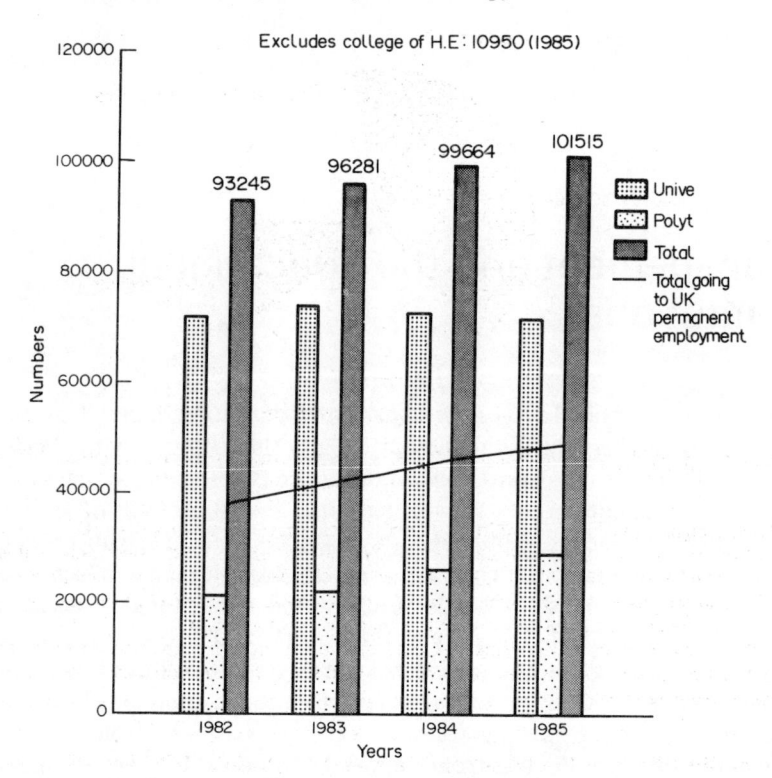

FIGURE 4.1. First degree graduates, university and polytechnics (*Source:* AGCAS)

courses, and of the 170,000 successful candidates in 1983/4, some 30,000 took diplomas and certificates, 100,000 first degrees, 11,000 higher diplomas and certificates and 23,000 higher degrees.

Figure 4.1 shows the trend in first degrees at universities and polytechnics. Only 49 per cent of graduates initially take up employment in the UK, although obviously most of the remainder do so at some time in the future.

Government action to control costs has had the effect of reducing the opportunities for school-leavers to attend universities. One by-product of this has been that standards of entry to higher education have risen, and many people who would have benefited from higher education have been shut out. Undoubtedly there is much waste of resources in the higher educational system, and this should be addressed. But at the same time if the proportion of graduates in British management is to be increased from the current 8 per cent, either more graduates must be produced or a higher proportion must be tempted into business.

Pearson[3] argues:

The next decade is likely to see a long term decline in the output of higher education due to the

Figure 4.2

First degree employment pie chart:
- Education 11.0%
- Public service 22.0%
- Other and unknown 10.0%
- Commerce 27.0%
- Industry 30.0%

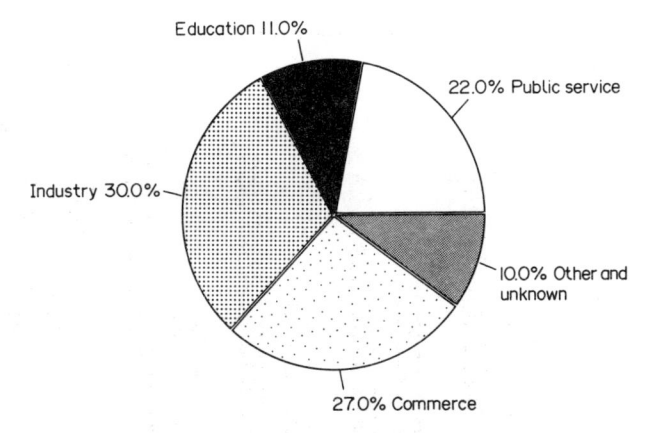

FIGURE 4.2. First degree employment, (54,932 graduates) (university, polytechnic, college of higher education) *Source:* AGCAS

cutback in higher education expenditure, expected to be reduced by up to two per cent per annum in real terms, and the 35 per cent decline in the number of 18-year-olds, the traditional entry group for higher education. The DES has argued that this decline will have a dramatic effect on the demand for places in higher education. Their assessment of the effect of this demographic trend on student demand can, however, be strongly criticised as unrealistic, in particular it does not take enough account of the rising demand from women and from mature students or of the potential demand for students from working class homes who represent only a tiny percentage of entrants to higher education.

The arguments of numbers of places and cost-effectiveness will be returned to later in this chapter, when attention will be directed at the MBA degree.

Lack of attractiveness of a management career to many of those that do obtain degrees

Figure 4.2 represents information already seen in Figure 3.2, from which it can be seen that only 57 per cent of first degree graduates initially move into industry and commerce. Public service still absorbs a high proportion of all graduates.

Not all of those who enter commerce and industry do so with management in hand. Many enter these employments as specialists and are not necessarily seeking a career in management. Figure 4.3 shows the broad employment categories of first degree students. At the time of writing, the more detailed statistical analyses were not available, but based on 1983/4 figures for polytechnics and universities it is possible to state that 37 per cent of those entering administration and operating management, 46 per cent of those going into buying, marketing and selling, and 58 per cent of those moving to financial work will have taken a degree in the administrative business and social studies grouping. These are not all management subjects, and include

FIGURE 4.3. First degrees 1984/5 – nature of permanent employment in the UK

	Administration and Operating Management	Scientific research design and development	Engineering research design and development	Scientific engineers support services	Environmental planning	Buying, marketing and selling	Management services	Financial work	Legal work	Information and library work	Personnel and Welfare	Teaching and lecturing	Creative and entertainment	Others	Total
Universities	3,159	1,716	4,318	879	1,148	2,667	2,852	6,394	131	675	7,569	1,290	739	1,762	35,309
Polytechnics	1,429	414	1,349	444	1,294	1,328	1,151	1,668	44	258	1,422	1,124	897	1,234	14,056
Colleges of further education	502	46	57	36	52	393	72	238	9	78	444	2,609	335	694	5,567
Total	5,090	2,186	5,724	1,359	2,494	4,388	4,075	8,300	184	1,011	9,435	5,023	1,971	3,690	54,932 (1)

The difference of 2 between the total figure and the total of each column is present in the published statistics.
Source: AGCAS

economics, geography, government, law, psychology and sociology, as well as business studies.

There is undoubtedly still some prejudice against business among many students. Equally, many firms have a reluctance to employ graduates.

Lack of interest by many employees in recruiting graduates

Not all firms seek new graduates as a matter of policy, and some are prejudiced against them. If the overall picture is that only 8 per cent of British managers have degrees, but a few large companies such as BP[4] have 80 per cent of their managers with degrees, it follows that many companies must have a very low proportion of graduates in management.

Unless the managers in such companies are particularly enlightened, they are likely to resent young graduates and be biased against them. This is even more likely when, as is the case in many companies, they themselves have received little or no management training during their own careers.

The only way to remove this prejudice is to change the outlook of the existing managers in the firm, through a programme of management development which removes the feelings of insecurity, and helps them to see that graduates can make a contribution.

The danger to these firms of denying themselves access to graduates is that they are closing the door on some of the brightest people in the population. As we have seen, many of the degree subjects are not directly related to a career in management, although some of the other subjects such as engineering are of prime importance to industry. The fact that a degree is educational, in the widest sense of the word, rather than vocational, does not mean that the person who possesses it is unsuitable for a career in management. To argue this way is to deny the real benefit that companies such as BP have attained by ensuring that they go for the best brains available.

"Wrong" subjects offered at centres of higher education

It is always easy to criticise a university or similar body for teaching the wrong thing, since there will always be areas of shortage. In Chapter 3 we discussed the cultural bias towards certain subjects, and there is no need to repeat this.

Currently there is a shortage of IT graduates. Is this the fault of the universities? To avoid such a shortage requires that it be forecast many years in advance, and even that may not solve the problem. Even if places are provided, they will only be filled if the secondary schools can turn out sufficient science and mathematics students to take them up.

The business schools

The business schools should be a leading force in providing qualified people for a career in management. In Chapter 3 we looked at the relatively small numbers of graduates produced annually, compared to the aims of the Franks Report, and at attitudes in British business towards the recruitment of MBAs. Ascher[5] states:

> Some have argued that people with MBAs are overambitious and overtly aggressive, often relying on theoretical rather than practical approaches to problems, and thus provide a source of friction within the managerial ranks of large corporations. Others maintain that the problem is one of tailoring business education to meet the needs of British industry, and suggest that the business schools are not providing the appropriate training for effective performance in the UK commercial environment. British business schools have, until recently, disagreed with these two diagnoses of the problem. Not all will admit that integration difficulties exist, but those that recognise them tend to point the finger of blame at British industry in general. They have suggested, both privately and publicly, that British companies are too traditional and conservative, and that it is their resistance to change which has made it difficult to adapt both to business graduates and to changes in the economic climate.

Until recently criticisms of the business schools have come from outside, and have hardly disturbed the cosy atmosphere that exists in the business schools. The paper by Griffiths and Murray,[6] which made a case for privatising the business schools, was unique in that the critics came from inside the schools.

The Harbridge House research[3] provided information about those who take the MBA and some of their views of their courses.

The MBA students

As indicated in the previous chapter, MBA programmes at the various UK business schools vary in terms of both structure and orientation. Similar differences exist among students undertaking the MBA course. Those who think of MBAs as a homogeneous commodity are clearly mistaken.

Our research enables us to provide a great deal of information about MBA students. First we give an overview of the types of students completing courses at the major UK institutions, based on information supplied by the schools. After that we look more closely at the experience, motivations and attitudes of students at four particular schools. Data for this section come from student responses to a questionnaire sent out earlier this summer.

UK graduates: background information

Any accurate portrait of the business school population in Britain requires significant input from the schools themselves. Although a number of schools were eager to help us, many others were reluctant to release information. We have compensated for major gaps in some schools' figures by using their primary data and biography books, but other schools have had to be omitted.

Not one of the British schools that require the GMAT entrance test would release a recent class average GMAT score.* This is traditionally one of the

---

* Two schools publish the general "range" of most scores, but these figures are not suitable for comparison.

TABLE 4.1. *Most frequent age at entry*

Younger (under 25 years)	Mixed (25–28 years)	Older (over 28)
Bradford	Lancaster	Aston
City	Warwick	Cranfield
Imperial	London	Glasgow
Edinburgh	Durham	Henley
Manchester		Strathclyde

best indicators of student ability, and we had hoped that it could be used to evaluate the frequent comments that British "business school students are second-rate". Defensive attitudes on the part of the UK schools contrasted sharply with the willingness of both American and European schools to produce this information.

The major British business schools produced approximately 1500 MBAs in 1984. Class sizes varied from 150 to two or three individuals. Fluctuations in class numbers over recent years have been small, with some schools showing slight growth and others remaining the same.

Most of the students who enter the MBA course are in their late 20s, and have had at least a few years of work experience. The range of ages in any one course, however, can be considerable; Aston and Edinburgh, for example, reported that their MBA class ranged in age from 21 to 47. Certain schools make work experience a condition for entry, and therefore tend to attract older graduates.

The "average age" of an MBA class is a figure often quoted by business schools, and generally refers to their mean age at graduation from the schools. This figure is in many cases a poor indicator of the ages of most students, as a few students in their late 30s tend to distort the average.

The same data problem exists with quoted levels of class work experience; averages are deceptive when a few students are significantly more mature than the majority of others. For example, at the time of the survey, Edinburgh's MBA class work experience averaged 3 years, although 45 per cent of the class had no work experience at all!

We have interpreted school statistics and raw data on individual MBA students to emerge with a rough classification of UK business schools in terms of student age. Younger students are more frequently found at schools in the grouping on the left of Table 4.1[1] and older ones at schools listed on the right.

British schools compare favourably with American schools in terms of student age and experience. The typical business school student in the UK might enter business school at age 26 with 3 years' work experience and graduate at 27; his or her American counterpart might enter a 2-year course at age 25 with the same amount of experience and graduate at 27. Pan-

TABLE 4.2. *Full-time MBA: class of 1983*

	No. of students	Percentage women	Percentage overseas students	Mean age (years)	No of Years[a] work experience
Aston	63	13	48	29.0	3
Bradford	115	19	28	26.6	0–1
City	142	30	38	27.2	2–5
Cranfield	153	11	21	30.0	7½
Durham	40[b]	32	48	26.0	2–5
Edinburgh	45[c]	20	47	n.a.	0–3
Imperial	80	30	44	n.a.	0–2
LBS	97	22	34	27.0	2–5
MBS	72	18	10	26.8	0–5
INSEAD	280	15	n.a.	28.0	2–5
Harvard	785	25	17	27.0	3½

[a] Most frequently quoted figures, except Aston, Cranfield and Harvard which reported average figures.
[b] 34 are full-time students.
[c] Number includes diploma students.
Source: School statistics.

European schools such as INSEAD and IMEDE attract slightly older students with closer to 5 years' work experience. A profile of the graduating class at 11 major business schools can be found in Table 4.2.

Numbers of overseas students are fairly significant on all MBA courses. At Aston, Durham and Edinburgh, foreign students account for close to half of the student population. Many of these individuals have completed a first degree at a UK university. It is likely that roughly one-quarter of all MBA graduates were born and brought up overseas.

British schools are presently trying hard to recruit more women into their programmes. About 1 in 5 MBA students (20 per cent) in the UK are women, although this proportion varies widely. At Durham and City Business Schools, women account for more than 30 per cent of the class, while at Cranfield they constitute only 11 per cent. American schools have had more success in attracting women; between one-fourth and one-third of American MBA students today are women.

Most students who undertake the MBA course have a graduate degree; indeed it is a requirement for entry at a number of schools. Overall, roughly 80 per cent have a recognised college degree; another 15–20 per cent may have a professional qualification in place of, or in addition to, a degree.

Most MBA students have obtained their first degree from a UK university, although the percentage of foreign degrees is high. A great number of students have completed degrees in engineering; social science and business studies are also frequent undergraduate concentrations. The proportion of Oxbridge graduates is significant only at LBS (16 per cent) and MBS (19 per cent). These business schools tend to have few candidates with professional qualifications; nearly all have completed a first degree. Table 4.3 gives data on the educational background of candidates at schools.

A number of both foreign and UK residents are sponsored to do the MBA course by their own organisation or their government. Sponsorship runs as high as 80 per cent at a school such as Henley, which incorporates work for the sponsoring organisation into its programme. Usually the figure is much lower, ranging from about 5 per cent at LBS and MBS to about 16 per cent at the City business school. Those companies that sponsor candidates expect the graduate to return to work within the organisation when the course is completed.

Surveyed students: four schools

Harbridge House felt that the experience and opinions of MBA students could offer valuable insight into the courses on offer. Our survey looked only at the attitudes and opinions of those students who would expect to receive the MBA or equivalent degree in 1984.

We selected four schools which provided a diversity of both people and course structure. Two schools, Manchester and Bradford, are located in the north of England; one in the Midlands (Aston) and one in London (London). Manchester and London run 2-year Masters programmes; Aston and Bradford courses are only 12 months in length.

We sent out approximately 315 questionnaires to these four schools and received 126 replies, which represents a response rate of 40 per cent. This was surprisingly high for this sort of survey, and even more unusual for one conducted during the run-up to final exams. A fairly even response rate across schools has resulted in what we feel to be a representative sample.

The students were asked to provide background information on themselves and their reasons for undertaking an MBA degree. We also asked them specific questions about the course, the school, and their prospective future in industry. The answers to these questions were both comprehensive and thought-provoking.

The information set out in the following pages comes directly from these 126 responses. It does not reflect the opinions of all the MBAs in the UK, nor does it necessarily reflect the opinions of all candidates at the chosen school. It is likely, however, that many views expressed here are widely held.

(a) Background

Our sample population seemed to be fairly representative of all MBAs in terms of age and background. Of the 126 respondents, 20 (16 per cent) were female. The great majority of both men and women fell between the ages of 25 and 35. A breakdown of our sample population by age and school is shown

TABLE 4.3. *Educational background of MBAs (1983)*

	Percentage with degrees	Oxbridge	Other UK university	UK polytechnic	Foreign university	Main subject	Second subject
Aston	62	—	34	47	19	Business/accounting	Maths/sciences
Bradford	88	3	69	15	13	Social sciences	—
City	88	8	63	19	10	Social sciences	Business studies
Cranfield	82	8	51	25	16	Accounting	Engineering
Durham	71	—	—	—	—	Science/engineering	Humanities
Imperial	—	4	62	10	24	Engineering	Maths/statistics/computer science
LBS	97	16	57	2	25	Social sciences	Engineering and technology
MBS	—	19	68	10	3	Natural sciences/engineering	Social sciences/humanities

Degree-granting institutions (percentage of those with degrees)

Source: Various school publications

TABLE 4.4. *Surveyed students: age and school*

	Aston	Bradford	LBS	MBS
Under 25	7	10	2	11
25–35	15	19	30	19
35+	6	2	2	3
Total	28	31	34	33

TABLE 4.5. *Surveyed graduates: educational background*

	Business school			
First degree origin	Aston	Bradford	LBS	Manchester
Oxbridge	–	2	9	10
The UK universities	15	21	16	20
Polytechnics	2	4	–	2
Foreign universities	4	1	9	1
No degree	7	3	–	–
Total	28	31	34	33

in Table 4.4. Most of our sample group had completed a few years of full-time work before undertaking the course. About half of our sample (49 per cent) had worked for over 5 years; many had at least 10 years of experience. Manchester proved the youngest group – 27 per cent of the sample had no work experience. Aston students were significantly older; almost half of all respondents had worked for at least 10 years before business school.

Most respondents held a first degree from a UK university. The educational background of these graduates is shown in Table 4.5. Our sample clearly reflects the absence of those without first degrees from LBS and MBS, and the tendency for both Aston and LBS to accept a relatively high proportion of foreign students. It should be noted that the response rate was slightly higher than average from Oxbridge graduates, and slightly lower than average from foreign students.

Surveyed MBA students displayed a wide range of backgrounds. Social and natural science degrees were most common, although Aston and Bradford had very high percentages of graduates in business and the arts, respectively. It is interesting to note that the percentage of people with a financial background was lowest at the school that is considered strongest in finance – LBS.

Just under one-third of the sample group had some sort of professional qualification. About 30 per cent of our Aston respondents held some form of financial or accounting qualification, while 12 per cent of the London students held engineering qualifications.

TABLE 4.6. *Surveyed graduates: primary reasons for undertaking an MBA (percentages)*

Primary Reason	Aston	Bradford	LBS	MBS
Improve job opportunities	36	50	31	50
Change career direction	18	34	29	24
More money	7	3	5	3
Obtain general business education	11	–	14	13
Intellectual stimulation	7	–	7	3
Increase self-confidence	4	3	7	–
Others	17	10	7	7
Total	100	100	100	100

(b) Motivations

The overwhelming majority of business students surveyed undertook the MBA course with a mind to improving job opportunities. This was cited as the foremost motive among respondents of all ages at Aston, Bradford and Manchester. London's 25–35-year-old age group indicated that a change in career direction had been the most pressing reason for undertaking the course. The main motives for enrolling in an MBA programme are noted in Table 4.6. The overwhelming reasons are those concerned with career improvements: more money, increased job opportunities, and a change in career direction. Personal reasons are such as intellectual stimulation or increasing self-confidence were very often secondary considerations.

Most respondents indicated that either the reputation of their school or its geographical location were key factors in their selection process. One-third of the students from Bradford, Aston and Manchester mentioned the course structure as a key factor in their choice of school.

(c) The academic experience

Most of the curent students felt that the programme had lived up to, and in certain cases, exceeded, their expectations. This did not, however, prevent them from suggesting course improvements. The most frequent comments about each school are summarised below.

Aston An unusually high percentage of students at Aston were unhappy with the course for one reason or another. Many felt that the 'selection criteria' for student admissions were inadequate and/or indiscriminate. Others stated that financial pressures on the school resulted in exceedingly large classes. There was a strong feeling that people without work experience should not have been allowed on the course.

The course itself was not stimulating or satisfying for many students. It was felt to be too broadly based, giving a shallow picture of a wide range of topics; many felt that a more focused or longer course would have been preferable. Some indicated that the school had adopted "flow-line techniques" in passing students, and that more rigorous assessment was needed.

Bradford Although Bradford students felt that the 1-year course was the ideal length, they also indicated the need for greater focus. It is interesting to note that Bradford was the only school whose students felt that both faculty and administration were outstanding.

Half of our respondents were disappointed by the intellectual abilities of their fellow-students. Like the Aston students they felt that all candidates should have a few years of work experience before entering the course. Many mentioned that assessment on the course was poor. The most serious comments from Bradford students concerned their difficulties in finding a job after the course. They reported that most interviewers were more impressed by their previous work experience record than their performance on the course, and that "some interviewers did not know what an MBA was". A large number of students felt that it was the school's responsibility to improve the marketing of its students to industry, and that increasing contact with the "real world" would be a step in that direction.

London The same feeling was expressed by recent graduates of the London Business School. They stated that more contact with "management practitioners" was desirable. It many cases academic tutors were criticised for their lack of ability or devotion to the course.

Although there was no doubt that students felt the course to be a challenge, they were critical of the method and frequency of assessment. Most felt that more careful grading was needed to distinguish deserving candidates. A number of students felt that grades and marks were somewhat random.

The most frequent concern mentioned by students was the heavy emphasis placed on finance and financial analysis. One student noted that LBS had prepared him for a "sacrifice to the God of money and exorbitant salaries". A number of students felt that manufacturing did not get sufficient attention.

Manchester Comments from Manchester and London students were very similar. Students at each school felt that "the course was not intellectually difficult, but very hard work". Both groups said that more emphasis needed to be directed at non-financial topics, and that contacts with industry should be strengthened. There was some feeling at both schools that the course is becoming increasingly orientated towards younger students.

Some Manchester students reported that the first year of the course was slightly congested and disjointed, but that the second-year project work was excellent. Many felt that opportunities to specialise should be increased, and that course assessment could be improved.

The preceding paragraphs indicate that students at different schools made many of the same comments. A number of these are highlighted below.

- Students at all four schools felt that the methods of selection and/or assessment of students were inadequate. In many cases, respondents stated that young and inexperienced students held up class progress. Others felt that course grading and exam structures did not sufficiently "discriminate the strong from the weak".
- Students of both 1- and 2-year programmes indicated that they would have liked more of a chance to specialise. Many felt that they had gained only a shallow understanding of a wide range of topics.
- A large percentage of students felt that they would like to see the business schools build more serious relationships with industry. They felt that the outside research activities of the tutors did not always keep them sufficiently in touch with "the real world", and that increasing use should be made of visiting lecturers from industry.
- Reaction to the course was in all cases very personal. Opinions very much reflected individual expectations and desires. In many cases the value of the MBA course to the individual was based on factors external to the course: what he or she was doing prior to it, what sort of job opportunities had been created by it, and how well he or she related to other students on the course.
- At all schools interviewed, a majority of students felt that some (but not all) of the skills learned at business school would be useful in their next job. A minority of older Aston respondents felt that few skills would be applicable.

The vast majority of the students did feel that they had made a wise decision in enrolling in the programme. Most felt that the course had been worthwhile for its contribution to their own personal development, and enjoyed the chance to interact with their peer group.

(d) Future employment

An overwhelming majority of non-sponsored respondents were going to new employers after finishing the course; just under 10 per cent intended to start their own business. Most of the students felt that the MBA course had increased their job opportunities significantly; this may explain why many who were critical of the course were not sorry they had undertaken it.

Two-thirds of the students at London, Manchester and Aston felt that their next employer would value the MBA qualification, while only 45 per cent of Bradford's students were convinced that their degree would be favourably received. Difficulties in finding jobs during the recruitment process came as a shock to many Bradford graduates.

Most MBA students felt that completion of the degree course had given them additional earning power. This did not, however, mean that finding a job was easy. Many students competed for jobs against members of their own or other graduating classes.

There is a unanimous feeling among business students from all four schools that British companies rarely understand or appreciate the MBA.

It signifies America, brash arrogance and salary profiteering (LBS student).

British industry is obsessed with superiority. To add fuel to fire, they are sceptical of MBAs. When the whole house is on fire, don't ask where the fire started (Aston student).

Companies prefer the "university of life" (Bradford student).

Companies view it as an unsuitable US panacea to UK problems (Manchester student).

An overwhelming majority of students stated that work experience was rated much more highly than the fact that they had completed the course. This lack of concern for educational qualifications by employers has been discussed elsewhere.

Conclusions of the Harbridge House study

The findings of the Harbridge House study, parts of which have been reported in this and the previous chapter, are followed by suggestions for improvement.

(a) The situation

British business schools have not expanded as rapidly as had been hoped. The Franks Report envisaged the business schools producing 2000 students annually by the late 1970s; they are only now approaching this target. Nevertheless, they have established a reasonably secure position in the field of management education. Full-time class numbers at the older schools remain stable, and incremental growth in the number of annual MBA graduates expected can be due to the expansion of part-time courses.

By and large, these schools promote the cult of the generalist, and indeed attract many students hoping to move out of specialist areas. The courses are broadly based and rely to varying extents on theoretical approaches to management practice. Much effort has been spent on removing the "American orientation" from those courses criticised in the 1970s for their indifference to the British and European context of business.

The percentage of business students who take a significant interest in the content of an MBA course prior to beginning it is small. Most students enroll out of a desire to increase job opportunities and achieve higher salaries. Business schools seem to recognise, accept and often encourage this behaviour.

The extent to which the students enjoy the course varies according to individual needs and preferences. The great majority of them are glad they have invested the time and money in it, although they admit that the opportunity cost involved in undertaking the course was extremely low. Most who regret their decision were dissatisfied with their particular school, and feel that an American MBA course would have been more worthwhile.

It is possible that many students' views on the utility of the course have been coloured by their experiences during the company recruitment and placement process. Some felt that the course had succeeded in making them a more attractive candidate, and received good job and salary offers. Others found that many companies were not interested in their degree, and felt that past work experience alone had helped them find a job.

Our interviews with companies indicate that the sentiments of both groups of MBAs are justified. Some companies see the MBA as something of a prerequisite for entry and recruit *only* at the business schools. Others have no interest in the MBA, and feel that an individual's background, personality and work experience are the best indicators of future performance.

Those companies that value the MBA do so highly, and offer outstanding salary packages. A high proportion of these firms are American by origin, and have carefully maintained the American tradition of paying a premium for MBAs. Top candidates from top schools compete against one another to land these jobs.

The remaining graduates are faced with British companies that are largely apathetic to their degree. There are exceptions, of course; each year a number of new companies try recruiting from the schools. But the number of graduates they need is small, and the majority of non-sponsored MBAs are left to both locate employers and convince them of their individual worth.

Nearly all of the students will have found a job within 6 months of graduating. Many, however, find that the environment in this job is not stimulating enough, and leave. Those joining dynamic firms with reasonably large MBA populations and fast promotion prospects tend to stay with their first postgraduate job a reasonably long period of time.

This results in a fairly heavy concentration of MBAs in certain industries, and very low MBA representation in others. Those firms who have experienced success with MBAs are increasingly committed to recruitment, while others who cannot retain the MBA graduates lose interest in the busines schools.

(b) Alternative diagnoses

One question that needs to be asked is whether the situation described above is in any way problematic. Does the mismatch between the goals and expectations of graduates and those of certain sectors of British industry really matter? Before presenting our own opinion, we document the feelings of the schools, the companies, and the students on this matter.

(c) Business schools

The business schools are pleased with the success of their MBA programmes. All of the schools have more applications than they do places; their only worry is finding competent staff. Some schools feel that the high salaries being paid by American banks and consulting firms attest to the value of their programme; others look upon continuous sponsorship or recruitment by a group of companies as a seal of approval. All are quick to point out the high ratios of students who find jobs soon after graduating.

Many business schools administrators state publicly that the relationship between themselves, their students and British industry is healthy. The fact that some companies do not utilise their service is attributed to a traditional and conservative British management's reluctance to change. They point out that the schools were intended to stimulate change, and that nobody ever imagined the change would come easily.

The fact that many people feel that business school courses do not reflect the needs of industry is not of great worry to many school personnel. Some schools say that they are preparing managers for tomorrow, not today, and that they can see the future needs of UK industry more clearly than profit-oriented companies. Others feel that their role is indeed one of reacting to industry, and that they are doing just that.

(d) Companies

A majority of companies would probably agree with the schools that the current relationship between themselves and the MBA graduates is adequate and little change is needed. To understand this, it is again necessary to consider the two different schools of thought about MBA programmes.

Those companies that recruit heavily from UK business schools are pleased with the programmes and the graduates. For them, the business schools provide a unique and highly valued source of young talent. Particular biases on individual courses often reflect their own internal biases.

Companies that have little contact with the schools and do not recruit there accept that these biases exist. The most traditional among them look upon MBA programmes as a training ground for graduates desiring a career in finance or consultancy, and are indifferent to the schools' existence. They feel that their own training needs are better met by technical institutes or in-house programmes.

Not all companies follow either of the above models; many rely on an occasional graduate to fill a specific post. A significant number of these companies said that they are interested in the individual, and not the degree, and that the whole issue of MBA usage was not relevant to their situation.

e) The students

Students are the only group that clearly recognise at least some of the dimensions of the problem. They are not at all content with the fact that the financial sector and a small number of forward-looking companies are eager to recruit them. Most feel that awareness and acceptance of the MBA has grown, but at much too slow a pace. Their feelings are that the complacency which both the schools and industry display toward the future of management education is dangerous.

Although some had experienced considerable success during the recruitment process, nearly all respondents reported that mainstream British industry does not yet fully appreciate the value of an MBA degree. They stated that awareness and understanding of the degree was limited to certain sectors of industry. Many companies do not trust MBAs; these firms are suspicious of non-technical qualifications and afraid that the graduates will not fit into a tightly structured organisation.

A few students accepted that some of the hostility from industry was of their own making. The award for humility goes to LBS students, many of whom saw more than one side to the issue: "Many MBAs believe that they can cure a company's ills on Day 1 between coffee and lunch. This immaturity reflects on the MBA rather than the person, and the degree suffers as a result." A high percentage of students felt that industry's outlook was partly a result of poor marketing efforts on the part of the schools. They stated categorically that the task of educating industry about the MBA course and student was the responsibility of the school. Marketing, in their view, is all about preparing both companies and graduates for a future together.

An objective assessment

It is sad that the biases of each of these groups – the schools, the companies and the students – are so obviously reflected in their assessments of the current situation. Indeed, the whole issue of MBA graduates and programmes is clothed in a suit of prejudice on the part of both individuals and institutions. Attitudes of students and schools towards industry, and those of industry towards MBA graduates and programmes, are often naive and poorly informed.

Many companies have made only futile attempts to make use of business school graduates. Some who had recruited one or two graduates 10–15 years ago found that they left the firm, and have never considered recruiting again. Others participated in a milk round at a few schools many years ago, did not like what they saw, and have never returned.

Business schools appeared equally culpable when it came to maintaining contact with companies. Some firms resent the fact that business schools claim to cater for British industry, when all the company ever receives is a glossy brochure through the post. Public relations on the part of the business schools received poor marks by many surveyed companies. All agreed that the schools should be more interested in their opinions and educational needs.

Students must also bear some of the blame for the present situation. Not all students appreciate British industry in the way they would like British industry to appreciate them; few have any interest in fields such as retailing or pharmaceuticals. Their expectations are often out of line with their own abilities and many are motivated solely by prospects of financial gain. As one MBA stated, "Most MBAs are seduced by City salaries and industry has no chance to learn what they are."

We would suggest that the blame for the mismatch between student expectations and those of many British companies cannot be laid on any one group; the behaviour of both individuals and organisations has reflected equal levels of self-interest. The real reasons why industry does not fully appreciate MBAs are complex, and involve company, student, and business school behaviour. Some of the underlying factors contributing to the present situation are summarised below.

- *The role of the MBA programme is unclear.* No one is sure if it should reflect the needs of its students, the needs of local or national industry, or the needs of future British management. Against what criteria can present programmes be evaluated?
- *Many business schools have fairly complacent attitudes towards their MBA course and students.* Marketing efforts are said to be poor, with more attention being paid to executive development courses. Does this mean that the same group of companies will continue to recruit from the schools year after year?
- *There is evidence that admission performance criteria at some business schools are loose.* Both students and companies feel that many MBA students are "2.2 candidates who went to business school to boost their record". What does this say about the calibre of MBAs being produced?
- *Increasing proportions of graduates are going into finance and consulting industries.* There is general agreement that MBAs remain alienated from many sectors of British industry. Is the MBA becoming more of a specialist degree for finance and strategy training?
- *Salary considerations play the largest part in determining where business graduates find jobs.* The salary differentials between industries are significant and an obstacle to wider recruitment. Is this free market approach likely to provide the most effective long-term solution to British management problems?

- *Many MBA graduates have extremely high expectations.* It is not clear that these expectations are really in line with their abilities or background. How frequently are these expectations met and what happens when they are not?
- *Many companies view MBAs as a homogeneous product.* The differences between a 22-year-old social scientist and a 38-year-old engineer far exceed their educational similarities. Are companies who recruit only MBAs and those who refuse to recruit any missing out on valuable sources of talent?
- *Not all companies desire clever and ambitious people.* Many companies feel that the nature of their business or organisation requires more low-key individuals. Is this really the case or is it simply a result of a devotion to process or tradition?
- *The increasing number of courses has led to a continuous growth in the MBA population.* Many different types of people are now attracted to a variety of full- and part-time MBA courses. How will this affect the content of the course and the attitudes of companies to MBA graduates?
- *Recruitment patterns across companies have changed little over the past decade.* Most large companies made a decision about MBA recruitment within the first 10 years of the schools' existence, and have stood behind it since then. Will the present reviews of recruitment lead to significant changes in policies?
- *There is no consensus as to the value of an MBA degree.* Some say it can increase self-confidence and business awareness; others feel that it is not possible to *learn* to be a good manager. Would today's successful industrialists have been more successful had they done an MBA course? Would there be more of them?

As noted earlier, not everyone would agree that the issues listed above deserve special attention. Many business school administrators feel that the present situation presents no cause for worry. Some look upon graduage placement patterns as an exercise in free market economics: excess demand for graduates has boosted their price, so that only those industries that really *need* the MBAs now pay to recruit them.

It is a fallacy, however, to think that only the large multinationals need, or indeed want, MBAs. These companies are likely to survive irrespective of graduate recruitment; it is the smaller national businesses, not always aware of MBA programme offerings, to whom future talent is most critical. Human resources are a unique commodity whose value is not always fully appreciated in the context of traditional economic theory.

The *laissez-faire* attitude which many business schools and companies have exhibited can only continue to aggravate the present situation. If some thought is not given to the major issues, the business schools and their MBA courses will increasingly be seen as training houses for US-based finance, consulting and manufacturing companies. This is not at all what the Franks Report had in mind when it recommended business schools for Britain.

The Griffiths and Murray Report

The Griffiths and Murray Report[6] suggested privatisation of the business schools as a means of curing the ills of the system, which they see as a failure to produce enough MBAs annually, and having a product which does not match the needs of business. Manley,[8] in an article defending the present system, summarised the argument: "The second system of malaise which Griffiths and Murray identify, and which is in itself, in part, an explanation of the first (low output) is that business schools are not supplying through their teaching the product which the market requires." MBA courses are, they suggest, too "academic" in content, and are taught by people divorced and sheltered from the rigours and entrepreneurial realities of business life and who, through institutional pressures within universities, channel their efforts into research rather than into teaching. In short, business schools are not producing the "right" product in the "right" quantities.

Griffiths and Murray believe that the business schools, because of public funding, have developed an ethos which encourages neither entrepreneurial activity or risk-taking. The argument is that exposure to free market forces would solve all these problems.

Some of the points of criticism were researched by the Business Graduates Association[9] among its members who are all in sympathy with the general aims of business schools. The sample was small (93), and the views are therefore not capable of precise statistical statement. Among the general findings were:

- A large majority believes that business schools should receive taxpayers' support.
- Most felt that tenured employment should be reduced.
- An overwhelming majority believed that the relationship between business schools and business was too distant.
- A small majority believed that courses were too academic.
- There was support for the Griffiths and Murray contention that the distate for the market place shown by British universities was a cause of the UK's relative decline.

There is also a post-experience educational role of the business schools, which at the London Business School, for example, amounts to 40 per cent of activity.[10] Part of this activity relates to open programmes for senior managers, and potentially this is one way to help redress the lack of academic training of British managers. Most business schools have also now moved into the closed programme, dedicated to a particular client. This is a generator of income for the business schools, but the question should be raised whether it is not also a diversion of effort away from the main task of increasing the quality and quantity of MBAs.

Accreditation

A current move by business schools to extend their activities and to get closer to industry is to give credit for internal training within a firm against the requirements of a part-time or distance learning MBA. The thinking goes a step further, in that the curriculum of the MBA may be modified to reflect the needs of the particular firm.

There is a lot that appeals in this line of thought, provided that it is not used as a Trojan horse to enable the business schools to take over the design and teaching of these internal company courses. Once this happens, switching costs could become very high for the company, making a change of vendor next to impossible.

It should also be recognised that this move is likely to be of value to that minority of managers who are willing to spend the considerable amount of personal time and effort needed to complete the course of study. The vast majority of managers would be untouched by such an initiative.

Much more remains to be done if management training is to be used as a competitive weapon, and accreditation will only scratch the surface.

Some issues we need to face

Whether the Griffiths and Murray argument is correct, and that privatisation would solve the ills of business schools, is a matter for conjecture. What is easier to specify is some of the things that need to be done to enable business schools to contribute more to the development of British enterprise.

- The number of establishments giving an MBA should be reduced to four or five centres of excellence. Note that the major US business schools have 5000 graduates per annum each, many more times the total from all UK sources.
- There should be an increase in the number of MBA graduates to around 10,000 per year. This would have the two-fold effect of creating a critical mass of more qualified managers in industry, while the increased supply would reduce the premium gained by those fortunate few who do complete an MBA. The extremes of salary paid to a proportion of the current graduates can hardly be in the public interest, and set a gulf between graduates and much of British industry.
- Salaries in business school faculties should be increased to commercial levels, but in return they should drop most of their sources of private income, particularly consultancy and teaching. It is hard to deny the conflict of interest that must occur between the corporate activities of a business school and the personal work of a faculty member. Any private work of this kind should be channelled through the business school.
- More effort should be made to attract faculty members out of industry, which would become a more realistic option were pay scales realistic.

- More information should be published about the activities and results of the business schools.

The business schools could be a great force to raise the competitiveness of British industry. Currently their potential is not being realised. In the immediate future there is unlikely to be any real improvement in the contribution that business schools can make. This means that business will have to find its own solutions to improving management performance.

References

1. Clare (1986): Streamed for failure in the name of equality and socialism. *Listener,* 5 June
2. Government Statistical Service (1985): *Educational Statistics for the UK,* 1985 edition, page iv
3. R. Pearson (1986): *Graduate Supply and Availability to 1987 and Beyond,* Institute of Manpower Studies report No. 114, page 8.
4. T. Glynn Jones (1986): *A New Look at a Multi-national's Training Needs,* 1986 World Congress on Management Development
5. K. Ascher (1986): Mastering the Business Graduate: *Personnel Management,* January.
6. R. Griffiths and H. Murray (1985): *Whose Business?* Institute of Economic affairs
7. K. Ascher (1983): *Masters of Business? The MBA and British Industry,* Harbridge House Europe
8. P. Manley (1986): Why public is preferable, *Transitions,* March
9. B. Lloyd (1986): *Whose Business?* Business Graduates Association
10. P. Moore (1986): Learning the B-school lessons, *Management Today,* May

5

Management Training in British Industry

General training practice

At a rough estimate there are two million people in management positions; the vast majority of them probably never receive any training at all.[1]

The story of management training in British industry can be summarised as inadequate resources ineffectively managed, and with most effort being devoted to the wrong things. The fault is rarely that of those who perform the training function in industry: it is with senior and top management who give little or no attention to the activity. If there is one area where amateurism prevails more than in any other it is in the management of training. There are exceptions, about some of which more will be said in later chapters.

Perhaps at this stage we should give some thought to the meanings of the terms management training, management education and management development. Peel[2] suggested two definitions of management education and management training. One was that long courses were education, short ones were training. The other was that education is to improve knowledge, training to improve skills. Rather than try to find the point where training becomes education I will use the words synonymously for the purpose of this book. If there is a difference for me it is that management education signifies breadth, and management training suggests depth. Certainly I would regard attendance at an MBA programme as management education, but beyond the clear examples of this sort I find so much blurred ground that it really does not seem worth the effort to try to separate the meanings.

Management development is a term that is wider than training and education, and would include ways of developing people in addition to these: for example, reading, job rotation, projects and other ways of trying to bring in the dimension of learning by experience in a managed way, rather than just assuming it will happen.

Before turning to some of the survey evidence on management training in the UK, we should examine evidence of the neglect of training overall. This is partly because management training is part of the overall training activity, and attitudes to training are likely to be similar whatever the nature of that training. It is also because there are blurred edges between management and certain other forms of training.

The Finniston report[3] commented on the failure of many employers to provide training for engineers, despite their bemoaning the fact that formal academic training was not producing people with the skills they required.

Much of the evidence submitted to us, and our own surveys, suggested that the quality of formal training obtained by engineers has progressively diminished over the last 20 years. The part-time route to qualification has declined markedly, and now provides only a fraction of past numbers. As far as graduates are concerned, their structured formation all too often ceases when they begin work. The Industrial Training Act established a number of Industrial Training Boards, part of whose remit extended to encouraging the provision of training to graduate engineers within industry. Their impact has been limited: for example the Engineering Industry Training Board reported that only 30 per cent of graduates from full-time courses – or 50 per cent of total graduates when sandwich course students are included – entering industries within their scope received training to their standards. Only a minority of those questioned in our survey of young graduate engineers stated that they had received formal training after graduation specifically for their first professional post. Many graduate recruits are 'thrown in at the deep end' without further training, almost always in technical jobs where their university experience is notionally relevant, on the principle that 'cream will rise to the top'. In fact the cream is often the first to get frustrated for want of encouragement and opportunities to develop their capabilities.

The Manpower Services Commission and the National Economic Development Office have jointly published a report commissioned from consultants Coopers and Lybrand Associates Ltd.[4] This examined the state of training within British industry, and found a disturbing state of ignorance and complacency. Compared with Germany, Japan and the USA, the UK companies provide considerably less training for their employees. Few companies perceive any link between training and competitive success and most, while agreeing that Britain did undertrain compared to other countries, thought that the amount of training they were doing was about right. At the same time few had any specific international comparisons to guide this belief, and indeed few had made any comparisons with other UK competitors. The report[4] argued: "This lack of concern might be regarded as reflecting confidence; we think it would be more realistic to regard it as reflecting complacency" (page 4).

Few British companies make training a board-room matter. The report suggested that management development was sometimes an exception, although our own research, which will be discussed later in this chapter, indicates that many such exceptions are more illusory than real.

Although many employers complained that the educational system does not prepare children adequately for the world of work, this did not stimulate any action to remedy the situation when school-leavers joined the firm.

In the USA a great deal of pressure to be better trained comes from the employee himself. This drive for self-improvement is largely absent in the UK, partly for cultural reasons, partly because few companies actively encourage their employees to train in their own time, or reimburse fees for such courses, and partly because few companies increase salary as a result of qualifications gained.

One of the things that gives me hope is the knowledge that not every individual is apathetic. Many do enroll in evening classes, correspondence courses, and part-time degrees, whether for self-satisfaction or career development. Chapter 13 deals with advances in distance/open learning which enables such self-improvement to spread to a wider number of people.

The Coopers and Lybrand report[4] drew attention (page 11) to the realisation of many employers that traditional apprenticeships which train for a single craft or skill are an anachronism in relation to modern industry's needs. This is one particular problem that is an industrial relations minefield, and requires management and trade union co-operation if a new system is to be developed.

Management education and training practice

The complacency Coopers and Lybrand found over training in general was mirrored in our first research study, published in 1983,[5] and confirmed in the Peel survey[2] published a year later. Both of these revealed a considerable amount of lethargy in the way in which companies approach management training. One ray of hope came through a survey of the market for tailored management training which we conducted in mid-1984[6] and which showed that half of the sample drawn from the more progressive companies was in the process of making a major reassessment of management training. Unfortunately we have no grounds for believing that this tendency applies to the whole of British industry.

In the following remarks about management training practice in the UK I must stress that I am discussing the general pattern. There are exceptions, and our research did identify some firms who have always done a first-class job. I know many from personal experience. There is evidence that almost all firms *think* they are doing a good job of management training and development, yet accept the general criticism of business in general. The reality is that most companies who think this way are in need of considerable improvement. All readers should therefore have an open mind when considering the research findings, as the statistical probability is that they are among the majority.

Organisation of training

The ways in which the management education and training function is organised vary so much between companies that they almost defy description. We found that roughly a third of our sample had a wholly centralised training function while the remaining two-thirds were either wholly or completely decentralised. Such a broad structural approach might be expected to bear a strong relationship to the nature of the firm's business, and its divisionalisation policies. No surprises so far.

In most organisations, ultimate responsibility for management training rested with the personnel director. However, in most companies very little top management time is devoted to management training, and there is very little involvement of the chief executive in the policies or actions of the training function. An interesting fact was that in that minority of companies which had recently shaken up their training initiatives, this was almost universally because the chief executive had become personally involved. It is possible to argue that this proves that chief executives become involved when it is appropriate, and delegate when things are satisfactory. Unfortunately all the evidence suggests that far too many companies are doing a bad job of training but are ignorant of this fact. Those who realised it, and did something about it, were indeed a minority.

In many organisations the status of the top training man is very low. Job titles are no guide. Although there are some senior training managers in some companies who are widely respected, and directly control large budgets, the majority have little power, and in some companies may be of low calibre. Some are allowed to take very few decisions and may not even control their own budgets. In only a very few companies are the top training executives likely to have access to information about corporate strategy to provide a context for training strategy. The majority are either too low in seniority or standing to have the confidence of top management and thus gain access to such important and sensitive information.

Our findings in no way contradicted the Coopers and Lybrand report[4] in its statement:

We formed the impression that training managers themselves tended not to view their activities as being the cutting edge of the competitiveness of their firm and nor do senior executives. *In consequence training managers and departments tend to have a relatively low status within firms*; they are rarely expected to be proactive in suggesting training activity, and in several companies they were not thought capable of determining the most cost-effective responses to business needs (page 9).

Management control of training

Few companies know what they spend on training. This is partly an organisational problem. For example one company I know has a corporate training function with certain international responsibilities. In addition most of its business divisions also have a central training function with some international duties. Each operating company around the world also has its training function, with in some cases further training activity at particular works and offices. Organisationally it is difficult to answer the question what do we spend on training in the UK, and to my knowledge the division of responsibilities gives no one in training the authority to collect this information as a matter of right. Since international training is sometimes carried out in the main training centre in the UK, and sometimes on sites overseas, a considerable system would be needed to separate all the costs into headings which would answer such a question. And for people whose responsibilities are global there may be very little interest in what happens in the particular country where the corporate headquarters happen to be situated.

In most companies the inability to look at training expenditure in statistical terms is, however, a measure of disinterest. Few companies approach the problem of controlling training expenditure in an appropriate manner, and as a result often take training decisions on the wrong economic basis.

There is a parallel with the concept of total physical distribution which was developed as a popular approach in the late 1960s. Many companies made improvements by taking a total view of distribution and its costs, whereas previously responsibility and costs had been spread across numerous managers. The decision to use air services to supply an overseas market became different when associated reductions in inventory and warehouse costs were brought into the picture. Economic sense did not come from just comparing sea and air freight rates without looking at other costs which would be affected, including the extra financing charges of inventory which had to be carried for a long sea voyage.

Our research showed that training decisions in the UK are in most companies related to the misconceptions which used to pervade physical distribution.

Although there are wide variations of budgetary philosophy, with a minority of trainers having to sell their courses on an internal company market and a majority operating as a free service, almost nobody ever looked at the full cost of training. Typically the training manager's budget will cover only the professional services (lecturing and course development), his own overheads and staff costs, and hotel and training centre charges. Travel to a course may fall on the budget of the departments sponsoring participants, as does the largest item the salaries of those on a course. In most cases these costs remain hidden. Peel[2] (page 24) found that while about two-thirds of companies included course participants' travel and subsistence expenses in the training budget, less than a quarter included the salaries of participants while on the course.

The pressure on the training manager is to do well against his own budget, which means that his motivation is to hold down or reduce those costs for which he is accountable. A much better economic decision would be a trade-off in terms of costs of a course and its effectiveness: in other words trying to maximise the return on the sacrifice of the opportunity cost, instead of aiming to minimise the out-of-pocket expenses. The control system in many companies forces decisions which are not necessarily in the best interests of the firm, and will often motivate the trainer to skimp on course development costs or use an inferior approach to tuition so long as he produces a reasonable course. What he should be doing is producing the course which makes the best use of participants' time, judged in relation to all the costs.

This split view of costs is another reason why companies do not know what training costs them. It is also why national surveys on training expenditure invariably end up with apples-and-pears statistics (which does not prevent some researchers from publishing tables drawn up from them!) I know one engineering company where even comparison inside the company is meaningless. All hourly paid people book time to a training number and the costs of their wages are thus included. No salaried people book time so their salaries are excluded from training costs.

Peel[2] (page 24) found that most of the 40 per cent of companies which had a cross-charging system for training services did not make a charge for overheads. "This being so, a rational decision, on the grounds of costs, as to whether to 'buy out' management training or to use internal resources must be difficult. The dice can be loaded against the external provider."

Training needs assessment

Our research asked respondents to describe the aims and objectives of their management training activity. It was encouraging to find that some companies felt that their need was for training that could be directly tied to the achievement of corporate objectives, but disappointing that this direct link was seen only by one-third. These respondents who claimed to relate to corporate objectives gave their answers in a general rather than a specific sense, and a much smaller number made any connection between training and corporate strategy. Thus our findings completely support the conclusion in the later research by Coopers and Lybrand[4] that few companies see a direct link between training and profitability, except in the negative sense of a cost.

In our survey we found that about two-fifths of trainers had a general belief that managers should receive skill training specific to each level, and all should be taught a general business background. A large minority, about one-fifth, argued that training objectives should be related to individual rather than corporate needs. With the main purpose to remedy defects, about 10 per cent focused their training activity on the preparation of people for promotion.

The predominant method used in the UK to assess training needs is an annual training appraisal, and this method is used by most organisations regardless of their training objectives. In theory a training appraisal is a formal review between subordinate and superior, where they jointly reach a conclusion on the training needs of the subordinate. In reality, this often becomes a boring routine in which the views of the superior predominate. Both parties are limited by their perceptual boundaries, which means that if neither is aware of a need, it will not be identified. This brings the danger that managers are all trained to plough the same furrow as their boss, which may not meet the strategic requirement of the firm.

In many firms training appraisals bring disillusionment, because many mangers are never offered the training needed to meet the identified needs. There are also many potential problems when training needs assessment is linked to performance appraisal system. Leavitt[7] observes that he knows no organisation that is pleased with its performance appraisal system. Handy[8] argues that the normal objectives of appraisal systems are not psychologically compatible, and some are "difficult to do well, even in isolation".

Peel[2] (page 27) found that 69 per cent of his respondents used the individual training needs appraisal method. Some 40 per cent, which means that there is an overlap, also use requests from line managers as a means of assessing needs.

All other methods are minority activities only. These include residential assessment centres, which offer the evaluators the opportunity of observing training needs away from the emotion and prejudices of the normal job, *ad hoc* surveys by training managers, and the very informal methods of self-selection based on published lists of available training courses.

Neither our surveys nor Peel's found any significant number of companies who added a top-down assessment of needs to the other methods. By this I do not mean the dabbling of an uninformed managing director, who without evidence feels he can decide the needs of everyone in the firm. I mean a careful attempt to identify the training support that is required to help implement new strategies, give effect to new policies or styles of management, achieve a desired change in corporate culture, or meet the challenge of changes in the business environment. In other words, a close linking of training with the corporate plan. Although companies which do this are a very small minority, they do exist. But most businesses in the UK are following inadequate (and often inappropriate) approaches to assessing training needs.

Most common internal management training initiatives

Subject areas of internal courses indicate an approach to management which is skills-oriented rather than integrated. Taking Peel's[2] findings (page 28), the subjects shown in Table 5.1 are run as internal courses by at least 57 per cent of all companies. Those asterisked fit the personal skill base of most trainers I know, which raises the question whether companies are getting what they really need, or what the training function is competent to deliver. It is not that these topics are unimportant, but that they represent a fragmented approach, and in any case there are significant omissions. It is hard to see how having fully trained managers in all of these areas will enable British firms to beat Japanese competition.

Even taking the less frequently mentioned internal courses, as well as all external training, into account, (and most companies make some use of external courses) there is the problem of penetration of the desired

TABLE 5.1. *Subject areas of internal courses*

Courses	Percentage of Companies
Personnel-related	
Health and Safety	86*
Employment Law	82*
Selection Interviewing	73*
Appraisal	72*
Industrial Relations	71*
Training Techniques	65*
Behavioural aspects of management	
Leadership	85*
Motivation	64*
Decision-making	63*
Delegation	57*
Other	
Computer Appreciation	85
Finance (for non-financial managers)	82
Microcomputing	64
Public Speaking	61*

population. The estimate given earlier in this chapter that most managers receive no training at all is by no means restricted to managers in the smaller companies. Our survey, which examined practice in 80 of the top 150 companies, found that most trainers were reluctant to estimate the frequency of managerial involvement in company courses. We formed the impression that few, if any, knew the extent to which the population group was taking up the opportunity to receive the training. Only one of the companies (in construction) felt able to give an estimate of training frequency of managers: one course every 3 years on average for each manager.

This suggests that the training function is unable, in most companies, to fully implement its strategies. Having assessed the need and provided the initiative, it is rarely in a position to measure the extent to which those with the need partake of the training.

One of the omissions from most companies' lists of training activity is the multi-disciplinary topic course. This is usually essential for an "implementing strategy" type of course. A change in market focus might, for example, require a course which covered marketing, strategy, control and the behavioural implications of change. Later chapters will enlarge on these ideas and will include some case histories. As I have frequently mentioned, there are sufficient examples from the minority of firms who do things well to give hope that the rest of British business is capable of change.

Lethargy

Our survey found considerable evidence of lethargy (or complacency) in training activities, which may in fact be a reflection of the fear of those in a function often held in low esteem to do anything that will rock the boat. We found trainers who boasted that proof of a good course was the number of years they had run it unchanged. Yet in view of the restructuring which most companies have gone through since the late 1970s a reasonable expectation would have been that individual courses would also need to change.

Yet the unchanged course is clearly a norm. Most training courses we came across in our research remained relatively stable from year to year. If major changes did take place they were initiated by top management.

In most companies top management did not get involved. When they did, the changes were often sweeping and fundamental. One plea of this book is that top management should be involved, and on a continuous basis. Most managing directors would find much to change if they took an interest in training, and most training managers I know would welcome such an involvement.

Training methods themselves are fairly static in many companies. Our experience is that most trainers will stick to an approach they know, and as a result are ignorant of alternative methods. This is partly a problem caused by tight resources, and partly by a lack of self-confidence caused by their status in the organisation.

As a result of these problems, more the fault of top management than the trainers themselves, training courses are rarely as effective as they could be. Many training initiatives could be considerably more creative and innovative, which in turn would make them more interesting to participants.

Options for internal courses

We formed the impression that many trainers do not know or do not consider the options when preparing a training initiative. These vary from courses, to workshops, use of distance learning, counselling and on-the-job training and many more. Within the course option are many different approaches, many of which have never been considered by some companies. For illustration a few of the different ways of designing and running a course will be explored. Some will be brought to life more vividly in later chapters.

(a) The course is designed and taught by the training staff

This particularly occurs with basic subjects such as interpersonal skills, communications, health and safety at work, and the like. A minority of companies also have a multi-disciplinary faculty at their own training college. For most this is inappropriate on the grounds of costs, utilisation, and objectivity. Most companies stick with the personnel and behavioural topics for this approach. My criticism is not that companies use their trainers for this purpose, but that the personal bias of the trainers often means it is the only training offered.

(b) An off-the-shelf course is presented by outsiders in house

The main advantage over sending managers on the same course outside is that the company has a bulk buying cost advantage. In all but a few situations the lack of relevance of the off-the-shelf course means that it rarely makes the best use of participants' time.

(c) The off-the-shelf course is purchased and run by company trainers

This is similar to the previous approach except that the company buys the standard material and teaches it with its own staff. This may give an opportunity for minor modifications in delivery which increase the cause's relevance, but basically it has the same defects as the standard course. If it happens to fit, it can be very cost-effective. It will not fit all organisations.

(d) The standard off-the-shelf course is "slanted" to the company

This, too, is similar to (b) above, except that the provider of the course spends a little time on cosmetics, so that company language is used and a few company examples are given. It is a little more expensive than the standard course, as some additional development is necessary, and it may be a little more effective. A combination of wishful thinking by the buyer and overselling by the vendor often leads companies to confuse this with a tailored course.

(e) The multi-lecturer course designed by the training staff

Typically the teaching slots will be filled by tutors from inside and outside the company. This sort of format has value in providing "how we do it" familiarisation from line managers, or in exposing senior managers to a host of new ideas. It is more frequently misused as a cheap way of putting together a course without regard for the teaching objectives. Line managers are often briefed to give a talk on what they do: outsiders are asked to give their standard talk on a subject or concept. This approach may also expand to a very expensive conference style, when leading authorities are flown in from various parts of the world. I personally dislike the multi-lecturer style for anything but an information course or a major conference. My experience of working with company trainers in this mode is that it is an excuse to avoid thinking: often they have no idea what a "new" lecturer intends to do or say, and give him no guidance on what they want.

(f)The true tailored course is by definition produced uniquely for the company

This is the only effective approach to a course designed to implement strategy or solve particular problems. Because the teaching material is developed around the company situation the cost of developing the course is higher than for other options, although it costs no more to deliver the course than with other options using external lecturers. Skills required in developing such a course include consultancy, creative course design, writing educational materials and teaching. Few companies have the ability to develop such a course without outside help; if they have all the skills they are often too close to the issues to develop the course with objectivity and detachment. Our most recent research suggests that this powerful and cost-effective approach is becoming more popular. It will be discussed in greater detail in subsequent chapters. For the present, it is enough to state that the companies which use it are in the minority, and that many do not even know of it.

The descriptions given above do not focus on the teaching methods within a course. Subsequent chapters will demonstrate the rich variety of methods that can be chosen within the broad heading of, for example, the tailored course.

Education

Our research found few companies who made any serious attempt at evaluating training initiatives, and we felt that our questions on this score embarrassed some of our respondents. Few were able to indicate the criteria by which programme success is measured, and only six of our 80 respondents were able to go into detail about their methods of evaluation.

Coopers and Lybrand[4] (page 10) found a similar picture of a failure to evaluate the cost-effectiveness of training in general, and like us saw this as a matter of concern. Peel[3] (page 35) reached a similar conclusion, but appears to condone it: "At best, management development and training must always be an act of faith", although he does agree that those authorising management training require to know whether the benefits exceed the costs. Most of the methods he identified as being used by those who attempted evaluation were inadequate. He somewhat contradicts his act-of-faith stance by arguing that sound evaluation could change the face of management training.

My view is that the failure to attempt to prove the benefits is one reason for the lack of interest by top management. Why should heavy expenditure be incurred, and top management time be given to, an activity which, although it may be perceived as "good"' appears to offer little return? Training managers fail to evaluate for a number of reasons. Firstly there is little top management pressure on them to do so.

Secondly, they recognise that out of a finite budget, money spent on evaluation cannot be spent on training, and fear that they will be able to do less training if they try to evaluate. Thirdly, much of the training is connected with the individual, rather than the corporate good. It is very difficult to measure changes in all dimensions of an individual's performance, although it might be easier to measure whether a corporate change (for example increase in market share) has occurred. As we have seen, few companies use training as a competitive weapon, and therefore throw themselves back to thinking only of the individual. Fourthly, the objectives of many internal training initiatives are unclear, as are the reasons why particular individuals attend. Fifthly, there is a measure of ignorance among many trainers about what can be done to evaluate: the tendency is to dismiss the whole subject as impossible, without considering that there may be benefit in focusing on those aspects where evaluation is possible.

A later chapter will explore some approaches to evaluation, including some of the methods identified by our research.

Conclusion

No one can look at the evidence and conclude that British firms are doing a good job of training. If this were a social matter only, the debate could be settled at a philosophical level. But although there are many social implications, the real issue is one of gaining competitive advantage.

Most companies are ignoring what is potentially one of the most powerful weapons available to them. Even most of those that give reasonable attention to training are deluding themselves that they are doing the right things.

What is needed in most companies is a mental shift from the common idea that training should be for the improvement of the individual because this will benefit the firm, to the concept that training should be for the benefit of the firm and this will benefit the individual. This change of emphasis is more than a play on words.

The general practice and approach to management training in the UK is entirely compatible with the analysis of the first three chapters. The question each company must face is whether to allow itself to remain a prisoner of our collective cultural history and all that reinforces it, or to forge from management education and training a new tool to achieve better economic results. The need is clear. The rest of this book will show the way.

References

1. C. Jardine (1985): Business schools learn their lesson, *Management Today,* December
2. M. Peel (1984): *Management Development and Training,* British Institute of Management/Professional Publishing Ltd, page 7
3. HMSO (1980): *Report of the Committee of Enquiry into the Engineering Profession,* page 85 (Finniston Report)

4. Coopers and Lybrand Associates (1985): *A Challenge to Complacency: Changing Attitudes to Training,* Manpower Services Commission/National Economic Development Office
5. K. Ascher (1983): *Management Training in Large UK Business Organisations: A Survey,* Harbridge House
6. F. Bateson (1986): *Tailored Management Education,* Harbridge House
7. H. J. Leavitt (1978): *Managerial Psychology,* 4th edition, University of Chicago Press, page 185
8. C. B. Handy (1981): *Understanding Organisations,* 2nd edition, Penguin, page 253

6
Strategy, People and Change

Our situation, in the UK, as outlined in the previous chapters, reminds me of the television adventure game, where teams of contestants are dumped in a tight spot, giving all the viewers the opportunity to urge "Now get out of that".

In our situation "getting out of that" will call for a great deal of painstaking, and sometimes painful, assessment and adjustment. Yet it is possible, and in this chapter we begin to move from the depressing truth about ourselves as a nation to ways of making the necessary changes. Much of the analysis so far has focused on the negative findings from the research. Subsequent chapters will include a number of philosophical arguments, and will draw on many of the positive findings from our various researches, and on some of the stimulating examples from our experience, and will weave these into some positive advice for management and, to a lesser degree, government.

Before plunging in to the many practical issues, I should like to explore some concepts around strategy, people and change which I hope will provide a background to many of the sbusequent arguments and suggestions.

Strategy

The words used to describe an activity have an element of fashion about them. Most companies would argue that they have taken on board some concept of strategy, and many would use the in-phrase strategic management. Gluck *et al.*[1] argue that very few firms in the world really practise strategic management, which is an approach which combines strategic planning with management into a single process. The focus is on managing all corporate resources to build competitive advantage. Basic requirements include: a framework for planning which is not inhibited by organisational boundaries and makes it possible to take strategic decisions about resources and activities; an approach to the process of planning which stimulates entrepreneurial thinking; a set of corporate values that encourages the commitment of individual managers to the strategy.

Ohmae[2] argues that the critical dimension in strategy is strategic thinking, which from rigorous analysis develops into a creative and entrepreneurial activity. He argues against the mindless bureaucracy of many large company planning systems. Creative insight is, he believes, the key to good strategic decisions, and this comes from individuals not systems.

Strategic thinking can be helped through the use of appropriate techniques of analysis, as has been argued in Chapter 2. Techniques are not an end in themselves, and do not make strategic decisions, but they can aid this process. For me one of their most important roles is to help change the perceptual boundaries of the strategic arena. Although they may throw new light on old problems, usually through the re-ordering of information into new patterns, they are effective only so far as people are willing to accept the possibility that the old views may be wrong. This is one of the first major behavioural issues in planning, and one that links directly as a possible objective for management education and training.

The problem of rejecting ideas which conflict with what we "know" to be true, and thereby closing our minds to other options, is by no means new. We all know the quotation "None so blind as those who won't see" (Heywood, 1546). Burton,[3] the famous explorer, wrote in 1856 about some views held by the Somali people. "The mosquito bite brings on, according to the same authority, deadly fevers; the superstition probably arises from the fact that mosquitoes and fevers become formidable about the same time." It took until 1894 for a serious theory to be postulated connecting the mosquito and malaria, and this connection was proved in 1897. Yet Burton, a brilliant scholar and self-reliant adventurer, was conditioned to dismiss the suggestion as "superstition".

Strategy is closely bound up with "people" issues, a theme which is receiving increasing attention in far-sighted companies.

Strategy and structure

The case for considering structure in the content of strategy has been well made, beginning with Chandler's[4] famous study of the evolution of some of America's major companies. This led to the birth of the massive research contribution from the Harvard Business School,[5] including the study by Channon[6] which has been extensively referred to in earlier chapters.

This stream of research explored how organisational structure changed as strategies altered. Some elements of this statement are self-evident. A new, major activity added to a firm would obviously require a structure to accommodate it. The research explored more fundamental changes, such as the move to centralisation or decentralisation as the nature of the firm's activities changed. Even without the research, few readers would have difficulty in accepting the premise that strategy can be frustrated if the structure is not compatible with the requirements of that strategy, and that when this happens either the structure or the strategy has to change.

Structures exist for the implementation of strategies, even when the strategies are implicitly rather than explicitly stated.

Further contributions were added by behaviouralists. Lawrence and Lorsch[7] developed the now famous contingency theory of organisation. Basically this stated that the appropriate organisational form was contingent on the circumstances in which the firm operated. Successful business in a rapidly changing environment requiring many non-routine decisions would be decentralised. A successful business in an unchanging, routine environment would probably be centralised. This leads on to the idea that success may also be influenced by getting the appropriate structures for the various sub-environments within an organisation. A newspaper had traditionally at least two such sub-environments: the turbulent world of the news reporters, with constant change and excitement; the routine world of the presses which have to print newspapers ready for placing in the distribution vans at the same time every day, regardless of the breaking of a new story.

Those who wish to follow these research programmes to a greater depth are referred to Galbraith and Nathanson,[8] whose book provides a valuable summary of the most important research findings.

Structure is usually clearly seen as something requiring top management attention, and many managing directors of my acquaintance seem to enjoy "re-organising". For most this consists of drawing new charts of reporting relationships, probably taking note of the individual strengths and weaknesses of key managers. They rarely do more than conceive of the organisation as a series of lines and boxes. In fact an organisation involves considerably more than this, as we shall see.

The "excellent" companies

Peters and Waterman[9] conducted their now world-famous study into what made the best companies so good. They identified eight key factors, some referring to strategy, and most consisting of behavioural factors such as style, values and culture. The basics are deceptively simple. Easy to list, but much more difficult to do.

1. *Getting things done.* All the successful companies had a "bias for action". This did not mean that they did not think, but they certainly got down to implementing the results of those thoughts.
2. *Staying close to the customer.* The customer is paramount, is served well, and is the source of many of the best product ideas. This may be what we have all learned to call the marketing concept, but knowing the buzzword is not the same as actually doing it.
3. *Leaders and innovators.* Innovation is encouraged, and there is adequate autonomy for the growth of entrepreneurial leaders.

4. *People and productivity*. People, at whatever level, are seen as the source for productivity. "We and they" attitudes are not fostered. The individual is important.
5. *Staying close to the business*. The best companies have managers who regularly, using the words favoured by the Industrial Society, "walk the job". Managers understand what goes on at the basic level.
6. *Staying with what you know*. I have trouble in fully accepting this point, but would agree that a company should know how it is going to manage any new area it decides to move into. Never to move from the business base is perhaps too conservative a view. Never to assume that you are immediately capable of managing *every* business is a very sensible point.
7. *Simple structures and small staffs*. All the best companies had simple organisational structures (no complex matrix organisations). Corporate staffs are very small.
8. *Mixed centralisation decentralisation*. Autonomy is pushed down about as far as it will go. At the same time the core values that the companies consider to be important are centralised.

Perhaps the key point from these attributes is that so many of them focus on corporate values based on a fundamental belief in the importance of people, whether they are customers or employees.

A different view of organisation

For most people the word "organisation" conjures up a vision of an organogram; in other words they think in terms of structure. In reality an organisation is much more than this, and consists of several interrelated variables of which structure is but one. Others, such as the tasks that have to be filled, the nature and skills of the people, the decision processes and the information processes, are equally important.

Most managers will be aware of situations where a new structure did not work because no one changed the internal systems so management information did not meet the needs of the new responsibilities, or when a particular person's performance made the defined structure impossible to work.

The reality is that the various components of organisation are interrelated, and a change in any one of the variables has the potential to affect any of the others. Most managers have first-hand knowledge of the impact on the variables as a result of the introduction of a new technology. The word processor, for example, can cause changes to every variable. Reward systems can affect the manner in which tasks are performed, and therefore the numbers of people needed, which in turn may modify the structure and information requirements.

Leavitt[10] began to clarify this interrelationship with his model which

Strategy, People and Change 75

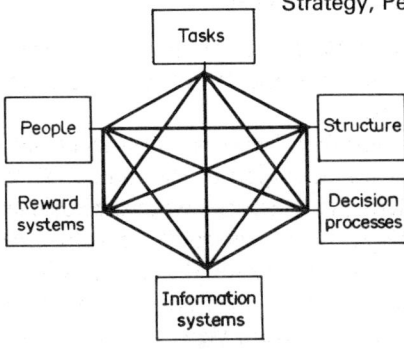

FIGURE 6.1. Organisation variables

showed the four components as structure, strategy, technology (tools), and people. This was the foundation of much of the subsequent thinking on this issue.

More well-known, particularly since the publication of *In Search of Excellence*, is the McKinsey 7-S model. This appears in Peters and Waterman,[9] (page 10) and links structure, strategy, systems, style, skills, staff and shared values.

There is some similarity with my own model, which also owes much to Galbraith and Nathanson,,[8] (page 2).

Figure 6.1 shows the first steps in thinking about an organisation, and has six variables, all of which have the potential to interact on all the others. There is thus the dynamic relationship between the various components of the organisation. It is worth discussing each of these boxes briefly, in order to ensure that the meanings are clear.

Tasks

The things that have to be done fall under this heading. We are also concerned with the degrees of certainty and uncertainty around those tasks. In the newspaper example given earlier, a reporter may not know who he will have to interview to get his next story, how he will do this, or where. Or he may have to interview no one. The printer knows that, regardless of content, he will have to perform his tasks in the same way today as he did yesterday, and will do tomorrow. Diversity of tasks will also be significant, as will their degree of interdependence: there is clearly more diversity in an editor's tasks than in a print operatives.

Structure

This is how the tasks are combined into jobs and put into reporting relationships. The structure shows how power is distributed (but not how it is exercised, which is a function of decision processes). Structure needs to consider division of labour against giving people responsibility for seeing an output to their work in which they can take pride and so achieve job satisfaction. Geographical factors have to be considered.

Decision Processes

This combines the style of the organisation with the levels at which various decisions are made. A firm with a participative style of decision-making will function differently from one with an autocratic style, even though their structures could look the same.

Information systems

The flow of information in an organisation has a direct impact on the other variables. Under this heading I would include budgeting and planning processes, integrative mechanisms and decision analysis, as well as the more obvious management information system. Disharmony between the budgetary system, the structure and the decision processes would obviously cause the organisation to function in an ineffective way.

Reward systems

Here we include both intrinsic (rewards which are internal to the person and come from the job itself), and extrinsic (rewards which are external to the person, such as salary), systems. The nature of the rewards themselves is important. Commission to salesmen will have a different impact on the other variables to a straight salary, for example. Ultimately, reward systems take us to ways of measuring individual performance (or in some cases team performance).

People

Under the people heading there are many factors, including items such as skills, recruitment, selection, promotion, training and development. Appropriate training can have as big an impact on the other variables as, for example, the basic selection processes. Training can therefore be seen as an important contributor to the total concept of organisation, having the power to cause changes in the other variables. Bad or inappropriate training will react negatively. Good, appropriate training will react positively.

The second element to the model is shown in Figure 6.2. This adds three new

Strategy, People and Change 77

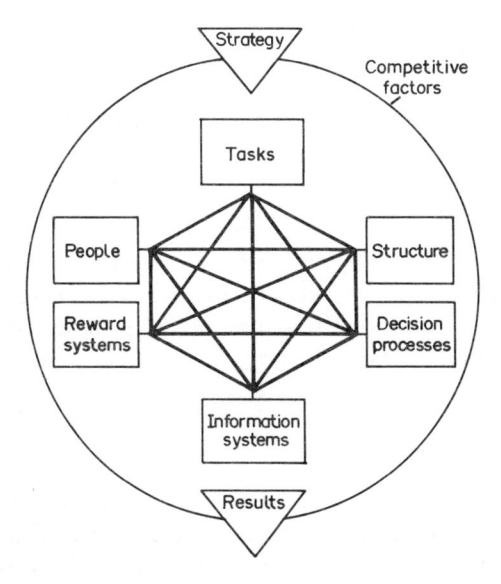

FIGURE 6.2. Strategy, competitive environment and organisational variables

features – strategy, results and the competitive environment. Strategy is shown as the driving force which, working through the organisation, aims to produce results. The actual results may be very different from what was intended (reasons for failure in the implementation of strategies will be discussed later). As we have already seen, a change in strategy may bring a need to change structure. The potential impact of strategy is in fact greater than this, and it may trigger a direct change in any or all of the variables, which in turn may bring a need to change some or all of the others. As there is nothing automatic about this model (changes come as a result of decisions, not as an inevitable consequence of strategy), the number of organisation variables that should be considered, in order to ensure that the right results are achieved, is significant. Training ranks high on this list, and management development, embracing management education and training, is in many situations the most important.

The competitive, or industry, environment has an impact on the strategy itself and on the people and reward systems variables. In some industries there is an unofficial "no-poaching" rule for managerial recruitment, which means that opportunities in competitor companies are reduced. In most industries it is a free-for-all. The most successful companies, those with the most attractive style, and those offering the higher rewards (which may be money, or may be opportunities for personal growth and development) are likely to be in the most favourable position when it comes to attracting and retaining staff. The competitive environment is an important force which cannot be ignored.

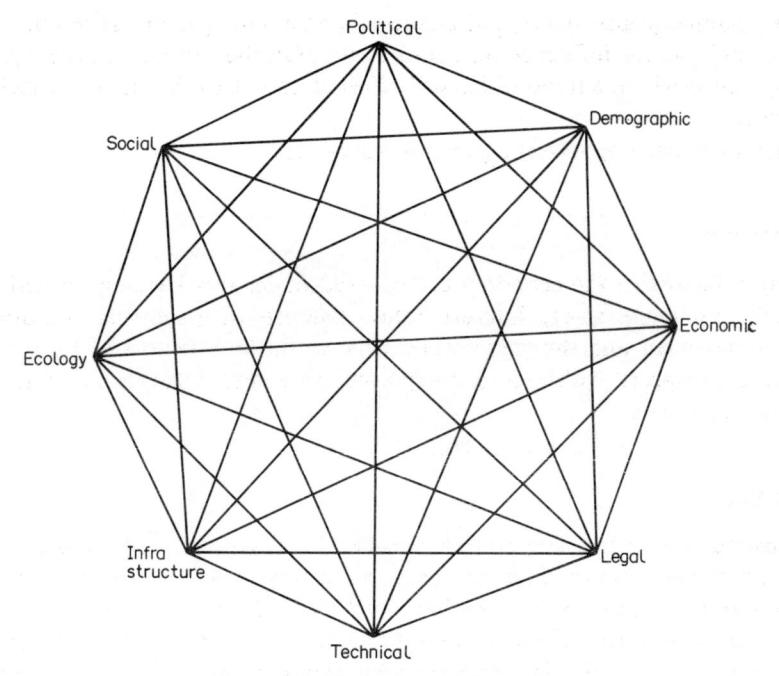

FIGURE 6.3. The business environment

The business environment

Competitor companies are not the only reference companies considered important by employees. In many industries there are groups of workers who compare the "fairness" of their own rewards to those offered by quite different industries. Thus the firemen might look at the police. Manual workers in one industry might compare themselves with similar workers in another industry. These outside reference groups may be more significant than other groups of employees inside the firm. An interesting dimension of this occurred in the US civil disorders in the 1960s. It was comparatively well-off black Americans who led the movement for reform, because they compared themselves to the white middle class and felt deprived. The poor people in the black communities compared themselves to those around them and were reasonably content.[11] For this reason alone it would be necessary to extend thinking beyond the competitive environment. In reality, the business environment has an enormous impact on the business. Figure 6.3 shows one way of thinking about it.

The environment is pictured as an octagon, each point representing a group of environmental factors. The lines inside the octagon, which connect each point to every other, represent the influence which changes in the factors have on each other. Nothing happens in a vacuum, although the degree of influence will not be the same in all directions. Changes in social values can, for example, cause significant changes in economic performance but may have only minor influence on demography. On the other hand the ageing population will be a trend which will affect almost all of the other factors in a significant way.

Each main heading covers a group of variables:

Economic

Major factors in the economy are covered under this heading: growth of GDP, exchange rates, interest rates, balance of payments, inflation, unemployment and the trade cycle. Change in these factors will not only affect prospects within a country, but may also change international competitiveness.

Social

Most businesses are affected to a considerable degree by social factors. The trends discussed in the first four chapters of this book are largely caused by the cultural values of our society. Included under this heading are the attitudes and norms of society and the social structure itself. Such things as attitudes to work, discrimination, perceived importance of higher education, attitudes to profit, and feelings about moral issues are among the most important. This is not to suggest that all social trends are ubiquitous. A particular company may be affected by minority issues, differences between regions, or may entirely escape any impact from some of the trends.

Legal

Legal factors are very clearly of significance, since there may be clear penalties for ignoring them. Yet many companies assume that other countries have the same laws as their home country. A UK firm expanding into Italy or West Germany would be very unwise to assume that employment legislation would be broadly similar to that of the UK.

Political

Political issues rarely stand alone from other aspects of the environment. They are important as a harbinger of economic, social and legal change.

Technological

The area of technological change is of the utmost importance, particularly when we consider that much of modern technology has come about within the working life of our senior managers. Banks and insurance companies are, for example, so affected by the development of electronics that they could operate in a very different way in the future.

Demographic

Both the population structure and its geographical distribution are factors of potential importance to business.

Infrastructure

This is critically important in a developing country, where absence of communications links may seriously affect the successful implementation of strategy. In the context of this book the availability of centres of higher education providing the training that is needed is a key matter.

Ecology

Last on the list are the numerous factors uner the heading ecology. This includes conservation, resource utilisation and anti-pollution issues, all of which are touching the affairs of more industries each year.

It is not difficult to see how environmental changes can affect corporate strategy. We have all lived through the recent recession, and have seen the great changes this has caused to most businesses.

Figure 6.4 places our organisational model within the environment, thus accepting that it affects not only strategy, but the environment and a number of organisational factors themselves. For example, if the educational system does not produce people with the skills business needs, it may be impossible to implement the strategy, unless business restructures so that jobs are done in a different way, or itself provides training to make up the deficiency.

Every company has a number of possible options in the face of an environmental issue. It may adapt its strategies and organisation to accommodate the change; it may deliberately seek opportunities arising from the change; it may discontinue an activity rather than face the change; it may seek to alter the environmental issue. The role of managing in a turbulent environment is by no means passive, and indeed the worst of all worlds is to be so unaware of what is going on that everything happens as a crisis.

Implementing strategy

Strategies are formulated to be implemented and, as we have seen, the excellent companies do turn ideas into action. But what happens in most companies when a strategy is formulated and the wrong results appear? The

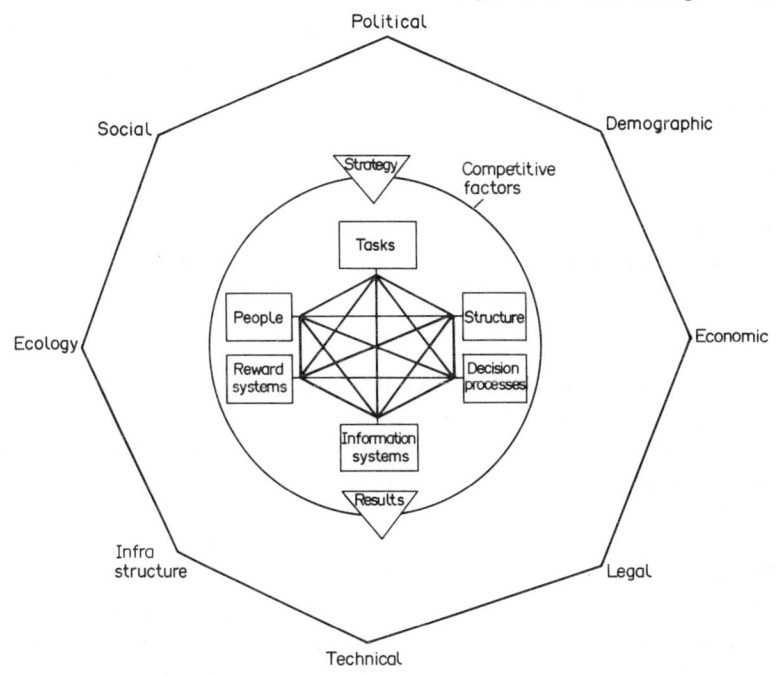

FIGURE 6.4. Organisation and the environment

automatic reaction is that the strategy is poor and has to be changed. An equally valid possibility is that the strategy is good, but the implementation is poor; therefore attention should be placed on implementation. Unfortunately it is not always easy for those at the top to sort out which of the two premises applies. The probability is that the strategy will be assumed to be at fault, because this may be defined in a neat package, capable of reformulation. An implementation problem may be lost in all or any of the boxes of our organisational model, and it may be very difficult to identify the problem and the remedy.

Alexander[12] found some interesting conclusions from his US survey into the reasons for failure to implement strategy. Nine of the ten top reasons for failure which he identified can be related directly to the organisational variables discussed above. The tenth refers to uncontrollable factors in the external environment. In addition, there is a direct connection with training (or lack of it) in a number of the causes. And this is without arguing the case that a better-trained management could well have avoided the other problems!

Table 6.1 shows Alexander's findings with my comments about training. I will leave the reader the task of relating the reasons to the other factors in the organisational model. Among Alexander's recommended solutions are communication and involvement. Strategy-related training, creatively

TABLE 6.1. *Ten most frequent strategy implementation problems as identified by Alexander[12] (base 93 firms)*

Problem	Percentage of firms	My comments
(1) Implementation took more time than originally allocated	76	This does not necessarily relate to training, but it can do. An appropriate initiative can cut down this time
(2) Major problems surfaced during implementation which had not been identified beforehand	74	Again training is not the uiversal answer. However, the right sort of course can be used to identify and remove problems
(3) Co-ordination of implementation activities not effective enough	66	Do not rely on training to solve all of these problems, but do not neglect the power of an appropriate training initiative to enhance co-ordination
(4) Competing activities and crises distracted management from implementing this decision	64	Training initiatives can be used to ensure the priority of a policy or strategy
(5) Capabilities of employees involved were not sufficient	63	This may be a recruitment problem, but is more likely to be a training issue. It is dangerous to assume that everyone can cope with something new, without giving appropriate training
(6) Training and instruction given to lower-level employees were inadequate	62	A straight training problem
(7) Uncontrollable factors in the external environment had an adverse impact on implementation	60	
(8) Leadership and direction provided by departmental managers were not enough	59	Perhaps they did not know how to do it better!
(9) Key implementation tasks and activities were not defined in enough detail	56	A training initiative can often help this to improve
(10) Information systems used to monitor implementation were not adequate	56	

designed, can be a way of providing both. We should not overlook the power of effective management training to forge a common will within the company, and to help establish a culture that contributes to success.

Strategic management

Earlier in this chapter I gave a definition of strategic management which included the concept of managing all the company's resources to build competitive advantage. People are among the most important of those resources, and training should be very high on the list of weapons which the company has to make the best use of the human resources. Yet, we have seen in the previous chapter, most British companies choose not to use training in this way, and do not see it as an important contributor to competitiveness.

In the next chapter we will begin to see how training, particularly management training, can become a major force in improving economic results. This chapter will also argue why management training should become a top management issue.

References

1. F.W. Gluck, S. P. Kaufman and A. S. Walleck (1980): Strategic management for competitive advantage, *Harvard Business Review* July/August (included in D. E. Hussey, *The Truth About Corporate Planning*, Pergamon, 1983)
2. K. Ohmae (1983): *The Mind of the Strategist*, Penguin
3. R. F. Burton (1856): *First Footsteps in East Africa* (memorial edition 1894), Tylston and Edwards
4. A. D. Chandler (1962): *Strategy and Structure*, MIT Press.
5. (a) B. R. Scott (1971): *Stages of Corporate Development*, Harvard Businessness School
   (b) R. Rumelt (1974): *Strategy, Structure and Economic Performance*, Harvard Business School.
6. D. Channon (1973): *Strategy and Structure of British Enterprise*, McMillan.
7. P. Lawrence and J. Lorsch (1967): *Organisation and Environment*, Harvard Business School.
8. J. R. Galbraith and D. A. Nathanson (1978): *Strategy Implementation – The Role of Structure and Process*, West.
9. T. J. Peters and R. H. Waterman (1982): *In Search of Excellence*, Harper and Row.
10. H. J. Leavitt (1964): Applied organisational change in industry – structural, technical and human approaches. In *New Perspectives in Organisational Research*, Wiley, New York; abridged version in Vrom and Deci, (eds), *Management and Motivation*, Penguin, 1970, page 363.
11. *Report of the National Advisory Commission on Civil Disorders*, Barton Books, New York. Referenced in W. W. Daniels (1975): *The PEP Survey on Inflation*, PEP, London
12. L. D. Alexander (1985): Scessfully implementing strategic decisions, *Long Range Planning*, 18(3), 91–97.

7

Management Training as a Competitive Weapon

It is clear from the evidence discussed so far that training in most British companies is neither used as a competitive weapon, nor is it seen as being a matter of serious concern to top management. The previous chapter showed that training should be a proper area of concern for all companies, and that much of the emphasis properly belongs in the board-room.

We know from the research that most companies view their training with a great deal of complacency. This is a pity, because it has led to the strange situation where most companies are not only underspending on management training, but are at the same time wasting much of what they do spend. This chapter will explore a solution to this bizarre state of affairs, and will show how management training can be developed into a competitive weapon. Some examples will be given to demonstrate that the suggestions are a practical reality, and these will be supported in later chapters by more detailed case histories, and an insight into some of the training methodologies which can help make this change of emphasis.

What is suggested here is not academic theory, but methods which are already used in a minority of more advanced companies. They are approaches which can be used to build competitive advantage for individual companies and, through them, for the country as a whole. All that is needed is for companies to come to them with an open mind, and not to allow prejudice to frustrate the possibility of using management training in this positive way. There is no need to take the ideas on trust. There is a need to be willing to consider the ideas, weigh the evidence, and be willing to experiment.

Management training: a top management perspective

My view is that management training must contribute to the attainment of the company's objectives, and that the only way to ensure that it does is to drive it from the top. This does not prevent the chief executive from delegating, but it does mean that he or she should take action to ensure that the right things are being done, defining the policy, and playing a key part in establishing the training plan. This means making a major departure from total reliance on the annual training needs assessment, or changing this process so that it measures needs against corporate requirements. More will be said about this later.

I can think of six situations when an appropriate training initiative can make a major contribution to corporate objectives: creating an awareness that challenges the perceptual boundaries; implementing a new policy: implementing a strategy; changing or maintaining the culture of the organisation (creating shared values); meeting a major environmental change; solving specific problems. The general tone of these headings hint that this training may be dynamic. We may set about improving particular skills, but we are just as likely to use the training initiative to help the firm identify what has to be done to overcome obstacles.

Training by itself may not be a total solution, and needs to fit neatly with the other actions needed to bring about the necessary change. Not all of these are behavioural. British Rail have recently been advertising that most of their employees have now gone through a course on customer relations. For most British Rail customers this is a cause of much hollow laughter: if the courses had worked they would not have had to tell us about them, would they? Maybe this training fits the image British Rail would like to have, but until other issues are dealt with, such as late trains and planned overcrowding, no amount of courtesy training is going to have any real impact on their operations. Maybe they are trying to get the rest of the act together. I do not know. But the example does show that the chief executive needs to pull all the strands together. Training should not be allowed to exist in a vacuum.

Contrast British Rail with British Caledonian. Their advertisements do not tell us that they have been training their staff, but reflect a friendly efficiency that is matched by what is found at the check-in desk or in the aircraft. Similar comments could be made about Singapore Airlines. I have no inside information on either airline, but can confidently argue that what is experienced by the passenger is the result of careful training of the staff involved, and that that training is not only compatible with the strategy of the companies, but is an important element in its implementation.

My six situations are all capable of leading to training initiatives with clear objectives. A seventh situation is also valid but moves into the twilight zone where almost all training currently exists, where training may be valuable but cannot be so easily related to a corporate end. There will always be some training activity in this grey area, but the redirection of training focus would, in most companies, reduce the perceived needs in absolute terms, since some would have been dealt with in the more specific context.

Challenging the perceptual boundaries

The need is to ensure that the management team does not fall into the trap of the British motor cycle industry, and misunderstand the arena which is the competitive battleground. Management training is not the only tool available to the firm, and indeed is unlikely to be successful unless accompanied by other initiatives. The force of a chief executive of outstanding vision, the intelligent use of modern tools of strategic analysis, and the development of a company culture which encourages innovation and the challenging of the *status quo* can all be important drives to the same end. Similarly recruitment from outside the industry of middle and senior management, or an injection of graduates and MBAs, can also be positive actions.

Training in this important area is likely to be required at all levels of the organisation, and is most needed at the highest levels, not just at corporate headquarters, but also in each business unit. Unfortunately, there is a tendency for many senior managers to view training as an admission of personal weakness, which is rationalised as being "unable to spare the time". There is also the fact that, given the actual or perceived status of the training function in too many organisations, few companies feel that their senior people can be trained internally.

One common response, which is declining in popularity but is still often used, is to place a senior manager on a public subscription course at a business school. This can have immense value, but will not necessarily change the perceptual boundaries of either the person or the firm. One reason for this is that it is rarely an experience shared with the rest of the management team. The one lucky person comes back with concepts and ideas that are alien to many of his colleagues and may be rejected by them. The experience is usually general, and rarely deals with the company or industry context. Because of this, and because of his long experience, the participant is likely to reinterpret concepts back to his original prejudices, or to dismiss them out of hand as "not relevant to us".

Some companies approach the problem with top management conferences, built around a theme, where leading world experts are brought in. The style is often a mixture of course and conference, and can be very effective in creating an awareness of changes in the business environment, or new ways of looking at current problems. This sort of conference has the advantage of being a shared experience which can contribute to the development of teamwork.

If managed professionally, with themes selected with careful reference to the company's situation, this can be a very useful tool. Unfortunately some firms, from ignorance or out of a false sense of economy, do not design or run these events well, and they can easily become a pleasant interlude in the country, where new information is endured in return for an interesting social programme. Another common fault is to cram too much into the conference, so that participants are bombarded with apparently unrelated offerings from different lectures. The lesson is do it well, and it may be worthwhile: if you cannot do it well, give up the idea.

A third approach, and one with which I have a good deal of personal experience, is the management workshop. This can run at any level, but is particularly appropriate for the top management team. A great advantage of the workshop is that it is education in disguise. Typically a workshop will be designed around a particular issue, usually strategic, and will involve work on the real situation, and using, for example, a new method of analysis. In both demonstrating the new approach, and actually using it, the facilitator works in the dual role of trainer and process consultant. This is a superb way of undertaking industry analysis or defining competitive advantage, or even examining the implications of portfolio analysis.

Workshops such as this can be run by a company with or without outside help. In either case there is a need for adequate research and preparation of workshop materials. The other important ingredient in both cases is that the facilitator be able to take an objective view, and be of a stature to challenge existing thinking, even though the thinking may be that of the chief executive.

The fourth method of changing the perceptual boundaries is through process consultancy. Few people would even consider this as a management development approach, but of course it can be if on a one-to-one, or team, basis the initiative provides coaching and counselling as the assignment moves towards the attainment of its objectives. Given an appropriate process consultant, this method can be even more effective than the workshop (or may be combined with it), as the fact that managers are being trained is rarely perceived. In their eyes they are working with the consultant to formulate a strategy, understand an issue, or whatever it is that is the purpose of the initiative.

Although these methods can have a strong bias to implementation, I have distinguished them from initiatives which are only concerned with implementation. The broadening element comes from re-thinking a business situation, or being more aware of forces for change and their potential impact on the company.

In common with other good training initiatives, the approaches can be used to obtain involvement, build commitment, and ensure good communication. None of them stand alone, and they can all be linked to action plans and reviews so that decisions become actions.

It would be hard to argue that training for this type of objective belongs anywhere else than with top management.

Implementing a new policy

There is not very much difference in methodology between training to implement policy, or training as a means to implement strategy, and in some situations the meaning of the two terms can become very blurred. One of the main differences is the degree of precision with which quantitative objectives can be set as the desired outcome.

One of the world's largest multinationals, always seen as one of the best-managed, identified that more attention had to be placed on competitor analysis both at top level and in the development of marketing plans by each operating unit. This was after careful self-analysis had revealed that much of the company's recent growth was without profit, because of weaknesses in the market place where competitors were proving more aggressive than the assumptions on which past plans had been based. Many companies would have issued a policy statement, in the form of an edict, that in future strategies should be formulated after more rigorous competitor analysis. Many would have failed to cause any change whatsoever, because:

- most people would be complacent about their own approach, while accepting that others needed to do better;
- some would believe the isue was unimportant and only pay lip service to it;
- others would not understand the policy;
- a few might not receive or read the statement.

Aware of these probable outcomes the chief executive of this multinational personally directed a world-wide educational initiative to bring the new thinking into life. He led top managers in a week-long introduction to the theme of "what about competition", and insisted that several hundred senior people should spend 2 weeks on a strategic planning workshop. He introduced an 8-hour audiovisual presentation to thousands more managers as a basis for discussion of, and commitment to, genuine strategic thinking. Many week-long implementation workshops have been held throughout the world, with practical training in competitor analysis which has led to the implementation of more realistic strategies.

Not surprisingly, this policy change has been made to work, and is enthusiastically endorsed by thousands of managers who are now convinced of its practical value. Unfortunately the group is not British.

Again it would be hard to argue that this sort of initiative be pursued independently from the board-room.

Implementation of strategy

It is often extremely difficult to implement a strategy even after the company has decided what to do. The reasons for this were shown very clearly in the previous chapter.

Trainers can be used as a tool for implementation, and an appropriate initiative can do a number of very positive things:

- a very clear understanding can be gained, of both the broad strategy *and* what it means to the individual in his or her job;
- commitment can be built, as people discover the reason for the strategy and decide for themselves that there is sense behind it;

- the implication of implementation can be explored and converted into personal action plans;
- appropriate training can be given so that the appropriate individuals are able to implement the strategy.

The L'Oreal case, given in Chapter 10, is an excellent example of this philosophy in action, although in this case history the initiative covered marketing management and the sales force, and was the same for each. In other situations, although the plan for the training initiatives should be devised as a whole, the initiatives might be different for different levels or areas of the company.

In my experience the best way to use a training initiative as a mode for strategy implementation is the tailored course. Because this is important, and is possibly the most important way of creating training initiatives that build competitive advantage, it is described in detail in Chapter 8.

One British company had previously supplied services in a relatively noncompetitive way to other firms in the same group. A downturn in the fortunes of its main externally marketed products caused it to decide on a strategy to market the services outside the group, and this coincided with a change of corporate policy which meant that in future it would have to compete with outside companies when selling to the group. The reason for the change of strategy was clear to all, but there was a great deal of cynicism about the chances of success, uncertainty over the future, and a measure of insecurity fostered by job losses as parts of the company had restructured.

Management felt that the managers in the company were capable of making the changes, but were inadequately trained to do so. Skill deficiencies were identified, and a decision made to provide training in them.

The training initiative followed the ideas of this book, and addressed the strategic issues at the same time as it provided the skills training. This made the whole concept relevant to those attending, as well as providing training that was essential to the success of the strategy. At middle management level the initiative consisted of two linked 5-day courses, separated by at least a month, and repeated as needed. The first week dealt in a practical way with marketing in the context of the firm, competitor analysis and a suggested approach to market planning. At this course top management assigned three or four projects, and between the courses participants worked in teams to collect the information needed to deal with the issues raised.

On the second course the teams worked on the projects, using the two tutors in a process consultancy role. The teams prepared presentations to top management, and at the appropriate time in this preparation tuition was given in presentation skills (a need previously identified by management but now realistically urgent). The rest of the week was spent on behavioural issues, helping participants to see how to implement the projects they worked on. All middle managers involved in the new strategy attended both sessions of these courses. After this a 2½-day workshop using the key concepts of the course was run for senior management.

In addition to the identified training needs, this approach provided focus, changed negative feelings about the strategy to positive ones, provided working tools for participants to use immediately, and through the projects took the company several steps further in the detailed implementation. It is noteworthy that the courses dealt with several management disciplines, according to the strategy implementation needs.

This sort of approach is, unfortunately, taken by only a minority of British companies, and the need for it simply cannot be identified in most companies because of the way they organise and manage the training function. It patently is an important top management concern, and one that should exercise the minds of all chief executives, whether at group, strategic business unit or subsidiary level.

Changing or maintaining the culture of an organisation

It is clearly a top management task to develop a culture which is appropriate for the company. Where the chief executive believes that the culture is appropriate, the task is to ensure that new people joining the firm become part of that culture. Selection processes and day-to-day management are critical elements in addition to training. The video *In Search of Excellence* clearly showed how Walt Disney Productions use training to create a common understanding of Disneyworld as a stage, customers as guests, and all employees (even those doing mundane jobs such as issuing tickets) as part of the show. Peters and Waterman[1] state that every new employee has to attend "Disney University" and take a course "Traditions 1". No one, at whatever level, is exempted from the course.

Changing a culture, or producing a shared culture from several sub-cultures, is a more wide-ranging problem. The need may come about because of a change of top management or as the result of a new acquisition. The chief executive can act in a monitoring role to ensure that a culture is maintained; he has to take the initiative if he wants to bring about a change. Training by itself will not be enough to change a culture, but what is perhaps unique is that it can act as both a change agent and a signal of serious intent.

Meeting a major environmental change

Although the cause may be different, training to meet environmental change has many similarities with the first four reasons we have discussed. Again it is a top management responsibility to manage the interface between the firm and the business environment, and therefore only top management is in a position to understand what needs to be done.

The British Petroleum case history discussed in a later chapter is in part an initiative to help the company cope with a variety of external changes that could be foreseen in general terms.

Solving specific problems

Problems come up at all levels of an organisation. It is not realistic to expect top management to be involved or even aware of all of them, and some of the training initiatives should be instigated at lower levels of the organisation. The top management role is to see that training is used for this purpose, and that the known major problems are included in the approach.

The Harbridge House Management Training Survey[2] found few companies who claimed to use management training to solve problems. There was one notable exception, an engineering company, whose approach was unusual in that it both dealt with problems *and* had the active involvement of top management. Some extracts from this company's approach as reported in the survey provide a neat illustration of what can be done:

The concept of in-company management development workshops

Managers employed in the same company participate in a planned development programme agreed with the chief executive, in which they work together on important company problems which are relevant to the achievement of business plan targets. Since the solutions are worked out by the managers themselves, their involvement generates a commitment to achievement of agreed objectives and improved management morale. The development programme is specificaly designed for each company after a careful diagnostic survey, and is agreed with the chief executive. The various stages in the operation of in-company workshops are set out later. The workshops differ from the traditional training course in that:

1. They are concerned with *"live" company problems*, identified by a survey and agreed with the chief executive, instead of lectures and simulated case studies.
2. They seek to influence the perception and attitudes of managers and are *action-orientated*. Implementation of agreed solutions is reviewed during the workshops.
3. The emphasis is on improving *effectiveness of management teams,* rather than individual managers. There is greater understanding of the jobs of other managers, and improvement in communications horizontally and vertically.
4. They enable managers to *determine priorities for achievement of their job objectives*, and they help integrate the efforts of the management team to achieve the business plan targets.

Benefits to the company

The ultimate benefit to the company must be improved effectiveness of the management team in achieving the company's business objectives. In addition, the following benefits will be evident:

1. Managers become better able, and more committed, to apply fully their knowledge and experience to improving their company's performance.
2. Managerial attention and effort is concentrated on the areas which will have the greatest impact on performance, instead of being dissipated on relatively unimportant matters.
3. Better teamwork and co-operation is achieved, resulting in "positive synergy", i.e. the effectiveness of the management as a whole becomes greater than the sum of individual managers.
4. Planned management of change instead of a series of "fire-fighting" exercises.
5. Mutual trust, candour and credibility are generated. A more open approach to the management of conflict is created.
6. It provides an excellent means of achieving a deeper involvement of managers at all levels in the running of the business. Managers' participation is an essential prerequisite for moving towards the company's objective of employee participation.

How the approaches work

1. A study is made of the company's accounts for the past 2 or 3 years, current budget and performance data, business plan and organisation chart.
2. Managers are interviewed regarding their jobs in relation to objectives, management style, strengths and weaknesses or the organisation. The confidentiality of the survey encourages complete frankness and open discussion.
3. A survey report, recommending workshops, if and where appropriate, is prepared and submitted to the chief executive. Agreement is reached regarding priorities, topics to be included in the programme, membership and timing.
4. Membership is appropriate to the problem being studied – i.e. directors, senior managers, junior managers or a departmental team. The managers selected have the authority, knowledge and experience to resolve the problem.
5. Workshops are based on live problems. Objectives are defined for each workshop and responsibility for action is clearly laid down. Workshops are supplemented, where necessary, by individual counselling or small group discussions. Each workshop normally meets weekly. No manager is

expected to attend more than once per week. The total programme extends over about 12 months. Workshops are not a training extra relevant to one small part of a manager's job. Unlike conventional training courses, there are no lectures. Emphasis is on joint problem-solving and learning by doing.
6. Throughout the workshop sessions, achievement is constantly reviewed against the objectives, both within the group and with the chief executive.

Making management training an economic force

The points made so far show areas where management training can be used as an economic weapon. They are so clearly a top management issue that I believe that any chief executive who ignores them is not doing his job as well as he should. In many companies this is likely to be because these particular uses of training have never crossed his mind.

It is one thing to urge that something is critical, but to be of value this advice has to be turned into a series of practical steps that can be taken. The rest of this chapter suggests a way to review what is being done in the company, with a view to changing it when appropriate.

The first step is for top management to review the management training that has been taking place, both the intentions for this year and the actual activities of the past two. Initially this is an information-gathering exercise, which in some companies will bring many surprises. Questions which need answering include:

- What training initiatives (internal and external have occurred)?
- What was the objective of each?
- Who was trained (numbers, levels, etc.)?
- What percentage were they of the people needing this training?
- What were the full costs?
- How does this spend compare with (a) UK competitors and (b) competitors from Japan, USA or West Germany?
- What was the outcome of this training?
- Were the objectives attained?
- How were the training needs established?

The next stage requires an assessment of training needs based on the objectives and strategies of the firm. In other words assessing training needs from the top-down against the six possible uses for training discussed above. All the research proves that very few companies will find that the analysis of what they are doing will match with the top-down strategic view of what they should be doing.

From these two exercises will come an understanding of the real needs of the firm. Bottom-up assessments, through for example the annual training needs analysis, should be studied against this view. In terms of topic there may indeed be some overlap, although the emphasis and context of the topic will usually be different.

It is desirable to make as detailed an analysis of training needs as possible in the light of the top-down requirements. Various options include:

- reorienting the annual appraisal scheme so that judgements are made against a more explicit view of the aims of the firm;
- management assessments comparing the critical skills needed to implement strategies – for example, with what they believe the company currently possesses;
- independent surveys, measuring against the corporate need.

My view is that it would be unwise to insist that every training initiative had to be proved to be of economic value in the sense described in this chapter. There will always be a measure of uncertainty around parts of the analysis. This grey area should be a modest proportion to the total training spend.

In most companies there will be enough savings from management training they will wish to discontinue, to fund at least some of the new initiatives. Care needs to be taken over how those new initiatives should be handled, and the next chapter will discuss one approach, the tailored course, in detail. It is unwise to generalise, but the research evidence suggests that the majority of chief executives who get involved in management training will drastically change the training programme. If they want to continue making management training a weapon for competitive success, they may have to change the way management training is organised and controlled, to redress the faults which were described in detail in Chapter 5.

The periodic sally by the chief executive into the training arena may cause a shake-up, but it may not give him a continuing system that will work for the firm's economic good. To achieve this he needs to think of the components of the organisational model of Chapter 6:

- Is the *task* of the training function properly defined?
- Are the *people* in training of the appropriate seniority level, competence and intellect?
- Is the function sensibly *structured*? Does the final reporting stand close enough to the top?
- Are the training *decision processes* adequate to ensure that the "right" initiatives are decided and run in the most effective way to achieve their objective?
- Is the appropriate *information* available for the training function to operate? Do they get access to his strategic thinking? Is there emphasis on monitoring and evaluating the results of training?

- Are the *reward systems* adequate to attract the right people into training?

In a modern company it is unwise for the training function to wait for the chief executive to weigh them in the balance. Those who sit and wait, and ignore the issues of this chapter, will undoubtedly be found wanting. Those who drive to get the right things done may well succeed in achieving more than would have been possible in the top-down investigation.

Many management training managers will find it hard to move, because of current status and lack of awareness of the options that are available to them. The chapters that follow, through example and analysis, provide further benchmarks against which training functions can measure themselves.

References

1. T. J. Peters and R. H. Waterman (1982): *In Search of Excellence,* Harper and Row, page 168
2. K. Ascher (1983): *Management Training in Large UK Business Organisations,* Harbridge House

8

The Tailored Course

Any company wishing to make management training a competitive weapon will need to think very carefully about the method of training chosen. There are many options open, but the discerning company will not use these blindly. While every option may be the "best" for some types of need, most are clearly unsuitable for meeting *all* needs. The appropriate option should be considered against the objectives of the training initiative and should evaluate the total costs against the expected benefit. Cheapness is only the most important criterion if it provides the same benefits as a more expensive option. The tired routes which some companies use for all their training should certainly be challenged, because many of the methods used are unsuitable for achieving the economic objectives argued in this book.

One of the most useful training options is the tailored company course, and this becomes almost the only option for senior to middle management training for at least one of the six key areas discussed in the previous chapter. It is difficult to imagine a successful training initiative designed to implement a corporate strategy, unless the training has been designed around the company situation.

It is possible to argue that the more specifically the objectives of the course are related to the corporate policies and strategies, the more likely it will be that a tailored course is the only valid option. It will also come into its own in an environment where managers are suspicious of training, since putting a course in the context of the company is a very good way of giving it relevance. Training that is in some way tied to the real world experienced by managers in the firm is likely to be better received by the hard-pressed or the cynical. The tailored course works well in situations where the exploration of concepts in the context of the firm facilitates learning. This may occur in all companies, and may be particularly appropriate for the vast majority of managers who have not had the opportunity to attend a business school.

The tailored course may be viable at the any level of management, varying from being *virtually essential* for senior managers to *possibly desirable* at supervisory levels. Where there arc large numbers of managers to be trained there may be only a small difference in training costs per head between the tailored course and other options. There is often value in a course which, with minor modifications, goes from top to bottom of the organisation, contributing to a common understanding, and helping to build a corporate culture.

When the prize is increased market share, successful implementation of a new strategy, the removal of a problem or something similar, the potential benefits may mean that it is economic even though comparatively small numbers of managers are to be trained.

What is a tailored course?

Our various surveys detected some confusion among some training managers over what a tailored course is. Some appear to think that any course run in-company is tailored, and this idea is reinforced by some vendors who overstate the virtues of their standard courses. I have been in competitive bid situations which called for a unique, tailored course, but where the contract was awarded to someone who bid on an off-the-shelf basis. In this situation had the specification been for a standard course, the unsuccessful vendors would have either bid on this basis or declined to propose. The confusion meant that the client was not necessarily awarding the tender to the most appropriate vendor, and the whole expensive process of preparing proposals was a waste of effort.

The tailored course by definition has to be designed specifically for the client situation. In my experience this means that the priorities and weightings of topics will be set in relation to the company need, and that all teaching material will be written or selected to fulfil the course objectives. This invariably means that any lecture sessions are prepared in the context of the company and with a good understanding of what is relevant to that company. Case studies are often written especially for the course, either to provide the particular experience needed, or to study a real company situation. It is not untypical for all teaching material to be specially prepared in this way.

Sometimes the objectives are not best served through a complete reliance on company-based teaching material. Occasionally material may be written around another situation, but it may also be appropriate to draw in a proportion of published material carefully selected to fit the need. This could take the form of case studies chosen from the glossary of the International Case Clearing House, or videos or films from outside sources.

There may be good reasons why some outside material should be considered. It may be better to approach a sensitive area via a neutral case study, so that participants are not inhibited by company policies or an unwillingness to criticise those involved in the real issue. Sometimes it is desirable for situations to be examined outside of a company context to give perspective. This may be of value, if only to demonstrate that the issue is not unique to the company.

What differentiates a tailored course using a measure of published material from an off-the-shelf standard course is that it is still a unique course, put together in a way that is unlikely to be run in this form for any other company. In my experience the necessary adaptation to the company situation means that the standard material context of a tailored course never rises above 50 per cent of the total content, and is nearly always much lower than this.

The standard off-the-shelf course, even if slanted to the company, is almost the same when run for another company. This lack of uniqueness means that it is rarely suitable for any initiative which is intended to operate in the six key areas identified in the previous chapter. There is one important exception where a standard course may become "self-tailoring", and this is in some of the behavioural subjects where questionnaires and assessments mean that the concepts are reinterpreted in the context of the participants. The main difficulty is to be sure that the particular concepts used are appropriate to the issue which the course is designed to tackle.

It should not be overlooked that many in-company courses which have been designed internally are not tailored to fulfil a particular economic objective. The fact that a senior marketing executive of the company gives a lecture on marketing does not necessarily carry the cause forwards (and in may cases takes it backwards!). Similarly the common mix of internal and external lectures in a sort of circus is also unlikely to achieve the results of a properly designed course tailored not only to fit the company but also to achieve specific objectives.

Developing a tailored course

A tailored course can be developed internally or by using external assistance. When the reason for the course is tied to one of the six key areas the internal option may become inappropriate on the grounds of objectivity or status. It may be very hard for a person inside the company to stretch the boundaries of perception, or to properly understand strategic options other than that being pursued. The internal person may be perceived as inappropriate for any course involving senior management, however competent he or she might be.

The internal option should only be taken if the design team is able to take a multi-disciplinary view. Company trainers may be excellent in behavioural topics, but may be unable to conceive of a course that intertwines several other disciplines in an integrated way. Another issue is whether the internal resource knows how to design a tailored course designed to achieve an economic objective. Few do, although the notes in this chapter may help.

Whether the choice is internal or external, the approach to the development should be similar and will go through a sequence of steps. These are shown diagrammatically in Figure 8.1.

The Tailored Course   99

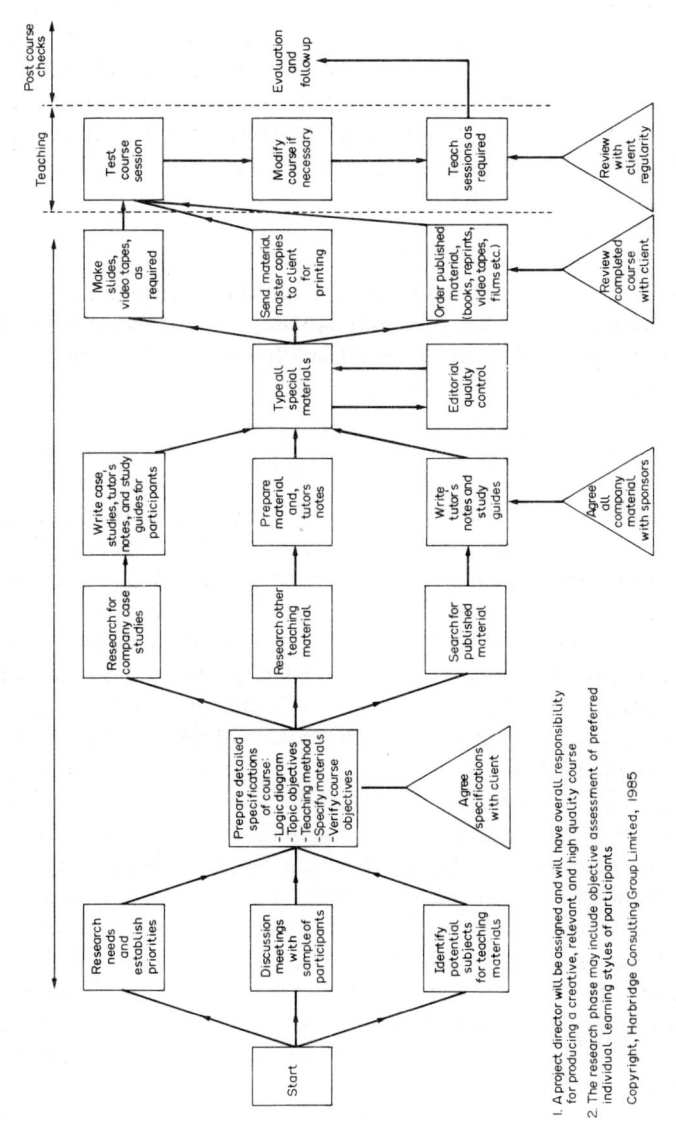

FIGURE 8.1. The Harbridge House general approach to developing tailored courses

1. Research phase

It is essential that the tailored course is designed in a full understanding of the company. Even when training needs have been clearly identified, the course designers will need to build on the statistical summaries by discussions with key manager and potential participants. The minimum aim is to understand the significance of course topics to the company so that priorities can be decided, and participants' requirements flushed out. Information may be drawn from individual interviews alone, or group discussions.

When the course is intended to address one of the six key areas, a greater depth of research may be required. A course to address a problem can only be designed if the problem can be properly defined in the context of the company's resources, skills, strengths and weaknesses. The implications of a new strategy have to be understood before a course can be designed to help implement that strategy.

The depths to which the research phase has to be taken will vary with the amount of work undertaken before the course is commissioned. The requirement is not to re-do everything that has been done already, but to gain a complete understanding of the situation for which the course is to be designed.

2. Design phase

The design and specification of the course follows naturally from the research phase. It is an opportunity for creative thinking, since the best way of dealing with a topic in a tailored course is rarely a matter of routine. A good specification should detail the objectives of the course, and should do much more than present a timetable. Priorities assigned to each topic should be shown, together with the expectations from the way each topic is to be addressed, the teaching approach to be used, the reason for the weighting given the topic, and a description of the teaching material that has to be designed or developed.

I find it helpful to draw a logic diagram for the course (not necessarily in programme order), so that the relationships of topics are clear, and can be seen in the context of the course objectives. Such diagrams are valuable for a single-subject course (for example, a model of the marketing concept which also shows how each course topic fits with the whole). They are invaluable for multi-function courses, which are intended to help the company achieve some state of change.

A major advantage of a carefully specified course is that it makes it possible for meaningful discussions to be held between those sponsoring and those preparing the course. It is cheaper to make changes at this stage than after all the material has been developed. The discipline forces thought to the design of the course, and in particular into the methods by which different topics can be integrated.

3. Development and selection of materials phase

By definition a large part of the teaching material, whether case studies, lectures, syndicate exercises or whatever, will be especially designed and written for the course. To write a case study around a company situation requires a measure of research, followed by the ability to translate the situation into a good teaching case study. Even the selection of published material is a matter for care. Although published case studies can be readily identified from the glossaries of the case clearing houses, specimen copies have to be obtained and studied both for fit with the course objectives and as a vehicle to teach the particular topic. Few case studies come with teaching notes, so these have to be prepared and a teaching plan worked out for the case study.

Not surprisingly, this is the most time-consuming stage in the preparation of a tailored course, and as a rule of thumb will take between 5 and 10 days preparation for each day of teaching (or longer, if computers are to be used which require new programes). This is real time. Elapsed time will be longer, as provison has to be made for clearing internal company material, interviewing appropriate managers during the presentation of material and reviewing all the materials before piloting. All new material has to be typed, and enough copies made for the piloting of the programme. As a rule of thumb the total elapsed time required for developing material will be about double the actual development time.

4. Testing the course

Sometimes there is only one session planned for a tailored course, in which case it is impossible to pilot it. Where several sessions are intended it is worthwhile making the first session a pilot, which means that an adequate gap must be allowed between this and subsequent repeats to correct any faults. Generally a pilot should be run in the normal way, except that a more thorough review of the course should be planned with participants, possibly a few days after the course. If the course is to have a large participation at each session it may be useful to restrict attendance at the pilot to a lower number.

If the course has been well thought out there will be no major problems at this stage. Typically the pilot will enable the course developers to test the assumptions made about the time needed for different exercises, check that the material is working in the way intended, and remove any ambiguities in instructions for syndicate exercises.

5. Delivering the course

After the successful pilot the course may be delivered as frequently as required. A common mistake is, once it becomes a successful part of the company's training programme, to run it without considering updating and adaptations to changing circumstances. A course that is intended to last several years should be reviewed annually to ensure relevance, and time spent in bringing it up to date if this is needed. A tailored course may well form part

```
           Concrete experience
          ╱                    ╲
Active experimentation      Reflective observation
          ╲                    ╱
          Abstract conceptualisation
```

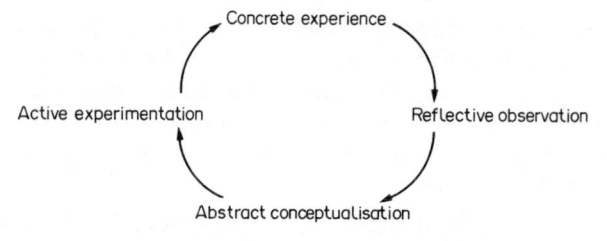

FIGURE 8.2. Learning cycle theory

of the regular training programme, but should not be allowed to wither from lack of attention.

The delivery method for a tailored course may take many forms. My preference is for the course to be taught by a team of two, selected to give coverage of the topics on the course, who work as a team throughout. This builds a strong rapport with participants. I have a strong bias against the ringmaster and circus type of course, where one person acts as co-ordinator and the presenters do their turn and go away from the course. This style of course, very popular with some company trainers, is considerably less effective as a learning mechanism.

6. Evaluation

Care should be given to evaluating any course, and as this is rarely done in the UK a separate chapter will discuss this important subject in detail.

Evaluation is easier when the objectives of the course can be defined in specific terms, and particularly when directed at corporate rather than individual benefits.

Learning cycle theory and the tailored courses

Learning cycle theory gives useful insight into how people learn. Figure 8.2 summarises the main stages of the learning cycle which have been identified. Individual learning is facilitated by an integrated process that includes all four elements of the learning cycle: *concrete experience*, or undertaking some form of activity to use the new knowledge; *reflective observation*, or the consideration of the information and the experience undergone; *abstract conceptualisation*, or the formation of statements, generalisations or theories that can be used by the individual; *active experimentation*, or applying the new understanding to different situations as a basis for moving to new experiences.

All individuals learn by some combination of these phases, and good course design will ensure that all four are present in the course. The concept helps to explain why for most people the lecture by itself is an inefficient

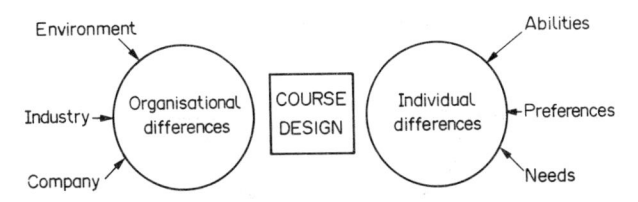

FIGURE 8.3. Designing the tailored course

learning mode, since it can usually address only one of the four stages of the cycle.

Unfortunately, individuals are not all the same in their preference for each of the four phases, although all four phases are present to some degree in each person. Such things as an individual's personality, his educational and career base, and his level in the organisation will affect his preferred learning style. It is possible to measure learning styles and to design courses which fit the learning style needs of individuals in the company. For practical reasons one course usually has to be designed, instead of numerous variants to suit groups with different learning styles. There is also a company benefit in mixing people with different learning style preferences, since this is more likely to allow for multi-functional attendance. The loss of efficiency to an individual, because the course does not completely mirror his learning preferences, may be compensated by the insight gained from seeing a problem through the viewpoint of a different function.

The tailored course draws on both organisational and individual differences, and can produce something which is uniquely valuable to both. Figure 8.3 illustrates this process.

Two other features which facilitate learning among managers are relevance and interest. The tailored course scores very heavily because of a high level of perceived relevance, and this is heightened when the course is intended to cope with one of our six key areas. It may be seen as relevant to study marketing in the context of the company, and this will be heightened if the course is clearly focused on a strategic change which will affect the future of those attending. Interest is helped by relevance. No one goes on a course to be entertained, but there is no reason why they should be bored. Bored people are unlikely to learn as effectively as interested people, if only because their attention wanders more frequently. If they are very bored, they may learn nothing. Attention to learning cycle theory is one way to ensure that there is variety in the course.

Learning cycle theory also illustrates one reason why individual assessment should not be made on participants' performance on a short course. Experimentation is curtailed if the personal risk goes too high. In addition, a course gives a lop-sided view of a person, and may be grossly unfair. When the course is tailored to achieve one of the six key results it is even more important to avoid individual assessment. A feature of the design of such a course might be to build commitment to a strategy by working through the reasons for it. A person who believes he is being evaluated may be reluctant to question a corporate decision lest this be taken as a signal that he is not a dedicated employee. If he cannot resolve his doubts about the strategy he is unlikely to become committed, and suppressing doubts rarely helps resolve them.

Case studies

Case studies are not the only route to a successful tailored course, but they are one of the richest, because they provide a vehicle that can be used to address each of the stages in the learning cycle. They can be written around a company situation to confront a problem or issue, or they may explore a parallel situation which is ostensibly occurring in another company, thus making it easier for participants to be critical.

For some people the image of case studies is a mixture of business schools, lengthy documents, and the 3 or 4-foot high stack of papers that greets each participant when he or she checks in at Harvard. In fact case studies provide a very flexible teaching tool, particularly when written especially for a particular teaching purpose.

It is possible to use a case study for individual use (questions requiring an essay-type answer), although this is unlikely to be appropriate on tailored company courses. More likely the case study will form the base of a small-group exercise, or be used in a plenary session in a participative manner.

Another imaginative approach is the development of an evolving case study, which is delivered to the class in sections, with one or more exercises around each section. This can bring a considerable economy in preparation time, since participants make a cumulative use of the case study information, and never have to master more than a few pages in each section. It is also valuable in showing how different functional issues may be brought about by a common core event. Such an approach may have something of the dynamism of a business game, withoug encouraging the desire to "beat the game" which so often occurs. It also leaves more educational control over topics than may occur with a business game.

Case studies may be used in a role-playing mode, although this demands a high level of case-writing skills.

It is also possible to make case studies multi-media, although this naturally increases development costs. Videos may supplement or replace written material, although any that require acting skills should be prepared by experts in that field. Programmes may be used on computers in conjunction with the case study.

Whichever method is chosen, the ability to tailor case studies to the exact requirements makes them one of the most useful teaching methods for company courses.

Sources of tailored courses

It is possible for a company to design, develop and run tailored courses from its own resources. Prerequisites are people with the appropriate educational skills and functional knowledge, who are able to be objective in their approach to company situations, have the status and courage to challenge company norms and strategies, are able to run courses at all levels in the company, including the very top, and have sufficient time to do the job well. In most companies one or more of these attributes are missing. The Coopers and Lybrand research,[1] as has already been mentioned, drew attention to the low status of the training function in many companies. Few companies have the skills to develop or teach a tailored course that seeks to deal with one of the six key areas. The probability is that the right solution is for the company to seek outside professional help.

This is relatively easy to obtain, although by no means all the purveyors of training who purport to offer tailored courses do in fact do so. There is a lack of knowledge among many vendors of both the benefits of the tailored course and how to do it, and the unsophisticated buyer can find himself using standard courses that do not in fact address his specific needs. There are, in fact, relatively few organisations that can offer these rather specific services, although there are literally hundreds that can fulfil other training needs. Some guidance to the professional services of capable organisations, and some hints on buying these services, will be useful to most people contemplating a tailored course, and particularly to those who have not used this approach before.

The Harbridge House research into tailored courses[2] sought information from both the larger companies which buy these services, and the leading vendors. There are really two main sources of help: academic institutions (business schools and management colleges), and some firms of management consultants. Not all business schools offer in-company training services, and not all that do provide tailored courses (although some confuse tailoring with other in-company courses).

In the USA the position is very similar. Dreybeck, Hampton and Byrne[3] report a survey of 46 leading graduate business schools which found that more than half had "jumped on the custom-programme bandwagon". Those that do not provide this service include the leading business schools Harvard and Stanford, whose traditional executive education programmes are the largest. The feeling in these business schools seems to be that the tailored course should be left to the consultants, since tying a course specifically to a company-need sacrifices some academic freedom, and departs from the advantage of exposing executives to peers in other companies and industries. In the USA the driving force that is pushing more business schools towards the tailored course route is economic rather than idealistic, as MBA classes have declined and new sources of income have been sought. Some US consultants are bitter about organisations with tax-free status competing in what has tradionally been their field.

In the UK it is also economic pressures which have forced more business schools and colleges to go this route, although some, like Ashridge and Henley, have always undertaken some work in the tailored areas. The pressures are declining enthusiasm for many of the traditional executive education programmes, coupled with increasing pressure on other sources of funds, and the overall debate about privatisation of business schools. One or two business schools have set up dedicated units to develop tailored educational assignments, but the buyer should be aware that courses he buys are not always staffed by the business school faculty. At least one of the leading British business schools relies heavily on part-time contracted labour to fulfil its contracts. Attitudes of individual business schools vary. One or two limit their involvement to top management projects or assignments that look interesting, and will turn down other work. Some are in it mainly for the economic return, and have no particular dedication to the value of what they are doing. Others are both dedicated and offer a good service.

The main advantage business schools have is that they are widely known, receive extensive promotion and publicity, and have an established alumni. Some moved in to the tailored education field partly because of requests received from potential customers, many of whom are not aware of other options. The famous statement that "nobody gets sacked for choosing IBM" applies here too. A well-known business school may be chosen because it offers less personal risk to the person recommending or making the decision: it may not be the least risky approach for the company, and may indeed not be the best choice, but the individual can escape censure by claiming that he went for the best.

The weakness of some business schools is that they do not really want to be in the tailored business. Staffing may be difficult. They have not all worked out sensible reward structures for the extra work put on the faculty (hence the use of contract tutors who are not on the faculty). Extra full-time staff cannot easily be hired because of controls on establishment size. In addition many faculty members may prefer to do consultancy or training work on their own account, and are thus often in competition with their employer. As a practitioner in this field I can perhaps sum up these weaknesses by saying that I believe that only about 10 per cent of the business schools offer serious concern to my organisation on a competitive bid, but despite this all business schools are likely to receive more requests to bid than any commercial operator in this field.

Outside of the academic institutions there are a few firms of management consultants which are expert in the field of tailored education; currently no more than half a dozen firms, although the expansion of the market is leading to new competitors. Those who can offer a good tailored service do not necessarily include all the well-known training names, and indeed being good in other areas of training does not necessarily imply competence in developing and teaching tailored courses.

Criteria for selecting a supplier

Good services in this field may be found in the academic and private sectors. Sorting out who to use requires a careful consideration of a number of factors in relation to the objectives of the initiative. Although particular situations will change priorities and add new factors, the following list gives a starting point.

1. Price

Price is obviously important, but should be looked at in relation to effectiveness and benefits. The approaches recommended by the suppliers may differ. If the price does not include a significant charge for developing and designing the course, you are probably not getting a tailored course.

2. Track record

Risk is reduced if you choose an organisation with a track record in tailored education, and in the type of situation you are trying to address. It is wise to ask for client references and to speak to those clients. Many organisations would respond to a request for proposals even though they may never have worked on tailored courses. Some would have the potential to do this work, but the buyer runs the risk that they will not understand fully what is involved.

3. Employees

The track record of the firm is one thing, and equally important is the track record of its employees. The key members of the consultants' or academic institution's team should themselves have a good record in this area. Tailored courses call for a mixture of consulting, creative development and teaching skills, and these are enhanced when backed by a record of achievement. Questions such as the standing and the quality of the people working on your project should be settled at the outset.

4. Activities of firm

The professional organisation offering to provide your tailored course is more likely to be able to meet your needs if it has a mix of activities. An organisation that does nothing but training is less well positioned than one whose employees work on a mix of teaching, course development and consultancy assignments.

5. Continuity

Some tailored courses are intended to solve an immediate problem, and the whole project will be over in a few months. Other situations may require the course to be taught for years. In the latter case the ability of the supplier to satisfy the buyer that he has the resources and competence to sustain the programme is of vital importance.

6. Flexibility

Many situations require a vendor who has the resources to be flexible to meet changing requirements. Where a course is taught; when; and how frequently should be determined by the needs of the client rather than the constraints of the supplier. Extensive programmes deserve careful planning by the client and the consultancy, but the consultancy should be in a position to meet all reasonable needs, and deal with the unexpected. A question to ask in selecting a vendor for a large or extensive assignment is whether the firm has this flexibility. Related to this is a different dimension of experience, that of working with people of different countries, cultures, and mother languages. It is not just a question of whether the firm can run two sessions of the course in Malawi, but whether they have any experience of the additional factors that become important in transferring a course to a different situation.

7. Commercial attitude

Another serious issue is whether the supplier has a commerical attitude and awareness. A reasonable course may be run for a general training need by a head-in-the-clouds academic (this is not to suggest that all academics are head-in-the-clouds), but as the company moves closer to the six key corporate needs, so it has to be sure that it is dealing with an organisation that can relate to the problems and empathise with the managers.

8. Creativity

You should also look for signs of creativity and innovativeness in the supplier you choose, signs which will be evident from the firm's track record and the suggestions made for dealing with your situation.

9. Teaching approach

Pay careful attention to the style of teaching to be used, and how the supplier intends to staff the course. Beware of the circus type of training, which does not allow any synergistic rapport between participants and tutors. Because the short course aimed at meeting one of the six key needs is different in objectives and content from the normal public attendance business schools short course, you should be suspicious of a solution which mirrors the public short course. Teaching approaches should be carefully related to the aims of the course.

10. Personal belief in value of work

Finally, try to choose a supplier whose employees have a personal belief in the value of what they are doing. It is possible to obtain a competent course from people who are cynical about the benefits of their work. An inspired course can only come from people who care.

What is going on?

The Harbridge House researches have revealed a resurgence of interest in the tailored course among the larger companies in the UK. About half of our admittedly small sample of 42 companies were re-evaluating their past pattern of training and giving more thought to the tailored course. All the suppliers of tailored courses interviewed, and this included almost all suppliers of significance, reported a resurgence of interest, and an increase in enquiries. Not all tailored courses address the six key areas, and the approach is sutiable for many other training situations. Interest in the tailored course is matched in the training world by a fascination with open learning approaches to management training. Findings from the Harbridge House research in this area, and suggestion for forging these methods into a competitive weapon, will appear in a later chapter. At this point I will do no more than suggest that for some large companies tailored courses and tailored open learning systems might be developed in conjunction with each other, particularly when addressing the corporate training needs.

Before moving to distance learning, it is valuable to look at the experience of others in using tailored courses, so that the skeleton of this chapter may be seen fleshed out in real situations. The next four chapters will present some examples from experience.

References

1. Coopers and Lybrand Associates (1985): *A Challenge to Complacency Changing Attitudes to Training,* Manpower Services Commission/National Economic Development Office
2. F. Bateson (1986): *Tailored Management Education. Myth or Reality?* Harbridge Consulting Group Ltd
3. K. Dreybeck, W. Hampton and J. Burne (1986): When companies tell business schools what to teach, *Business Week,* 10 February

9

Coopers and Lybrand: Choosing an Outside Supplier

Background

Large contracts with outside suppliers to develop and teach courses are not all that numerous. Because of that, there is little experience in how to evaluate and compare proposals from different vendors.

Some companies will instinctively go to a business school, because of the past connections of a senior manager, the image of business schools as centres of excellence, or ignorance of any alternative.

This case study, which was originally published in the Harbridge House survey of tailored education, [1] provides information on the way in which Coopers and Lybrand reached a decision on what must be one of the major tailored management education contracts awarded in 1986. This was a large contract. The lessons can be applied to much smaller contracts.

Harbridge House was awarded the contract, on a competitive bid against five business schools and one other commercial firm. Coopers and Lybrand provided the information for this case history of the bidding and selection process, although names of the competing organisations have not been attributed to the data. The data itself are real.

Coopers and Lybrand sought a supplier who could design, develop and teach four linked management courses of 3-4 days each to their professional staff (the majority of whom are accountants) from immediately after qualifying to the stage before promotion to partner. Each level of course was designed for a different grade, and the total concept moved the knowledge from operational at the lower levels to strategic at the highest. This business knowledge programme needed to position management as an integrated activity, since each course had to cover four to five different functional topics.

The business knowledge courses were to be a key part of a broader approach to post-qualifying training. Other aspects would include behavioural skills and product knowledge.

Coopers and Lybrand prepared a careful and lengthy brief which described the background to the firm, the aims and objectives of the total management development approach, the purpose of the business knowledge programme, and an outline requirement for each course.

A key paragraph in the briefing document was that Coopers and Lybrand were seeking an external resource "who can demonstrate the breadth of knowledge, understanding, and creative thinking" needed to help achieve the overall aim.

The advantage of the document was that it made Coopers and Lybrand's expectations clear, but left considerable scope to the supplier for creative thinking. One of the challenges to the supplier was to develop linkages among levels, and across each course, so that the result would be an integrated whole.

Pre-selection of bidders

Coopers and Lybrand spent some time deciding who to invite to propose, and eventually produced a list of seven organisations. These were visited and the project discussed with them. A formal invitation to bid followed.

The bid process

Suppliers were given about a month to prepare proposals, which had to reach Coopers and Lybrand just before Christmas 1985. The brief made it very clear what was needed in the proposal. The intention was to invite all bidders to make a presentation of their proposals in early January, which would lead to a short list who would make presentations to the top management group. A decision would be reached in February.

A team of three senior human resourses people was set up to evaluate the proposals and the first presentations. In order to make these reviews effective a set of evaluation criteria was drawn up.

The only flaw in this was the assumption that the span of prices bid would be narrow and that price would be fairly low in the decision criteria. The reality was that prices quoted varied enormously and commercial sense meant that it had to be given more consideration.

Evaluation criteria

The evaluation criteria developed for this project appear in Table 9.1. It would not be ethical to publicise the scores attributed to each supplier by name, but the range was from a low of 22 to a high of 41 (the ultimate winner).

Although an initial assessment was made based on the proposals received, the selection criteria score sheet was used principally for making the final assessment after the presentations. By then the suppliers had had the

TABLE 9.1. Coopers and Lybrand evaluation criteria

	_____Criteria/Rating_____				Raw score	Weighting factor	Total score
	0	1	2	3			
Previous experience							
C & L's market sector	None	Relevant but limited	Quite relevant	Highly relevant	—	—	—
Tailored programmes	None	Some Interesting but uncertain	Quite a lot	A lot	—	2	—
Design concepts	Not attractive	Interesting but uncertain	Quite interesting and may work	Very interesting and likely to work	—	2	—
Price competitive							
Development	Very expensive	Expensive	Average	Below average	—	—	—
Delivery	Very expensive	Expensive	Average	Below average	—	—	—
Note: relative to each other							
Commitment (ability to deliver on time)	Low-key interest with reservations	Low-key interest	Enthusiastic but with reservations	Enthusiastic	—	2	—
Willingness to develop tailored programme	Unwilling	Slanted off-the-shelf, not tailored	Probably tailored	Definitely tailored	—	3	—
Relate to us as a client	Does not relate	Relates OK	Relates well	Relates extremely well	—	3	—

TABLE 9.2. *Prices of the seven suppliers bidding (Coopers and Lybrand assignment.)*

	Total costs: development + 1 year teaching	Type of proposal classified by degree of tailoring
1	£141,330	Slanted, off-the-shelf
2	£214,375	Highly tailored
3	£218,600	Off-the-shelf
4	£324,500	Substantially tailored
5	£337,275	Moderately tailored
6	£368,000	Moderately tailored
7	£435,950	Highly tailored

opportunity to explain their approach, and the evaluation team gained the opportunity to probe and clarify statements made in the proposals.

Nature of proposals

Despite the fact that the brief called for a response which was unique to the client, only three of the vendors actually proposed significant tailoring of the programme. However, this did not mean that those who bid on a standard material basis were cheaper than those who offered a tailored approach, as in many cases their teaching price was higher.

Among those who bid for a tailored form there was a considerable difference in approach. This was genuinely helpful to Coopers and Lybrand in making their decision, and illustrated the richness and variety that can be brought into the tailored solution.

Price was also affected by the way in which each supplier proposed to deliver the courses. For example the *daily rate* charges of the highest price bidder were actually lower than those of the successful bidder, whose overall price was the second cheapest.

Span of prices

Table 9.2 shows the prices for developing, piloting, and teaching the first year's sessions of the courses. The enormous variation in price, coupled with differences of approach, suggest that great care should be given to the choice of supplier in any large assignment. The key is not cheapness, but cost-effectiveness.

The lessons

The first lesson that can be drawn from this is that in order to evaluate suppliers' bids the brief has to be well-thought-out. Ideally it should leave room for the supplier to suggest approaches to achieve the objectives. How else can you separate creativity from an echo chamber?

If the brief is clear it is possible to draw up criteria, against which to evaluate the suppliers. The second lesson is that the care is needed in preparing these criteria. The more objectively this can be done, the more likely is a sensible result likely.

The third lesson is that the general reputation of a supplier is no guarantee that it can respond to the problem you are facing.

The fourth lesson is that prices quoted may vary widely. They depend not only on the daily charge-out rate for consultants used on the project, but on the staffing levels required by the solution. Thus there may be major differences in price because of different approaches.

The fifth lesson is never to assume that a business school is the only solution.

Reference

1. F. Bateson (1986): *Tailored Management Education. Myth or Reality?* Harbridge Consultancy Group Ltd.

10

British Petroleum's Business Management Programme: Management Education for Future Growth

The problem

It would be easy to dismiss some of the suggestions of the previous two chapters as unworkable in the real world, and for this reason I have included in this book a number of case histories which substantiate my views. One of the highlights of my personal career has been a long association, through Harbridge House, with British Petroleum, an association that has given me much friendship, intellectual stimulation, and the opportunity to develop and make real many of my own ideas. A great feeling of satisfaction has come from the changes that have resulted.

In the mid-1970s BP began to think about some of the organisational issues caused by the environment in which it operates. Until 1973 this had followed a predictable path. After the OPEC initiatives of that year the relative stability was succeeded by turbulence. It became clear that the world of the future was going to be very different from the past, and that one of the requirements would be for managers who could cope with changes, many of which could not even be visualised.

At the same time BP was changing as a business, moving in new directions and becoming more diversified. This again overlaid a different pattern of managerial needs, making limited function experience within one industry alone inadequate for the successful operation of the BP of the future. It was not that BP would overnight become unrecognisable, but that it could start to draw away from many of the experiences and characteristics that had made it successful in the past. In fact the pace of change has been fairly dramatic, and the BP of today has many significant differences with the BP of 1978 when I was first involved. It also has many cultural values and skills which were recognisable in the "old" BP, and it is these which have played an important part in helping BP adapt to new circumstances.

In thinking about these issues it was realised that modern managers in BP would have to be able to manage in a very different way from their predecessors, and that the pressures on them would intensify as BP underwent future changes. It was not just that the managers of 1977 faced a different situation from managers of 1973, but that the situation would change many times as their careers developed. It was in 1977 that BP began to look seriously at the management educational implications of the diagnosis, and whether an educational initiative could be used as a means of ensuring that the younger managers of the day would be in a position to manage effectively when they became the senior managers of the future.

BP is an organisation that tends to retain its employees, and it was a reasonable bet that most of the future general managers and managing directors were already employed. Historically, BP has always given a lot of attention to training, and has a professional approach to this function. It was almost a natural evolution for the management training advisor, Tom Glynn Jones, to be charged with the task of developing and implementing a solution.

The magnitude of the task was easy to define. In the UK alone there was a pool of several hundred managers, in the approximate age range of 28 – 35, and there was a fast flow into and out of this pool. What was required was a business school type of programme, something like the 12-week Advanced Management Programme of Harvard in scope, although the peer group would be younger and in more junior positions than the AMP would accept. The initial aim was to help participants be more aware of change and potential change, be multi-functional in their thinking, and better equipped to manage now and in the future.

Discussions were held with many business schools, but the problem was insoluble in the way it was defined. BP could not release so many people for such a lengthy period, particularly as it already sponsored a significant number of managers of all levels in business schools, either on short courses or to obtain MBA degrees. In any case no one business school could allow its public courses to be swamped by representatives from one organisation. However, the fact that BP could not release hundreds of people, nor the schools accept them, made it even more important that some internal solution was found so that those senior managers and high-fliers who did go away to external programmes did not get too far away from their staff in skills taught or new thinking made available. It was important for the critical mass of trained managers to be vertical as well as horizontal.

The solution

Harbridge House worked with BP to rethink the problem. Tom Glynn Jones, recalling the decision to use Harbridge House, said "My choice fell on them because, apart from the numbers issue, the business schools did not seem to understand what I was getting at, or did not want to. They saw it as taking away their market, instead of seeing it as an extension of the market. Harbridge House understood right away." The required solution needed to be flexible in order to deal with the issues of time away from work and variations in individual needs. A breakthrough came when it was recognised that to benefit from this type of initiative an individual did not have to undergo a period of continuous training, and that there were quite significant benefits in spreading it over a period of up to 5 years. In turn this led to the idea of breaking the programme down into 1-week modules carefully linked and organised by topic. Within each topic, subject priorities could be adjusted to suit the needs of BP, and changed as the needs altered. The modular concept reduced the project to manageable proportions. It reduced the risk, by enabling the project to be initiated on a phased basis. It created a flexible solution which enabled the participant to match the training to his available time. The eventual design of the programme meant that participants could enter on the topic most important to them, progressing through the others in a manner best suited to their own needs. Those already expert in a topic could miss that module from their personal agenda, a flexibility not available in the normal business school programme.

Individual modules could also be used by persons with limited training needs. There was no necessity to go through every module.

From this basic rethinking of the problem the Business Management Programme was born in late 1978, and the pilot session of the first module was run in May 1979.

The nature of the programme, with inter-module links and numerous entry points, meant that it had to be tailor-made. Standard off-the-shelf material would not have come together in an effective way, and in any case, without tailoring, the sub-topics would not have been weighted to meet BP's needs. A further advantage of a uniquely designed programme was that much of the teaching material could be written around BP situations. In the event some 60 per cent of case studies and other material was written for BP. The remainder was published material deliberately chosen to broaden perspectives, bearing in mind that one objective of the course was to help people deal with different situations. These case studies were selected from normal academic sources. All material was taught in a BP context.

The BP case studies were chosen to fulfil the needs of the course, and to reflect something of the geographical and product diversity of this enormous company (now among the largest in the world). Researching, conceptualising and writing the case studies took the case writers to Australia, Canada, Sweden, Denmark and Germany. Subsequently, case studies have also been written on situations in Zambia and Zimbabwe as the basic BMP modules were modified for use in Africa. One suite of cases covered some of the major strategic decisions faced by BP Canada from the period 1953 - 1980: later material brought this series up to date to 1983. Another case writer found herself on an oil rig in the North Sea, preparing a case on role conflict between a driller and a geologist. Some case studies illustrate situations which have clearly gone very well: others show things which have been more disappointing. The whole provides a rich pattern which, apart from being a vehicle for teaching the programme, helps participants to learn a great deal about the company of which they are a part.

Implementing the solution

One advantage of the module approach was that the development could be spread over several years. There was no need to offer all modules initially, which meant that the concept could be tested on an evolutionary basis. Development costs were spread by this approach, which had the advantage of reducing risk (in the sense of exposure) on a concept which was new to BP and, as far as we were aware, to any firm in the UK. The development, piloting and integration into the programme of each module thus became a process that was manageable.

The order of development followed the priority of needs in BP assessed by Central Training, and took the following course:

Managerial Economics
Marketing 1
Marketing 2
Management Information and Control
Strategic Management
Business Policy 1
Business Policy 2
Creative Decision-making
Organisation and People
Finance and Accounting

The last course, which in fact is one of the favourite entry points into the programme, was only developed last because initially it was intended to add an existing internal course in this topic to the programme. The careful linking of the courses and the common style they followed left the existing course increasingly isolated, and eventually BP took the decision to scrap it and have a new version developed.

Each module followed the development path outlined in Figure 10.1. A sample of potential participants were interviewed to gain their perceptions of the subject and their needs. More detailed interviews were held with various senior managers with a functional interest in a particular topic. In this way it became possible to amend the proposed list of sub-topics so that current BP needs and priorities were addressed. These interviews were undertaken in a pro-active way, which explored why certain issues were not seen as significant, and sought to adjust for any blinkered vision which might have existed. Thus the fact that BP did not use, for example, a particular strategic analytical tool became a cause for debate with corporate planners, and in one

BP Business Management Programme

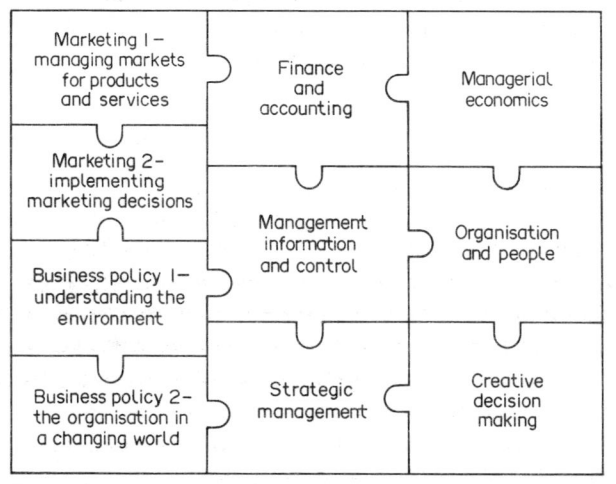

```
┌─────────────────┬─────────────────┬─────────────────┐
│ Marketing 1 –   │                 │                 │
│ managing markets│ Finance         │ Managerial      │
│ for products    │ and             │ economics       │
│ and services    │ accounting      │                 │
├─────────────────┤                 │                 │
│ Marketing 2 –   │                 │                 │
│ implementing    ├─────────────────┼─────────────────┤
│ marketing       │ Management      │                 │
│ decisions       │ information     │ Organisation    │
├─────────────────┤ and control     │ and people      │
│ Business policy │                 │                 │
│ 1 – understanding│                │                 │
│ the environment │                 │                 │
├─────────────────┼─────────────────┼─────────────────┤
│ Business policy │ Strategic       │ Creative        │
│ 2 – the         │ management      │ decision        │
│ organisation in │                 │ making          │
│ a changing world│                 │                 │
└─────────────────┴─────────────────┴─────────────────┘
```

FIGURE 10.1. Extract from BP's internal brochure showing the overall concept of the BMP

or two cases this initiative itself helped to change views in the functional departments.

Course outlines were drawn up with detailed specifications which were discussed and agreed with BP before the courses were developed.

Evaluation

Apart from normal end-of-course assessments, attention was given from the beginning to the thorny subject of evaluation. BP financed some experimental work to measure the learning that actually took place on a course, although this was abandoned when it was realised how much time would be needed in order to be able to interpret results for management use. Two leading US business school professors (George Cabot Lodge, Harvard, and George Steiner, UCLA) critiqued the material which provided an outside quality assessment.

After a few years of operation a complete review of the results of the whole programme was made by a British university. At this point no one had been through all modules, although many had attended several. This meant that some participants had experienced the cumulative effect of the deliberate linkages and reinforcement built into the programme design. The review led to a very useful report which endorsed the concept and the results it was achieving.

Periodic reviews continue, the latest being an assessment of the benefits of the programme to BP Zambia, and such careful assessment should remain a feature in the future.

A new opportunity to continuously monitor the knowledge gained by

120   Management Training and Corporate Strategy

Contents of the Course and Links to other Modules

Creative Decision Making
- Creative-decision making techniques
- Applying creative decision-making to work

Organisation and People
- Organisational structure
- Organisation and its boundaries
- Matrix organisation
- Effective organisation management

Business Policy 2
- People and Change

Finance and Accounting
- Acquisition valuation and consolidation

Strategic Management
- Objectives
- Creativity and innovation
- Strategy and structure
- Strategy and the environment
- Strategic options: methods of analysis
- Pre-acquisition strategy
- Post-acquisition strategy
- International competition
- Strategic choice

Business Policy 1: Understanding the Environment
- Impact on business
- Strategic information
- 'Futures' techniques
- Analytical approaches
- Changing the environment

Business Policy 2: Organisation in a Changing World
- How business copes with change (research studies)
- Scenario planning
- Specific issues

Managerial Economics
- Industry structure analysis
- Cost analysis
- Project evaluation (DCF)

Managing Markets
- Marketing strategy
- Competitive reactions

Finance and Accounting
- Financial policy
- Financial strategy

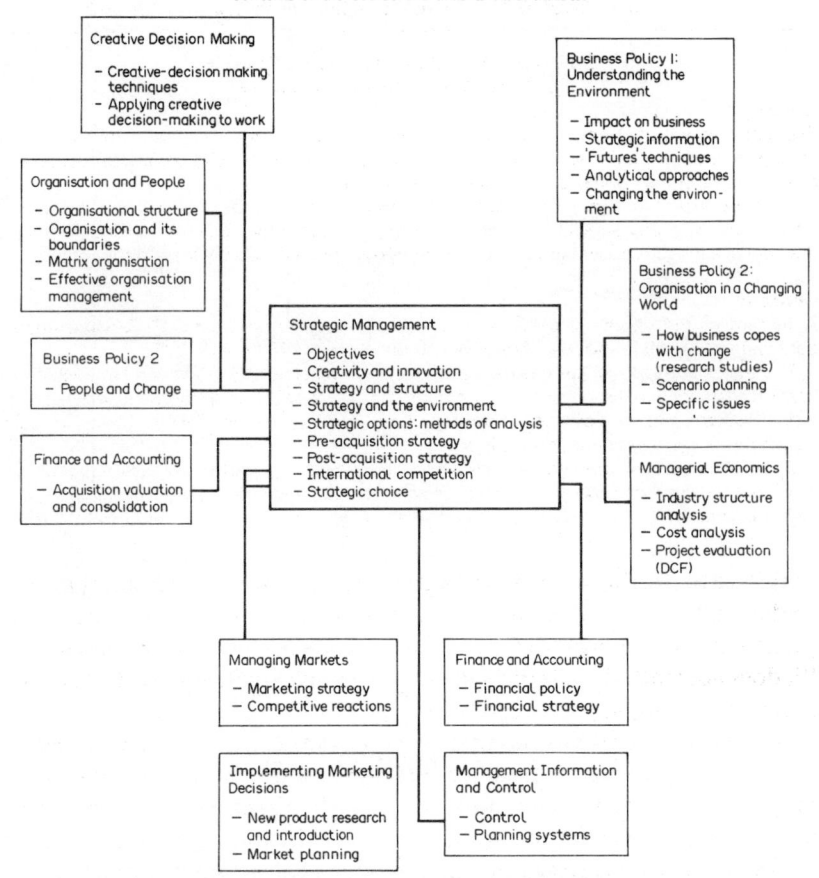

Implementing Marketing Decisions
- New product research and introduction
- Market planning

Management Information and Control
- Control
- Planning systems

FIGURE 10.2. Extract from BP's internal brochure showing how one module links with others

individuals will occur if negotiations with business schools fulfil their promise. The outcome would be an assessment by the business school with a view to giving exemption from the first year of a distance learning and part time MBA to "graduates" of the BMP. Not all participants would want this, but all would be pleased that programmes they had attended had this potential. Those who go through this assessment process will provide a useful example of learning by the rest. There should be a motivational value for those who do not choose to take the MBA route.

Review and updating

BP were always aware that their priorities would change over time; that external events incorporated into course material would have to be brought up to date and would not remain the relevant issues to study; that advances in

FIGURE 10.3. Broad description of the module illustrated in Figure 10.2

BUSINESS MANAGEMENT PROGRAMME
Strategic Management (One Week)

Objective

The management of strategy is one of the most important corporate tasks. Knowledge of the principles of strategic decision-making is essential for any person who wishes to progress and one objective of the course is to provide this knowledge.

At the same time participants will acquire knowledge which will be direct value in their present jobs. There are many parallels between corporate and individual decision-making. In addition the course aims to broaden and strengthen individual powers of analysis and thought.

Content

A feature of the course is a series of case studies written around BP Canada, enabling participants to explore various strategic situations between 1972 and 1980.

The topics studied include business purpose and objectives, creativity and innovation, the relation of strategy to the external environment, the analysis of strategic options, acquisition and diversification, and the contrast of strategy between Japanese and British firms, using the British motor cycle industry as a vehicle.

Some techniques of strategic analysis are demonstrated (e.g. portfolio analysis), but the main emphasis is on understanding the principles which lead to good business decisions at corporate and individual level.

---

subjects would bring a further need to change courses. In addition, when case studies are based on company situations there is more pressure from participants to say what happened next. The normal academic answer that "it does not matter" falls on deaf ears, because to these people it does matter as it is their company.

At the beginning it was accepted that the programme would stagnate unless it was regularly reviewed and updated. An annual review is made of all the programmes, and a list of necessary modifications is made, graded into priority. From this it is possible to select the most important work within the constraints of available funds. Minor modifications are made to the material by the tutors while teaching programmes. More significant alternatives require a more dedicated effort, often with research in BP to confirm priorities or write new case study material.

When the need is to know what happened next, the easiest approach is to invite an appropriate senior manager to a question-and-answer session after participants have studied the case study. A video is made of this session, and is used on subsequent occasions.

Some of the earliest courses have undergone significant variations over time, and although in an evolving situation it is never possible to be completely up to date, it is fair to claim that the BMP remains relevant to BP's needs.

Delivery

Some 18 1-week sessions are now held in the UK each year, and are attended by about 20 people per course. On the most popular courses, which are those used for skills development as well as fulfilling the broader aims of the programme, this may rise to 22, with a waiting list. The courses were designed to accommodate no more than 20, and the occasional excess is usually the result of a milder urgent need. Breakout groups are kept small in number of participants, six being considered a maximum and five much preferable. This prevents anyone from opting out of discussion in the smaller groups.

Each course is taught by a pair of consultants, who between them can cover all the topics. Because the consultancy recruits people with general, as well as specific, skills, the same consultants are able to teach most courses. A team of 10 people is used, in various combinations, although the bulk of teaching is handled by four or five people. A real advantage for participants is that they meet some of the tutors several times as they pass through the BMP, building strong relationships.

Tutors are in residence with the course the whole time, and work as a team. This means that both are always present, giving continuity.

There is also a cost advantage over the alternative approach of using an anchorman and a series of different lecturers for each course.

As a follow-up to the courses the consultants offer a support advisory service for participants who wish to review a topic of the course, or attempt to apply a concept new to his or her own business area. This is used by a small number of participants, but the fact that the opportunity exists is a practical demonstration of the commitment of the consultants to the programme.

The teaching approach is so robust that it has even survived the intrusion of a BBC sound recording team. Syndicate discussion of a BP case study on the Sohio Acquisition and the financing of North Sea production, and the resultant plenary, were incorporated into the schools programme "Business Matters". Harbridge House had been giving the producer some assistance with this programme, and introduced the BBC to BP on the grounds that hearing management training in progress was likely to be more effective than listening to someone talk about it. BP readily agreed, and part of a finance and accounting module thus became immortalised and presumably will remain in the archives indefinitely.

BP's business approach

BP uses a market philosophy to define its requirements for supporting services. This means that even a programme like the BMP, designed in response to a defined corporate need, has to be wanted by the rest of the organisation to the extent that they are willing to buy places on it. Whatever the strength of the reason for running a course, Group Training have no power to direct participants to attend. A course which is uneconomic in these terms, even though all payments come from inside the company, will face closure.

Group Training thus have to market their programmes within the

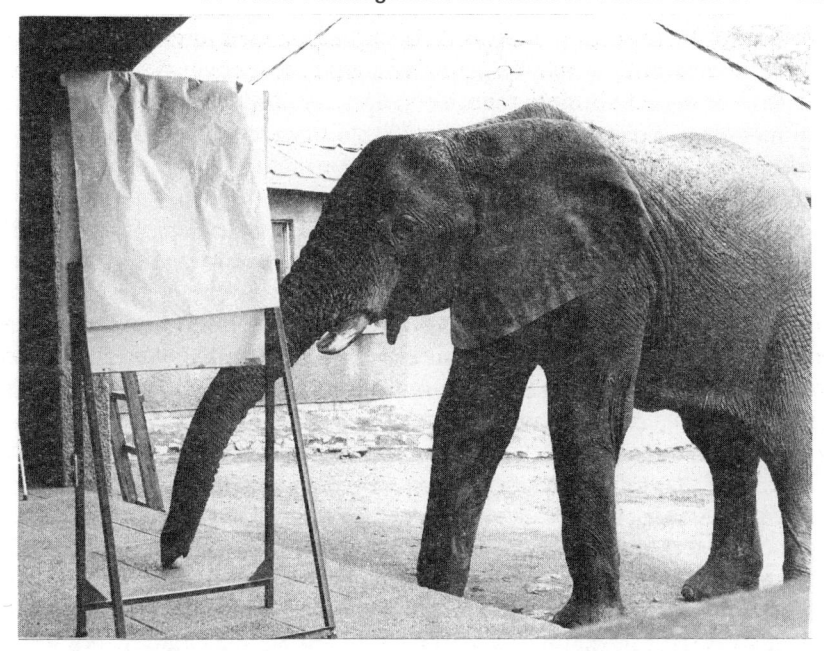

FIGURE 10.4. An unexpected visitor to a syndicate discussion during a Zambian session of the BMP. The elephant is an outcast from the herd (note broken tusks) and although wild and dangerous, is a periodic visitor to the hotel where the course was held.
Photograph: Expendito Chipala, BP Zambia Ltd.

organisation, convincing business stream managers of both the need and value of their products.

The advantage of this philosophy is that it prevents staff and service departments from proliferating and offering services which the "sharp end" does not want but otherwise would have to support. The disadvantage is that a great deal of time has to be spent gaining the commitment of senior managers to the courses and to the BMP as a solution to the original problem. This becomes a continuous process as people change jobs within the company. Over time it is becoming an easier process, as some of the original participants are promoted to positions of greater influence.

Inevitably much of the pressure for places on the BMP comes from participants who, after attending one module, become determined to follow the programme through. Word-of-mouth recommendations lead to many more of the requests for places.

The international BMP

In 1983 the first sessions of the BMP were run outside of the UK, at the Victoria Falls in Zambia. To reduce the impact of air fares the same course was run twice, each session attended by managers from various African countries. Slight changes were made to the course to suit local needs, and some African case studies were written to add relevance.

This pattern has been repeated twice a year, with the variation that sometimes two different courses are taken out and taught by the same pair of consultants. Case studies have been written around real situations in Zambia and Zimbabwe.

Because of exchange control problems which beset this part of Africa, Zambia always provides the majority of participants, who have gone through the BMP modules as a team. Other participants come from Zimbabwe, Zambia, Malawi, Mozambique, Tanzania and, on one occasion, Ghana.

One advantage of the Zambian concentration is that there is a shared experience which has led to changes. There have been occasions when ideas which emerged on one course have been implemented by the time of the next course, 6 months later.

Zambia has offered some strange experiences to the tutors. On one occasion a participant was stung by a scorpion. On another, an elephant wandered into the hotel grounds (this time in a game reserve) and poked its head into the verandah where minutes before a syndicate group had been in earnest discussion. The photograph, which shows the elephant by one of the flip charts, reveals that not all participants waited to pick up their books.

The second international step was taken in 1984 when three different sessions of the BMP were run back to back in Singapore. This is now an annual event (although the location might shift within the region), and draws participants from Malaysia, Singapore, Indonesia, Hong Kong, Japan, China, Australia and New Zealand. It would be difficult to find multinational courses with more cultural disparity than these sessions.

Taking stock of the BMP

The BMP is interesting because it came about as a result of considering corporate needs. A bottom-up study of training needs as perceived by individuals did not identify this requirement at all, and there was little overlap even with individual topics. This is by no means surprising as the individuals surveyed were rarely in a position where they could see the broader picture.

There is no doubt that the programme has played its part in helping BP adjust to and shape its future. In addition to the evidence of the formal reviews there is much anecdotal evidence of individuals who have taken different actions because of what they have learned on BMP modules.

As with other training initiatives mounted by BP, the BMP illustrates a clearly defined liked between management training and competitive advantage. And because of the regular remoulding of the programme to BP's needs it should continue to contribute for a long time to come.

11
L'Oreal: Implementing a Corporate Strategy

The second case history I have chosen is interesting because it provides a good illustration of the validity of the diagram in Figure 6.2. L'Oreal altered their corporate strategy, one of the key support actions of which meant changes in the channels of distribution they used. In order to reach these channels, new tasks were identified which in turn led to a careful re-structuring of the sales organisation. L'Oreal was concerned that the people involved should accept, understand, and be capable of working in the new structure. It was recognised that an appropriate training initiative could provide the means of making the whole thing work.

In concept there is no difference between this approach, which was primarily directed at sales representatives, and what has been done in other companies where the participants are all managers. It is an excellent illustration of a use of training which could be beneficial to hundreds if applied in other companies.

This particular case history was written by my colleague Lyn Wilson, and was originally published in *Marketing* (March 1979). It has been slightly edited, and is reproduced here by permission of the author and the editor of *Marketing*.

How L'Oreal learned to accept change

In spite of heavy advertising and subsequently high consumer awareness, the penetration of L'Oreal's products was not matching increased demand. Blame was levelled at inadequate distribution. Lyn Wilson describes the company's investment in the education of the sales force to secure new opportunities.

The Consumer Products Division of L'Oreal grew rapidly between 1975 and early 1979. However, in 1979 a marketing study into distribution revealed that the company's products were unavailable in many outlets, although heavy advertising had created high consumer awareness.

This unsatisfactory situation was viewed as a challenge. But to take advantage of the opportunity for increased distribution through the chemist trade, required the sales force to undertake new responsibilities. L'Oreal and management consultants Harbridge House Europe worked together to introduce to the marketing and field sales staff an appreciation of why a change in organisation was essential, so that the new and profitable opportunities were exploited with understanding and enthusiam.

L'Oreal is a French international toiletries company which is well known in the UK for Ambre Solaire, and hair care products such as Allurell and Elnett hair sprays, conditioners and colourants. These are widely available in hair and beauty salons and are also sold direct to the public through independent chemists, Boots, F. W. Woolworth and other multiple retailers.

Since 1975 sales volume had increased substantially in the Consumer Division; the investment in TV and Press advertising had been heavy, and had been rewarded by high consumer awareness and brand loyalty. The result was that a somewhat sleepy company of the 1960s and early 1970s had been developed until it was recognised as being among the leaders in the hair care market.

This growth was the result of a careful marketing strategy which concentrated on selling to consumers through non-grocery outlets – chemists, drug stores, department stores such as Selfridges and Fenwicks, and Boots and Woolworths. The company employed a direct sales force of some 40 representatives which, until the restructuring, operated on a functional basis. National accounts, for example Boots, and Woolworth, have been handled from head office while territory representatives have concentrated on direct orders from independent chemists and drug stores. Selling to the wholesale trade has been, by and large, a managerial responsibility.

During the previous two years the L'Oreal sales force had developed the business volume successfully, but in a somewhat haphazard manner, which left gaps in the national distribution – especially among the chemists which were supposed to be the main base of the company's distribution system. Increasing volume sales and turnover bred a euphoria which was exciting but exhausting, and the weakness in distribution was unacceptable for developing the business in the future.

The Chief Executive of the Consumer Products Division, Franklin Berrebi and his team, recognised that in a changing environment – where L'Oreal was winning more tricks than it was losing – the company as an organic body could not stand still but must itself change in order to achieve its growth targets.

L'Oreal is a company which pays a great deal of attention to management training and development. Senior people are often business graduates, and many are involved with the CEDEP programme at INSEAD.

The need for direction

While visibly successful, management did not rest on its laurels and recognised that to avoid stagnation and decay the enterprise had to move forward. As professionals they subscribed to Drucker's view that "the results of the business do not exist inside the business", and therefore they carried out a careful study of the UK market to assess the trends and potential for L'Oreal over the next few years.

This analysis revealed a great deal, from which one element will be extracted for the sake of example. The chemists trade was increasing volume turnover but the number of pharmacies was decreasing. Published Nielsen figures show 12,200 chemists in 1971 and 10,900 in 1976, thereby confirming the move to larger retail stores, and the increasing power of groups. But the study also revealed that almost three-quarters of these retailers were not called on by the L'Oreal sales force.

Theory and practice stress the importance of market share for company security, and financial benefit; it was clear that L'Oreal's advertising was successfully creating awareness, but distribution improvements could be made.

Balancing the business

Ideally, wider distribution would lead to more product displays, greater recognition, increased sales, and then more advertising and the introduction of new products. The end result would be a more balanced business, with a range of products at various stages in their life cycles and with the accompanying cash generation or cash needs.

Following the market study and analysis, management decided to develop their business in "new" chemist outlets, i.e. those not called on previously. This they decided to do by indirect orders using the country's 100 wholsalers to a greater extent than in the past when they had been "sold to" and the L'Oreal team had focused its main attention on the major retail chemists.

The incentive scheme encouraged representatives to seek the big orders – in wholesale and retail accounts – and the distribution of smaller lots to chemists was neglected. Yet superb TV advertising was creating brand awareness among many potential customers who relied on the local chemist, while many of the L'Oreal products remained in the wholesalers' warehouses.

The new approach required each representative to be responsible in his or her territory for developing the total business with all possible wholesalers and retailers – excluding grocery – and merchandising in Boots and Woolworths where sales had been negotiated at Head Office.

A change of policy

There was a clear change of policy: indirect orders must be increased – to gain distribution – with close co-operation with the wholesale trade. This was a move from "selling to" retailers to merchandising L'Oreal's products in retailers and "pulling through" the channels of distribution.

The analysis and the policies were logical and clear. However, to implement the new policies required the support and understanding of the 40 sales representatives and area managers, and clearly such changes would create uncertainty unless handled wisely.

Organisations and dynamic bodies

The analysis of the problems and the solution required a change in the organisation, but change in one part of an organisation affects other parts. This simple and obvious statement has not been recognised for very long, and there are still plenty of companies which introduce change without thinking through the possible implications. Top management may "formulate strategy" and rely on somebody else to "implement the strategy" and then be surprised at the resulting chaos.

In L'Oreal's case, senior management was well aware of the vital significance of its sales force and appreciated the hazards of introducing unplanned and often misunderstood changes. So the new tasks and the reasoning of management had to be comprehended fully by the sales representatives and sales management.

Educating the sales force

The solution to the problem was an investment in education. Harbridge House Europe was asked to study the problems and the needs associated with introducing the change in organisation and then make recommendations for working with the sales force so that the reorganisation and the new tasks for individuals were fully understood by all concerned.

"We were confronted by the necessity to prepare and equip our field-force personnel to cope with a new organisational structure and changes in their responsibilities", said Brian Sullivan, Head of Human Resources. "In addition, there were working relationships, especially those between our regionally-based sales personnel and the National Accounts Sales function, which needed to work more harmoniously. How should we do this? By the traditional way through group presentations and subsequent consultations, followed by field accompaniments to train them in their new tasks, or should we try to ensure they fully understood the "why" underlying the reorganisation? Essentially it was an issue of trust. Management believed that the company was at a stage where we had to involve people in contributing to the future of the Division and appreciating the rationale for the various changes necessary to move forward.

A highly risky exercise

"We needed an educational exercise to support our Head Office plans and that was why we turned to Harbridge House. We wanted to simulate for each representative the dilemma confronting management prior to the reorganisation. It was a highly risky exercise. The field-force could have come to very different conclusions and as a consequence strongly resist the change. But we considered that if that were the outcome it would probably mean there were important issues we had not explored and that maybe our strategy was not as perfect as we would like to think."

The L'Oreal assignment

Harbridge House Europe assigned to L'Oreal David Hussey, well known as an international authority in corporate planning, and Lyn Wilson – experienced in marketing and management education. Both delved into the L'Oreal files, posed questions to the marketing staff and chief executive, branch managers, market researchers, and worked in the field with some sales representatives. In this way they attempted to design and construct a 2½-day training course – to be repeated four times – for some 60 L'Oreal sales and marketing staff.

These discussions revealed that most L'Oreal personnel were running so fast that standing still and thinking were neglected arts. The new approach to the business, where each representative became in effect "Managing Director" of his region, required management at all levels to think about and determine objectives, structure, lines of communication and responsibilities, remuneration and incentives, and gain a much clearer understanding of the buying motivation of the various categories of retailer.

Hypothetical case study

From this exploratory work David Hussey prepared a hypothetical case study about a French toiletries firm wishing to enter the UK market and compete with L'Oreal, Beecham, Wella, Elida Gibbs and the others. Real L'Oreal and Nielsen data were used in the case. The course participants – salesmen, sales managers and marketing personnel – would be asked to develop a marketing plan to tackle the UK and, secondly an organisation structure for their imaginary French merchant venturer.

The resulting programme was called "The Selling Challenge of L'Oreal's Growth" and it studied change in the environment and the need for a positive response by L'Oreal.

There were five phases. First, some general observations about changes in technology, society, population, politics, fashion, family life and so forth. Second, work on the case study was directed at issues of distribution, selling and product policy within the decision framework of the marketing mix. The response by groups at all levels to the work involved in preparing the case and agreeing on a strategy was outstandingly good.

These two elements of the programme resulted in individuals being convinced about the need for change in the real world of L'Oreal, so half the battle was won.

Concentrated study of distribution

Third, there was a more detailed study of L'Oreal's channels of distribution and real marketing strategies. Fourth, audiovisual and live studies of some of L'Oreal's major customer categories were used to give new knowledge to the sales force about their tasks after the reorganisation. Fifth, they studied the real L'Oreal organisation change as a management response to the new marketing needs of the company.

The programmes involved concentrated and heavy learning, not without humour, which demanded the active participation of all concerned. The educational material, the roles of course members and the pace varied: heavy meals and wines were avoided – with salads and occasional beer in the seminar or conference room providing adequate and non-soporific nourishment.

The intensity of the courses, often involving work for 12 hours a day, was not ideal, but all concerned accepted that time in a 2½- day programme was at a premium, and so it was used to the utmost.

Some comments on highlights may be worthwhile.

Sales force did not believe the figures

The sales force was suspicious of the Nielsen data used. This was also a problem for Unigate (*Marketing*, February 1978, pp. 22-26) and in the L'Oreal example a considerable amount of time was devoted to explaining the methods of data collection and interpretation. These exercises enabled the sales force to appreciate how and why management introduced tactical changes to the field operation.

Hussey and Wilson also used company records of sales calls and volume sales for a particular southern town which was mapped for the participants and showed the 18 possible retail outlets available, ranging from small independent chemists, to Woolworth and Boots.

Aggressive sales plan

On each course the participants agreed on an aggressive sales call plan to exploit the market directly and through indirect orders from wholesalers; they were staggered when it was revealed that in the past L'Oreal's territory representative only called on two of the retailers. The response was, "Things must be changed. We're missing out!"

Some of L'Oreal's major customers responded enthusiastically when asked if they would address the first course (and be videotaped) on the subject of "What I expect from a L'Oreal representative!" These sessions and the tapes provided valuable material for sales people to study and develop methods for marketing a positive response to satisfy the customers' needs through understanding "the customer frame of reference". Interestingly, some brand managers on the courses commented that the buyer presentations had substantially increased their respect for their own salesmen.

L'Oreal and change

Brian Sullivan of L'Oreal said that management "believed that the company was at a stage where we had to involve people in contributing to the future... and appreciating its rationale for the various changes necessary to move forward".

Hussey and Wilson, as outsiders, saw L'Oreal as an exciting company where there were very few levels of management, no enormous hierarchical pyramid, and where ideas for improvement were welcomed from any quarter and the ideas evaluated by managers with open minds and objective analysis.

The educational exercise was part of the change and it was not "one off". It was positioned as part of a programme for developing a resourceful sales force in which individuals would assume wider responsibilities and accept greater challenges.

L'Oreal personnel recognise the constancy of change but, as any truly marketing-orientated company must do, people adapt the enterprise and their roles within it to respond to identified needs in providing improved services to customers.

The company comes first

Sales and marketing staff on the Harbridge House course moved from "the here and now with which I am familiar" to "the company success means there's a new and bigger and different job to do. Now I can see why, and I can see what my role is and the skills I need to tackle the new task."

The individual and change

As part of building for the future the course ended, after the fifth phase studying the L'Oreal reorganisation, with syndicate discussions and feedback by individuals on their new tasks and what these would mean in personal terms for the territory representatives. Elements of the new job were listed (itself a useful reinforcing process) to allow management to build appropriate systems.

This added further information about the sales force's needs and expectations to which management could make a constructive response. The major concerns were further education, information sharing, team building and personal development – not forgetting rewards and incentives.

This paper describes the response of one company to change. The company strengths were really represented by the employees of which the sales force was a vital element. When it was essential to build on growth by undertaking a major reorganisation in the sales force, L'Oreal recognised that the changes must be studied, recognised, explored, and explained – not merely by managers using a dictatorial top-down style but by all concerned.

Therefore, in conjunction with consultants Harbridge House Europe, intensive $2\frac{1}{2}$-day educational programmes were designed as an introduction to a continuing investment in the training and development of the company's human resources.

Morale is running high

"As a result of the 1978 reorganisation", said Peter McFarlane, General Sales Manager, "morale and enthusiasm among the members of the sales team have substantially increased. There is now a much greater degree of stability among the staff. In marketing terms the most important effect has been achieving higher levels of distribution, improved point of sale displays and merchandising effort which has created more impact with the customer. This activity, associated with quality products, impactful advertising and high consumer awareness has had a very favourable effect on the company's brand shares."

12

Otis Elevator Co. Ltd: Implementing Change

Management training played a small but essential part in changing the economics of Otis Elevator's Liverpool factory.

Background

The factory, at Kirkby, was custom-built in 1956 for the manufacture of escalators and lifts. It was designed to serve the UK market and those Waygood-Otis overseas companies that had been established from the UK, mainly in the Commonwealth or former Commonwealth countries. At that time there was little standardisation of product, and each order taken was especially designed for the building into which it was to be installed.

At that time the UK company earned what profit it could on all products made in the factory, and set its own prices on sales to other companies in the group. To this extent it operated more as an independent company rather than as a subsidiary in a multinational group.

In the early days it was a sellers' market, and long lead times or high costs did not impair the ability to earn good profits. By the mid-1970s many things had changed:

- The market was now a buyers' market, to the extent that all manufacturers sold new equipment at a loss or low profit, relying on subsequent service sales to achieve profitability.
- The UK company had moved closer to the Otis companies in Europe, and operated under a regional strategy.
- Profits were earned at the marketing end. The task of all factories was to supply products at breakeven so that those close to the markets could set total margins in a way that took note of the market situation. Thus all factories became cost recovery centres.
- Production was rationalised on a global basis. Escalator manufacture moved to Germany: a range of standard lifts ("models") was introduced into all companies in the region; these were made in France. The Liverpool factory concentrated on "traditional" lifts (those applications that could

not be met with "models") and supplied to Otis internationally, but in competition with other designated Otis factories and outside vendors.
- Standardised components, internationally made or sourced, began to become a feature. This trend accelerated as, during the 1970s, electronics were gradually introduced into lifts.
- Otis Elevators International Inc. was acquired by United Technologies Corporation.

After the mid-1970s there were a number of market changes. The building boom collapsed, ending the demand for speculative high-rise buildings. There was a general move to low-rise buildings, indeed some high-rise residential buildings have been demolished. Market emphasis has changed to installing lifts in existing rather than new buildings, which require shorter lead times. Overall the market for lifts in the UK had halved over the decade up to 1983, and the average size of lift installation had shrunk. The combined effect of the changes meant that in 1983 the factory at Liverpool was operating at less than 25 per cent of physical capacity. Lead times were unacceptably high, and in any case 60 per cent of contracts were delivered late. Cost pressures and falling volumes meant that the operation was rapidly becoming uncompetitive compared to other Otis factories in other countries.

Main elements of a lift

An electric lift consists of a number of major units:

- the architectural products (car, door, door surrounds, etc.);
- a controller;
- a machine to drive the lift.

These major units were made in the Liverpool factory, who would arrange shipment to the building site (if a UK installation), in theory on the required date, where the field staff would begin to install it. In a complex high-rise building, involving many lifts, it might be necessary to schedule several deliveries to fit the building schedule. In addition to the manufactured items, cable and guide rails would be purchased from outside vendors. At the Liverpool factory there was also activity of making one or more of the above items for lift modernisations. Frequently this work would be put out to outside vendors, and the factory tended to be used only when a vendor could not be found. This was because on cost and lead time Liverpool was not competitive, and salesmen believed that the factory would always let them down. There was also a service workshop, producing or arranging spares for service operations. Frequently these would be abstracted from the main production area, often illicitly.

Overall the Liverpool factory had a floor area of 400,000 square feet, supported by 50,000 square feet of office and 20,400 square feet of canteen space, and standing in a site of 25 acres.

The different activities in the factory were subject to different forces. Lift cars often had special customer requirements that had to be specially engineered for that contract. There were often delays in settling these details. However, once settled, there was usually little difficulty in obtaining raw materials; sheet metal was available, for example, on 24-hour delivery. The need for customer specials meant that this sort of product needed a higher level of industrial engineering support than other products.

Machines had fewer customer specials and details could be finalised earlier, but many of the components had to be purchased, and some had long lead time (up to 6 months for castings). Efficient operations required a high quality of planning to avoid stock-outs or over-stocking. Manufacturing processes include grooving or drilling castings, winding copper, assembly, and testing.

Architectural products involve operations to bend, shape, drill, give special finishes to, weld, and assemble metal into various products such as cars, entrances, and lift doors. Because metal moves from one location to another it is more difficult to keep track of these products than with, for example, a controller where all the work is done in one place. Controller manufacture is labour-intensive, assembly mainly bought-in parts, and consists of electrical wiring and testing. There are few customer specials for controllers.

The zone workshop made all of these products, often for small contracts, not always requiring more than one product. Because products were made for existing buildings, usually to replace old or broken equipment, almost everything was a special.

Organisation

The factory had been well laid out for the tasks it was originally designed to fulfil. All stores were centralised and historically had achieved only 65 per cent stock accuracy. Stock control and materials planning was through a material requirement planning system which was batch-based, worked on a weekly cycle, and highlighted all physical errors in stock. No one person was responsible for inventory, and the annual stock-take took 14 days, involved most of the factory, and caused production to cease.

The factory was supported by extensive computer systems at a cost of £500,000 per year to operate. However, it was difficult to track down where in the factory were the various elements of a contract, and whether progress was according to plan.

The factory was laid out by machine type, and organisational structure followed this concept. Where possible a flow-line principle was followed. A lift car, for instance, would be moved on a wheeled platform to five different points, and five people would each carry out one stage in its production to speed up the throughput.

A piece-rate system had been operated for some time and, in order to maintain earnings, components and semi-finished pieces were manufactured for inventory. The agreement with the unions allowed flexibility, but earnings had to be maintained. Thus a switch of a man, from his normal job of cutting metal billets, to a drill, meant that he had to be paid at his metal billet rates regardless of output on the drill. There were numerous grades of labour and rates of pay. The system was very costly to operate.

Union negotiations were not simple, as there were 13 unions representing hourly paid workers. There was a works committee, and three separate committees representing the staff.

As is so often the case with a business whose objectives and products have changed over time, much of the equipment was not ideal for the purposes it was used for, although new plant had been added over the years. For example £1 million was spent on INCA machine tools in 1975.

Time for drastic action

Incremental solutions had not worked, and management knew that drastic action had to be taken. Volume reduction caused unit costs to rise, which in turn led to loss of orders from other Otis companies. The further loss of volume caused unit costs to rise even higher, while action to reduce manpower in line with volume falls caused further production and lead time problems. One solution being explored was to completely relocate the factory, away from Liverpool, in a much smaller plant designed for the new situation. Not surprisingly, this option was not liked by the unions and employees at the Liverpool factory.

In fact this solution was not implemented, although the feasibility study on the relocation was completed and a new site had been chosen.

However, in February 1985 the Managing Director of Otis UK was able to give a presentation at an international conference in Singapore showing a complete turnround in the Liverpool factory. He demonstrated how Liverpool's costs had shrunk: for example, it could now produce a particular popular gearless machine 18 per cent cheaper than Taiwan. Lead times had been reduced and the proportion delivered on time had increased. This dramatic improvement was the result of considerable hard work by the Liverpool management team, implementing a major new strategy in the Liverpool factory.

The focused workshop approach

The foundation of the strategy was the breaking down of the Liverpool factory into a number of workshops, physically united, each of which could be managed as a business unit. The manager of each would be responsible for all aspects of his operations. To facilitate this the central stores were broken up, each workshop operating its own, and the white-collar staff associated with each operation were moved from the office block and housed in custom-built offices adjacent to their manufacturing operation.

This released 114,000 square feet of productive space which was separated from the rest of the factory by a brick wall, and sub-let to another organisation, Masons. (This also reduced the rates bill.) The wall was used as a symbol of the project. At the start, plaques were inserted by leading ETO managers bearing their names. On completion, Francois Jaulin, then president of Otis worldwide (and formerly head of the European region) inserted a plaque signalling completion of the project. John Miller, the new director of manufacturing who was the architect of the new strategies, said, "It is important to have a definite end to a project such as this, so that people know that the changes have been completed and they can concentrate on making them work." This was just one of the behavioural actions which contributed to the successful implementation of the strategy.

The workshops were organised around the major elements that make up an elevator, plus the field workshop. The elements are Machine, Architectural Products, and Controllers.

From being a "vendor of the last resort" the field workshop was turned into a focused activity which could be used to help salesmen gain modernisation orders; it is now frequently visited by customers, and the employees have a close association with the field activity. A fifth workshop is Consolidation and Shipping, which is the link between the other workshops and the customer. Each workshop, in addition to having a product focus, has its own technologies.

Service spares are no longer produced at Liverpool. This activity was transferred to be close to the service warehouse in London, removing from the premises an activity which had little in common with the remaining operations.

The results of the strategy

There is no doubt that the focused workshop approach has produced significant financial improvements. Lower costs, shorter lead times, and a better record for on-time delivery have resulted in an increase of orders to Liverpool.

For the first time in memory the number of indirect staff fell below the number of direct workers. Despite lower hours per unit of production, standard hours of production began to rise as orders from Otis companies overseas started flowing back to Liverpool. The field workshop began capturing work previously given to outside vendors. Despite the intention to run the factory as a cost recovery centre, a considerable contribution has been made since the implementation of strategy. The over-recovery came about as the improvements during each year exceeded the amount budgeted (largely because neither the accountants nor top management believed that the improvements would happen to the extent planned, and insisted that historic costs be used for budgeting, not future promises).

Lower lead times allowed a faster response to customer needs, and costs of product (which on the cost centre concept of Otis is the works price) have fallen in *current* money terms.

John Miller summarised the reasons for the approach as follows:

> The advantage of the focused approach was that workshops could be established from a zero base, allowing a break with past practices and the previous culture. A manufacturing resource could be created to suit the specific needs of each workshop. Smaller focused units made it easier to use a team approach to problem-solving and contributed to job flexibility. Above all, it was possible to give people something to identify with, which they could run as a business and see the results of their efforts.

The dedication to teamwork is manifested physically in the conference facility built into the offices in each workshop. This gave the workshop managers the ability to bring people together quickly and easily.

Steps in implementing the strategy

In order to implement the new strategy a number of tasks were identified and undertaken.

Payment scheme

The existing piece-rate system for hourly paid employees, which encouraged the production of unwanted inventory, was abolished, as were the numerous grades that previously existed. Instead four bands of pay were established. The distinction between skilled and unskilled workers vanished, and flexibility was obtained to move people to different jobs, even when these might be of a lower skill.

Information and systems

A new manufacturing management system was selected and implemented. John and his team drew up specifications of what they wanted, and laid out the manufacturing systems operations. They examined six outside packages which they narrowed down to three which were technically acceptable. Fund selection was then turned over to the workshop managers who were going to operate the system: management insisted that they made the final choice. The system chosen was MANMAN by Scicon, costing £180,000 per year to run (compared with the £500,000 of the previous less effective system).

Controls

The new system gave the ability to interactively control at the level of the workshops, and to a degree never before possible at Liverpool. In addition, rules were set up so that it was very clear what each workshop would and would not do. Decentralisation of stores meant that it was possible to measure inventory performance by workshop.

Unnecessary controls were eliminated. For example, the "front end paperchase" was cut on orders for standard equipment, thus helping to reduce lead times. In one case a production order which used to take 4 weeks to raise was reduced to 4 minutes.

Capital equipment

Under the new concept, subcomponents were made for contract, not for stock, which meant that the workshops needed flexible equipment with low set-up time. In fact a number of orders for equipment judged as inappropriate were cancelled. In their place Otis bought flexible numerically-controlled machines which met the new requirements.

Charter

A charter was developed for the factory, agreed with the unions, and issued to every employee.

Management

The jobs of workshop managers were new and difficult, and would make redundant some of the previous factory management and supervisory jobs. John decided to advertise the new jobs internally within the Otis group in the UK. This not only made the positions competitive, but forced applicants to consider the new jobs against their own skills and ambitions. All positions were filled from within Otis.

Changes in methods

Manufacturing methods have changed. Sometimes this has been because of the new equipment, sometimes because the grouping of activities under the workshop concept has made it possible to change, and sometimes because different methods aid a closer identification with the product and workshop. Now, for example, a lift car is totally assembled by one person. All his component requirements are delivered to his workstation and he is wholly responsible for building the car.

Workshops differ by product and technology, and also by mix of labour.

Changes in attitudes

The successful implementation of the focused factory concept required changes in attitude and behavior throughout the Liverpool site. Among the aims of the workshop approach were a restoration of pride in a job well done, and identification with a business unit and the commercial factors which would make it a success or failure.

Brochures were prepared which describe each workshop, its business and mission.

Each workshop has a different colour for its overalls, to assist in creating a feeling of identification, and the integration of office staff into the workshop area helps to create a total identity within the unit.

Management training played a vital part in helping to change attitudes and provide managers with the new knowledge needed if they were to play their part in the new concept. The method used was not elaborate, and the case study is included to demonstrate that relatively standard approaches can work well when they provide a solution to the needs of the company.

St Helen's Management College was asked to design a training programme for managers and supervisors in the new workshops. The focused workshop approach meant that people needed new knowledge to make the system work properly; knowledge which had not been essential under the previous manufacturing concept. For example, cost accounting, marketing and various management skills became essential if the project were to work.

A series of weekly evening programmes was devised, starting at 4pm and continuing until about 8pm. Although designed for the managers and supervisors they were thrown open to anyone at the factory who wished to come.

The broader invitation was a part of the strategy for changing attitudes at Liverpool, and would have not been considered before the focused concept was introduced; nor would non-management employees have viewed the invitation with anything except suspicion. As part of a new climate at Liverpool, it was received enthusiasticaly by a number of shop-floor and office employees, and probably was seen as evidence of a new approach even by those who elected not to attend.

The managers and supervisors received training which undoubtedly benefited them personally. However, the need for the training was corporate, and essential for the implementation of the focused workshop strategy.

Those who are interested in the broader aspects of management education might care to know that John Miller is both an MBA and an experienced manager. He has successfully combined industry experience with the development of his education, beginning as a undergraduate trainee with Tube Investments after A-levels. This led to a B.Sc. in 1969, which was followed by an M.Sc. in computing science. He worked with Kenning Motor Group after gaining the higher degree, becoming management services manager. A NATO scholarship took him to IMEDE in 1978, where he completed his MBA, appearing on the Dean's honours list in all four terms.

After the MBA he joined Plessey Aerospace, where he was involved in rationalisation and reorganisation, and in addressing the problems of linking manufacturing and marketing strategy. It was at this period that he first used the concepts of Professor Wikham Skinner, later used in Otis as a stimulus for the "focused workshops".

One of his first actions on joining Otis was to arrange a conference for his senior managers at Liverpool to introduce them to the concepts, and where an outline plan was prepared for their introduction. Thus the changing attitudes and the gaining of commitment began at an early stage in the project.

13

Distance Learning

The nature of distance learning

So far the examples in this book have looked at ways of forging traditional methods of training into a competitive weapon. Traditional is not used in the sense of being "old-fashioned", and the bringing together of people on a course has many advantages beyond the purely educational. Such initiatives may have indirect results, such as improved co-ordination or better communication between different parts of the company, which are as valuable as the actual training itself.

There is another completely different approach to training which is undergoing something of a revival in the UK. This is distance learning.

Peel[1] found in his survey (page 38) that there was an emergence of interest in distance learning, particularly in firms employing more than 1000 people. At the time of his survey (1984) there were few firms actually using these methods, but almost a quarter of respondents were in some form of development or evaluation mode, if not already making some use of the approach. Part of the interest could be put down to the availability of computer and video, which altered distance learning's image to something more flexible and modern than the original correspondence courses.

In some ways the terms traditional and distance are something of a misnomer. Not all traditional education is older than distance learning, and certainly the tailored course is a newer development than the correspondence course. It is also not necessary to have an either/or approach, and both methods can be used to achieve a single purpose. The best-known example of this is the Open University, which supplements its distance learning with tutor groups and summer schools.

Distance learning implies a physical separation of the student from the tutor, epitomised in its original form by the correspondence course. However, a distance learning initiative is more than private study, in that material is provided by an educational organisation, and the student has two-way communication with the tutor (who he may never meet). In the original format this communication consisted mainly of the marking of completed exercises, although faster response communication now features in some of the newer approaches to distance learning. People are taught individually; in the original correspondence course format students never came together in groups.

Open learning is another term which has been variously defined, and may be applied to both traditional and distance learning. It implies a responsiveness to individual students' learning needs. Although some proponents of distance learning argue that it overcomes the lack of "openness" of the traditional classroom situation, this is not necessarily so. Some distance learning is decidedly "closed", and some traditional approaches may be open. In any such discussion one must be careful not to compare the best of one system with the worst of another.

Distance learning and personal development

Peel[1] (page 19) states: "The Open University concept is now seen as more relevant to management development", and certainly the addition of radio and television broadcasts to written material, supplemented with summer schools, has been a powerful example of high visibility. In fact the Open University was not the world's first degree-conferring distance learning establishment. The University of South Africa pre-dated it by many years as a university entirely dedicated to external students, and claims to be the pioneer of distance education in the Western World.[2] This university had nearly 76,000 students in 1985, compared with a little over 20,000 in 1970, and is planning for 130,000 by 2011. (This compares with 300,000 students of the Open University.)

Distance education for the benefit of the individual at his or her own desire is a very different thing from distance learning in industry, although there may be some areas of overlap. Certainly the attainment of professional qualifications or a degree should be encouraged by business.

It is noteworthy that the Open University now has an Open Business School which offers a number of courses, and that there are now two distance learning MBA degrees available:

(a) Strathclyde Business School MBA

Students must satisfy the same entrance requirements and sit the same examinations as those enrolling full-time, but they study with the text at home. The course involves five foundation classes, three general electives, one final elective and one project. Each course is divided into units requiring 1-2 weeks to complete. On the full-time course this would involve approximately 2-3 hours of lecturing. The package includes study guides, a conclusion in each unit and a lead into the following unit, and guided reading. Overall, a distance learning MBA student is expected to take up to 4 years to complete the programme.

To avoid the inevitable problems of isolation there is a support programme comprising personal tutors and weekend and summer schools. A summer school prior to starting the degree is required, plus two more weekend schools during the course. Each student is assigned a tutor to assist with difficulties in course progress. In addition, evening tutorials can be arranged, when the tutor goes out to the students, rather than vice-versa, thus overcoming the problems of geographical diversity.

Strathclyde also offers the Open Executive Programme (OEP), which is a home-study programme featuring off-the-shelf, university-level training without examinations. Aimed at middle-ranking managers who want to improve career prospects, the OEP offers subject modules that contain reformatted material taken from the existing MBA programme:

- Accountancy and Finance
- Quantitative Methods
- Manufacturing Management
- Marketing
- Management of Human Resources
- Economics of the Business Environment.

The OEP requires no previous academic qualification.

(b) Wolsey Hall and University of Warwick

This well-established correspondence school and the university have recently joined forces to produce an external MBA programme. The University's School of Industrial and Business Studies has an excellent record in the field of management education, and Wolsey Hall is publishing and administering the programme. The external MBA programme, which commenced in January 1986, is designed as a self-supporting initiative expected to serve 200 students in its first year.

Employers were surveyed during the programme's design phase to determine if potential students would receive company support, and the response was very favourable. The programme set-up cost has been between £15,000 and £20,000.

Candidates should have obtained either an honours degree awarded by an approved university or the Council of National Academic Awards, or a final qualification of an approved professional society; candidates who meet certain requirements such as a minimum of 4 years business experience will be considered as well.

The course presents all the modules for the full-time MBA over a 4-year period. Examinations take place in the first 3 years, and a dissertation must be submitted in the fourth year. The student receives a package, designed around current management texts, that include case studies and audio tapes. One can expect to study between 12 and 15 hours a week. A further requirement to combat isolation is a residential period at Warwick in

September of each year. Classes are held, and students and tutors have the opportunity to exchange views, which also provides the tutors with useful feedback.

Each participant has a personal tutor to mark assignments and provide assistance by telephone. There are also counsellors available at Wolsey Hall for administrative queries, as well as an MBA "hotline" outside working hours.

The use of distance education for personal reasons is a very different motivational situation from the use of distance learning systems at the behest of the employer, which is the subject of most of this chapter. Much of the text is drawn from Harbridge House research,[3] which is used without specific acknowledgement.

The survey covered 28 suppliers of distance learning and 55 users or potential users. Because the intention was to learn about the benefits and problems of this approach most of the firms contacted were known users, with a few non-users included to give perspective.

The tools of distance learning

Text, video and computers are the three most common course media, and they are often linked in various combinations. One could argue that the linkage of personal computer and video disc to produce interactive video results is a fourth medium which is uniquely different.

Although text-based distance education programmes still dominate the market, the largest and most significant growth in any one medium has been that of the computer. Computer-based training (CBT) is fast becoming prominent in the distance education area, and if technological advances continue at the present rate the possibilities appear endless. There is a wealth of CBT materials on the market – hardware, software, laser disk and interactive video – available either as complete packages or in any combination. The majority of packages involve tuition in keyboard skills, computer applications, and specific technical skills, but courses dealing with management skills are beginning to appear as well. Many CBT packages are designed for use with the increasingly popular microcomputer, and interest in interactive video systems is growing. The focus on CBT in the area of management is fairly new, however, and generic packages are only beginning to gain interest. Alec Keith, general manager of Maxim Training Systems Ltd, notes in his article "CBT for management development"[4] that few training organisations possess sufficient computer skills to develop professional material, and that many trainers remain sceptical about the potential of CBT for providing staff with effective management skills.

One advantage of CBT is that the training department, senior management, and learners can be assured of standard quality of tuition and uniformity of course content. Further, CBT materials can be carefully evaluated and validated well in advance of actual training, unlike teacher-based courses, which rely as much on the instructor's delivery as on course content for their success. Many companies are opting to develop or buy "authoring packages" that provide instruction for the creation of original software for CBT courses. Authoring packages allow for subsequent updating or modification of the content, and for customisation of training. To effectively design the educational materials in a distance format, however, requires special skills, hence the preference of many companies for "off-the-shelf" packages.

CBT can solve a number of training problems. It can accommodate a diversity of knowledge backgrounds, and can be used in conjunction with conventional courses as a preparation, supplement, reinforcement, or even a replacement.

CBT does not, however, solve all problems. If approached without awareness of its pitfalls it can create more. There is a danger of the technology becoming out of date very quickly, making heavy investment unprofitable. Alec Keith, in describing his firm's management training package, CALM (Computer-Assisted Learning for Managers), cautions that CBT for management education can have the following limitations:

- *Lack of individuality*. It offers a consistent approach to management training, and does not accommodate individual requirements and/or knowledge levels; personnel familiar with course issues cannot "branch" to higher levels of sophistication. Future developments in the field may make this possible.
- *Lack of personal contact*. Participants who have difficulty understanding concepts cannot ask specific questions of a computer as they could of course a tutor. This lack of personal contact may detract from the learning experience.
- *Individual reactions to technology*. Despite continued expansion in the use of microcomputers, individual feelings towards new technology remain mixed. While some individuals are keen to utilise the latest training concepts, others may find it trivial and gimmicky. Encouraging non-computer users to participate may prove difficult.
- *Limited skill development*. CBT for managers is most effective when used in conjunction with other training methods. It has only limited use as an independent training resource.

Some companies have found themselves with incompatible hardware and software, and others with sophisticated equipment that gathers dust because staff have not been adequately prepared and trained for its use. Because of such dangers, the wise user will investigate all possible options to ensure maximum compatibility and cost-effectiveness, possibly combining different names in hardware and software for the best of end-products.

Both those who supply and those who use CBT agree that it will never completely replace standard forms of training, and that not all companies will find it of value, even if they can afford the initial outlay. Investment into CBT is not for the uninitiated and unaware. Extensive investigation of company needs and available materials must be undertaken before CBT products are purchased, and users must have a strategy for long-term CBT applications, lest they find themselves with incompatible hardware and soon-to-be-obsolete software.

Video is frequently used in traditional training initiatives. It has a new dimension in distance learning, given the widespread ownership of video recorders and the ability of the visual image to replace or supplement the printed page.

It is probably unwise for any course designer to think in terms of using one medium only. As best results are more likely from an intelligent combination of whatever is appropriate for the particular training situation.

Advantages and disadvantages of distance learning in companies

In theory, distance learning offers a cost-effective way of reaching a mass audience. When a large audience is scattered geographically, and the need is technical training which may be difficult to duplicate in the classroom, this advantage may be very real. There are now examples of interactive video to provide technical training to service engineers in, for example, the lift industry and dealers in personal computers.

In circumstances such as these, other advantages are also very real: the flexibility of distance learning makes it possible to provide training that goes at the pace of the trainee and which can be scheduled to avoid interuption to work.

Whether such advantages transfer to management training is a different matter. The lack of human interaction has proved to be a severe disadvantage in some subject areas, and is difficult to imagine some of the strategic-level courses described in preceding chapters being effective if run by distance learning methods. Any course which is trying to create a common corporate culture is likely to require traditional approaches, and many have found weaknesses in distance learning in behavioural subjects.

There are situations in management training where distance learning methods could well be used to provide basic skills which might later be taken to greater heights in a seminar. Basic accountancy taught by distance learning could well make traditional-style courses on finance and management accounting more effective. In my experience the course is more likely to be slowed down by individual learning speeds at the basic level than with what most of us would consider to be the more interesting aspect of accountancy. Similar approaches could no doubt be developed for many other subjects, so that the effectiveness of training is increased.

Even at this basic level distance learning has some other problem to face. If the course is long, it may be difficult to maintain commitment, unless there is a strong personal motivation as with a qualification. It is also difficult for the trainer to ensure that the distance learning course is completed in a reasonable time span. Although hotel or study centre costs may be saved, it is still necessary for time to be spent on a distance learning course, and it is naive to believe that, unless for personal benefit, this will occur in personal time. Indeed, less personal time may be spent on a distance learning course than on an intensive residential course where there is evening work.

And distance learning is not cheap. Hardware has to be purchased in adequate quantities, and may require computer and video equipment. Software is relatively expensive, although it may serve many people, and is particularly costly if it has to be customised for the firm.

It is also fair to claim that distance learning material has to be written more carefully than ordinary material. There is no opportunity for the tutor to explain, add examples from his or her own experience, or probe to ensure that participants understand. This brings another advantage for distance learning: that the course is always the same. Any tutor will vary in the quality of his performance from time to time. On the other hand, a never-varying course may become stale, because there is no opportunity for the tutor to update by new examples, or to modify approaches as he goes. So what may be good in one sense may be bad in another.

Some examples of distance learning in business

As noted earlier, distance education techniques are generally well known to industry trainers. The majority of those surveyed by Harbridge House use them in some form (including pilot programmes) for either technical or management training; some are researching the application of such techniques to existing training needs, while a few do not consider it suitable for their needs. Of those using or considering it, roughly half emphasise management courses and half technical. A great number, however, have invested in both.

Of those using distance education for technical training, many develop their own materials. Far fewer companies develop their own management training materials; the main reason is that there appears to be a respect accorded to outside bodies with a good reputation, especially for senior management development. Many companies feel that they lack the expertise to produce materials to the same standard as Henley or Cranfield, or any of the business schools. Others say that they have not the time necessary to do the subject justice. For this reason – institutional credibility – the majority of the companies we spoke to have turned to the Henley and the Open University courses rather more than to others. When asked why, typical responses included: "we know the name", "we have used their courses before", "we had read/heard about their recent ventures". Effective marketing, coupled with proven capability, has contributed towards the high ranking on many lists. Indeed, the means of selection cited above confirm the findings of Peel [1] on management development and training, which reveals that the primary criterion among large companies (over 1000 employees) for selecting a supplier is "previous experience with provider" and among smaller companies it ranks second behind "provider's knowledge of industry".

Shell chose Henley initially because it was aware of Henley's substantial commitment of resources to develop basic but detailed courses which coincided with the company's needs. Their first choice was Finance for Non-financial Managers, selected for those managers with 10 years experience who required training in this area. Shell re-did about 30% of the package – including a whole workbook – to tailor it to their own requirements. From the original pilot scheme, in Sarawak, courses are now run in up to 25 countries. Results vary between regions, but Group Training has sold about 60 packages.

Shell finds this to be a cost-effective approach; it would cost about £750 to tutor a Shell manager on a 1-week residential course at a Shell training centre, but the distance education packages range from £100 to £350 each. Shell is also using distance education in its training centre in Holland, from which it is providing personnel training to Shell staff world-wide. The material, developed from a standard package originally produced for the Institute of Personnel Management by Kingston Polytechnic, is modified for company needs. Shell intends to step up its distance education effort over the next 5 years in areas where it is seen to be appropriate. Many hundreds of Shell executives are currently using distance education materials, and many more will participate by the end of the 1980s.

Henley has by far the greatest name recognition, but companies are also considering the offerings of other institutions. Cranfield's area of expertise is marketing, while institutions such as Strathclyde and Warwick have largely restricted themselves as yet to one product, the MBA. Such an academic qualification, requiring a deep level of commitment on the part of the student, tends to rule out corporate-level affiliation with the programme. Certainly, companies will sponsor an individual through, or give their blessing to, a course (as with Jaguar and Warwick), but a corporate distance MBA policy is, and seems likely to remain, a rarity. (Note the linkage of a distance/part-time MBA with internal courses by British Petroleum as described in Chapter 9.)

As one of the few companies developing their own management material and researching extensively in this field, *W. H. Smith* intends to use a blend of generic and tailored material, and is currently identifying training needs most appropriate for distance education. The training department is also planning to prepare students for the impending changes. Following senior management approval they will demonstrate how it will work by conducting seminars to explain the open learning process to management. Managers will then individually brief staff members embarking on open learning packages. Reaction so far has been positive – and one of the reasons for this is that study time will be given to the student. It would not be acceptable to reduce the availability of residential training and also insist that students give up their own time to study.

Many organisations who have or are successfully implementing pilot programmes assert that adequate preparation of staff is essential. They recognise that an open learning system will work if it is "sold" to their staff; companies in the pilot stage of distance education programmes report good acceptance of the new techniques, but often find course administration initially burdensome.

With a view to testing the water, as it were, a large percentage of companies have run or are running pilot programmes. During these, many trainers investigate motivation, learning styles, as well as effectiveness of material content.

Metal Box plc, for example is intending to offer two Henley packages – financial skills and marketing – to six managers on a pilot basis; the managers study in their own time and assist trainers in evaluating the materials.

Investigating distance education as a training enhancement, *British Rail* has engaged a firm to convert a 1-week conventional course – Effective Speaking – into a distance package. The package will be used as an introduction; participants will then attend a 2-day residential course to practise the skills they have learned. An estimated 600–1000 managers have been identified for this course. Technical training is also being considered for distance education formatting.

Jaguar Cars Ltd's Open Learning Programme is designed to encourage employees at all levels to develop their abilities in their own time; 25 per cent of the workforce (more than 2000 people) are enrolled for 80 different courses.

Electrolux Ltd stresses the value of employee preparation for new training methods. A pilot programme is soon to be run for managers (based on an Open University course), and the training department is discussing the course with them in detail. Coursework will be done in office time. In the future, distance format management courses will be given at the individual's request, but technical courses will be by nomination. The pilot programme will last 1 year. If successful, more distance education components will be added to company training. Off-the-shelf materials will be purchased; there are no plans for CBT in the near future.

Some companies well along in their pilots have observed that a number of students flit from one course to another, while others stick doggedly to one until finished – no matter how long it takes them. Of critical importance is sustained motivation, which can be accomplished through effective tutorial support, interest of supervisors, group learning, and good "marketing" of courses.

It has become clear through the pilot schemes that a time limit has to be set against which performance can be monitored. Although distance education courses should be self-pacing, the absence of a benchmark means that problems can occur with students taking too long, or not finishing one module before starting the next. Difficulties encountered in monitoring or assessing performance were cited by those who chose either to reject open management education, or limit its use to short skills-based training.

British Gas, however, devotes considerable time to assessing distance education materials and reports considerable success. Most packages are validated before use and are also evaluated in terms of their contribution to improving job performance, determined by measuring established objectives (based on known needs) against post-training results.

CBT Examples

Although this report is primarily concerned with management education (some CBT is management-oriented), our research revealed more CBT in skills areas. The technological revolution has added a new dimension to training and many companies are investigating appropriate equipment. The figures for investment are large; Lloyds £4m is probably among the highest. Computers, audio, and video equipment, alone or combined, offer standardised training opportunities to personnel world-wide.

The numbers investigating or using CBT are not quite comparable with the previous section. Well over half of the respondents have invested in this area, some to a greater extent than others, but any venture into this arena requires some considerable commitment of resources. The applications varied among organisations, but most expressed a wish for staff at all levels to be computer-literate. Many CBT courses teach the use of computers themselves, particularly the systems of the organisation in question. Deltak, among others, supplies a number of companies with CBT and video packages for training data processing personnel.

Black and Decker has used distance education for several years as part of the sales training programme, and is now exploring these techniques for management and technical training as well. A small on-site open learning centre has been established, initially for technical and supervisory training as well as CBT training at the work place. Packages are off-the-shelf but tailored. Further, staff take advantage of distance education packages at Control Data centres. In the future, distance education techniques will be increasingly integrated into overall training.

Sun Life is looking at CBT with a view to teaching its staff computer basics.

British Airways relies on CBT in ticketing and fares operations since these operations are performed on computer.

At *Hewlett-Packard* most personnell have a terminal on their desk, and can key in at any time to learn about the electronic mail system or, for example, Lotus 1-2-3. For engineers there are technical self-paced packages, and there are a number of packages comprising sales skills and accounting for management.

Although CBT is not at present a major training resource, it is used extensively at the *British Rail* Travel Centre, which uses microcomputers in operator training in the rules and regulations affecting their jobs and the industry in general.

Lloyds Bank offers little management training using these techniques at present, but the company's large investment into interactive video reflects confidence in the medium. Shortly, 1500 kits will be distributed – a "training trolley", using laser disk technology. It will include micro, video, disk player, and TV monitor, plus the first five programmes in such skills as selling, induction programmes, and group communications.

Of these companies currently using CBT or interactive video in some form, most produce their own programmes, as opposed to buying off-the-shelf. Certainly there is greater scope for tailoring a course to specific needs if developed in-house, provided the resources are there to update as necessary. Updating is an extra cost frequently not taken into consideration during initial planning.

Many software houses are developing authoring software. This allows them to develop their own tailor-made courseware, using "authoring" software such as P/CAN or PLATO. The danger is that an inexperienced author or course writer will produce courseware that is inappropriate for the medium and ineffective in the long run. A point to consider when buying is the development time, which differs dramatically among various types of courseware. Some are far simpler than others. P/CAN, for instance, requires a great deal of complicated language to produce one line of text, while others use "plain English".

The vast majority of companies are aware of the risks; some, like Abbey National, are researching into the area, but are monitoring the results of other pilot programmes before investing heavily in their own.

Tutorial support

One of the chief disadvantages cited by numerous companies was the lack of human interaction inherent in any distance education system. The main suppliers, particularly of management material, have recognised this, and provide residential periods, hotlines, personal tutors, local group interaction, and so on. However, Henley reports that the hotline and tutors are not used as much as might have been expected, which may indicate that students are turning to their own peers or superiors in an organisation. The majority of respondents do provide tutorial support in some form – either systematic or an as-needed basis – but many admitted that tutor support, an indispensable motivational resource, could be better administered. In many cases tutors are also employees themselves, and tutorial activities must be co-ordinated around work activities.

On-site centres

A great many companies have developed an open learning resource on-site, providing access for staff to open learning materials. Some have courseware and programmes of various media, but all centres maintain library sections and study areas. Well over half of the respondents have these on-site facilities, and most claimed that they were well used and worth the time and money invested. A few firms allow time for study at work, particularly if the subject is directly job-related. Many trainers commented that self-development facilities enhance job satisfaction and make for a happier, more productive environment.

Smith and Nephew maintains an on-site centre that features the Open University's Effective Manager course, which is offered to selected groups of both junior and senior managers who go through the course together to share experiences and practise skills. Also available is a Technical Education Council (TEC) course for maintenance personnel, and a communications skills course. Employees use the centre on their own time. In the future the focus at the centre will be technical training rather than management development. Educational materials will continue to be stand-alone.

British Gas's facilities include interactive video, audio/tape, workbooks, and library facilities. Deltak is one of their suppliers. CBT does not currently play a major part in the centre's activities, but this area is expected to receive more attention over the next 5 years.

At *Land Rover* employees have access all day and evening to the on-site centre, which offers CBT, reading materials, video, and slide/tape facilities. Among the offerings are Henley programmes such as Marketing for Managers, Accounting for Managers, and The Effective Manager. Fifteen packages in all (some developed in-house, some purchased) are available, plus a borrowing arrangement with another company that owns 500 programmes. In addition to general management development materials, specific skill building packages are also available – BASIC programming, value engineering, network analysis, and speed reading, to name a few. The centre has been open for a year and is proving popular.

Britoil plc maintains a centre for operator and supervisory grades; management training is currently being investigated. For technicians and professionals (e.g. petroleum engineers) some technical courses are mandatory. Interactive video packages are available; content is determined in-house and the material is formatted by an outside software developer. Packages are designed as stand-alones or as components in conventional programmes.

British Caledonian's centre features video, tape decks, several computers, and a reading room. Twenty-five internally developed packages are available in such areas as basic management skills, network analysis, communication skills, and some languages. The set-up costs were not high, as a portion was covered by a government grant, and response has been good. The offerings are aimed at individual, not company, needs and are viewed as introductions to subjects, not as rigorous training. Employees may use the centre during working hours for job-related training (supervisor approval required). While distance education packages are generally intended simply as introductions, they are also used for several specialised applications; sophisticated, self-paced sound/slide packages designed as refresher courses for engineers facing CAA examinations and packages designed to familiarise pilots with landing procedures at various airports are available.

Austin Rover opened its first open learning centre in 1983. Since then, open learning centres have been introduced on each of the nine major sites in the company. High utilisation is reported both during working hours (for job-related training) and after hours for personal development. A wide range of packages is available, including valve engineering, statistics, BASIC programming, keyboard skills, robotics, hydraulics and word processing. Computer-based training courses are also available to aid training in topics such as effective meetings, report writing and time management. Packages range from 4 to 30 hours. Courseware is largely developed in-house, but software is purchased when it meets company needs. Substantial resources are currently being allocated to expand the range of training available through open learning centres and through the introduction of interactive video into courseware.

The *Association of British Ports* is presently developing on-site distance education resources aimed at their four levels of supervisory personnel. Formerly residential courses are being translated into a supervisory programme designed to meet the same needs and using the same basic content. Eventually, there will be a centre at each of the several port groups for supervisory (rather than management) personnel. A combination of technical and management courses will be offered.

Some suppliers of distance learning packages

Because there is a revival of interest in distance learning, new suppliers are being attracted into the market and there is something of an explosion of available packages. Many appear to be developed because of infusions of funds from the Manpower Services Commission, or because of the interests of suppliers. It is debatable whether all have considered the market.

An indication of the range of products available is given below. It is by no means a full list.

Control Data Ltd

One of the largest companies in the area of CBT is Control Data. In addition to their numerous off-the-shelf products, Control Data also offers PLATO courseware. Using a PLATO authoring system a company can build a complete course tailored to its needs. Control Data centres in Britain provide on-site facilities for the study of a variety of courses using PLATO ready-made lessons, plus workbooks and laboratory exercises, audio, and video.

In addition, Control Data has worked in co-operation with other bodies to produce off-the-shelf courseware. As a result of the MSC's small business initiative, Henley, The Management College and the Certified Accountants Educational Trust (CAET) have worked in conjunction with Control Data and others to develop marketing and finance courses. The CAET package includes Cash Flow, Balance Sheet, Profit and Loss, and Management of Working Capital. (Control Data also has two titles of its own: Pricing for Profit and Business Planning.) Henley marketing titles include: This is Marketing, Know Your Market, Marketing Plans and Control, and Managing the Market Way. Courses comprise 30–50 pages of text and a CBT lesson on floppy disk, which includes test sequences covering the text and an interactive simulation that reinforces key learning points. At £95 these packages can be a cost-effective asset, serving as a stand-alone introduction or as a component of a larger training initiative.

Deltak Ltd

Deltak's focus is on analytical management and personnel skills. The firm believes that staff are the most important resource within an organisation, and typically the most neglected. Using a combination of CBT, video films, text, graphics, and lecture-supported workshops, Deltak offers a "core curriculum" in the following subject areas:

Leadership	Management Strategy
Organisation and Planning	Personal Skills
Delegation	Motivation
Problem-solving/Decision-making	Communications
Interviewing, Selection and Training	Safety and Industrial Relations.
Coaching and Counselling	

Deltak offers to design and deliver a training solution tailored precisely to suit a company's needs, one which comes complete with a training consultancy service to help define needs and select the best resources.

Caet

The CAET, as part of the Chartered Association of Certified Accountants (CACA), has long recognised the average manager's need for financial training, and has produced courses in various forms over the years. Today, in addition to the CBT package mentioned above, there are four full courses available, which together comprise the Certified Diploma in Accounting and Finance: Financial Accounting, Management Accounting, The Principles of Management, and Financial Management.

There are three methods of study: R, reading only (£20 per subject) involving study books; P, correspondence (£46 per subject), which adds work packs; and W, correspondence plus one weekend of live tuition (£230 including tuition, per subject). Additionally, short revision courses are available prior to examinations. Although the CAET found the "live" tuition essential, some companies were reluctant to spare managers for a week, so in many cases a compromise was devised whereby the employer releases the employee Thursday afternoon and Friday, and the employee devotes the weekend to study.

The diploma awarded does not afford membership to the CACA, but holders are encouraged to subscribe to the Association and to take part in public presentations. CACA also offers a series of short courses and public presentations to supplement the main body of professional courses, which can be studied by correspondence.

IPM

While the CAET diploma caters for a wider audience (non-financial specialists in a variety of disciplines) using distance education, the IPM offers home study options aimed at IPM membership. The National and Local Government Officers Association and the International Correspondence Schools Ltd feature among others as approved institutions offering correspondence tuition for the IPM examination, although special regulations apply for students opting to study by this method. A new condition in qualifying for IPM membership is that students who have successfully completed the Open University course The Effective Manager may claim exemption from Stage 1 and proceed directly to Stage 2 of the IPM programme.

Further options are available upon completion, notably studying as an independent student (the IPM must be satisfied of a student's ability to undertake this method of study), which involves taking the work home and going it alone. Here again, Open University courses – Personnel Selection, Interviewing, and Improving Personnel Performance – are recommended as satisfying Stage 2 assignments and the residential/sequential element.

Manpower Service Commission (MSC) Open Tech programme.

The MSC's response to industry's growing emphasis on mangement education, and indeed on skills training at all levels, has been remarkable. The MSC appears almost everywhere as a key provider of funding for various training initiatives. The Open Tech programme, which began in 1983, has promted many industries to re-evaluate their training along the lines of its goal of "seeking to widen opportunities for mature students through open access to learning, using new technology both as a teaching and learning tool". We have not attempted to examine this programme in any great depth, as some of the courses have not yet been launched, and others are still fairly new.

We must note here that MSC funding is a limited offer only, in that the money is available to launch and assess such material but after that it is expected that the programmes pay for themselves. Part of the MSC funding is intended to help industry validate the various Open Tech schemes through in-company pilot programmes. For example, Trusthouse Forte has recently piloted a number of units from the HCITB (see below).

The Centre for the Study of Management Learning at Lancaster University has embarked on a more comprehensive study of the MSC projects and has produced a number of positional papers and reports, which are readily accessible. As the largest and possibly the most publicised initiative, the success or failure of MSC programmes will have far-reaching effects on the whole spectrum of management development programmes in the UK.

Hotel and Catering Industrial Training Board (HCITB)

Aimed at the untrained manager rather than potential members of the Hotel Catering and Industrial Management Association (HCIMA), these distance education packages are targeted at the estimated 75 per cent of hotel and catering managers who have had no formal training. Following the MSC initiative, HCITB researched and developed a series of 10 distance education modules, covering such areas as food and beverage management, personnel management in practice, and practical approaches to marketing. Several have yet to be launched.

Each module has a self-instructional text; some also include audio materials and textbooks, while others add the use of a computer (for hands-on exercise of computing, as opposed to CBT). So far, the average cost is around £75 plus the cost of renting a BBC microcomputer; an optional tutor (available at additional cost) is available only to mark the assignment at the end of each module. Most units are divided into four or five sections that take an average of 3-4 hours each to complete.

On successful completion of a unit the student is awarded an HCITB certificate. The Board is presently negotiating with the HCIMA and Business

Technicians Educational Council (BTEC) in the hope that accreditation points may be awarded to those in possession of these certificates. Recognising the importance of a support structure in sustaining student motivation, the Board is also considering the establishment of local delivery centres at colleges where students and tutors can meet.

Bristol Polytechnic

As part of the MSC initiative, Bristol Polytechnic has developed its Open Tech for Technical Supervisors in collaboration with Plessey plc. The modular packages include:

Introduction to Management Skills
Planning
Information Handling (Statistics)
Computer-based Information Systems
Introduction to the Electronic Office
Business, a Systems View
Signal Processing Systems
Quality
Problem-solving and Decision-making.

These packages are particularly suitable for personnel training in high-technology business. However, the design of the modules allows them to be customised by the insertion of company-specific case studies, examples, and exercises. Currently, all the material is paper-based, but expansion into other media has not been ruled out.

Materials are designed to be purchased by companies and passed on to individual students. They are willing to train trainers, prepare tailored company-specific materials, and provide tutorial support. The cost of such support will be negotiated with each customer.

British Institute of Inkeeping (BII).

The BII has produced a series of five titles under the heading of "Pub Business." This Open Tech-sponsored programme is marketed as a means of withstanding the competition of wine bars and off-licences, which threaten this bastion of British life.

The five courses are: Marketing, Product Development, Staff Development, Finance and Accounting, and Business Information for Control. Each contains two illustrated workbooks and an audio tape, and is designed for those who wish to study specific topics (e.g. sales and profits) and also for those who want a more integrated development programme. For the latter, the BII awards a Business Management Certificate upon successful completion.

As with some other MSC-sponsored initiatives, several colleges are supporting this programme by developing short courses and providing tutorial back-up and postal assessment and feedback. However, the BII advises students to take advantage of the support available and work with a mentor – someone of the student's own choice to guide him through the course.

The BII and the HCITB are supportive of the MSC Open Tech initiative, but they believe that, while their respective programmes are available to individuals, corporate purchase and distribution will be more common. Both see the Open Tech in particular and distance education in general as enhancing existing training, not replacing it. The units, they stress, are for *development* and not training – a subtle but important difference. Trusthouse Forte used the HCITB materials *between* its own training sessions with the aim of maintaining the level of knowledge and developing skills further. Individual managers use them to supplement their knowledge base.

National Examinations Board for Supervisory Studies (NEBSS)

Although officially begun in October 1984, this project is very much in its early stages, with only a few of the planned 47 modules presently in the pilot stage. The programme, originally funded by the MSC, is managed by NEBSS in conjunction with the Northern Regional Management Centre and the Northern Consortium of Colleges. The units, which are available directly to individuals or to companies for internal distribution, cover the following areas:

Principles and Practice of Supervision
Technical Aspects of Supervision
Communication
Economic and Financial Aspects
Industrial Relations.

Each unit is expected to take 6–8 hours of study and comprises a blend of text and audio material. Support services are provided, and extensions and recommendations of relevant TV programmes, videos, and books are included. There are no academic entry requirements.

Southtek

Southtek was devised by the head of the Learning Resources Department at Brighton Polytechnic, who saw the need for people to gain competence in computer technology. The project provides training in such subjects as basic digital electronics, fault-finding, and computer-aided design – all packaged so people can learn at work or at home at their own pace.

Southtek was launched by the MSC, which has awarded a grant of £1.7m to be administered by East Sussex County Council. Its administrators hope it will be able to go independent when the grant runs out.

The training packages will be developed by a staff of 30 at Southtek's headquarters in Brighton Polytechnic, with the help of outside specialists. Their average cost will be £40–£45 a course and involve about 16 hours of study. There will be no final qualifications, but students who sit a test will gain a certificate proving they have completed the course.

Cranfield School of Management

As a result of research into current management needs, the Distance Education Centre at Cranfield produced one course, Effective Marketing Management, building on existing courses at the school. It was priced uncompetitively at £12,000, which may explain why it failed to make significant inroads into the market.

Cranfield later produced a smaller, less expensive package, and involved Bell and Howell (manufacturers of audio-visual equipment) in marketing and selling it. This course – Marketing Plans: How to Prepare Them, How to Use Them – takes a step-by-step approach, using text, video, and workbook. The course is directly related to the 2-day residential course at Cranfield. The distance education package is estimated to take 60 hours to complete (12 modules at 5 hours each). In addition to the course material, a tutor's guide is available (at extra cost) so the package can be run by companies as a traditional teacher-based programme. The more competitive price of £350 plus VAT has prompted greater success than that achieved by its predecessor.

Another popular course is Effective Industrial Selling, which sells for £750 and consists of a textbook, video summary of each chapter in the book, case studies, role-play exercises, mini-cases for each chapter, tutor's guides for each of the above, a tutor's training guide, and training material for five salesmen. This resource is being used in 40 countries and has been translated into five languages.

Cranfield also produces tailor-made distance teaching resources for a number of multinationals, including National Westminster Bank. Specially designed courses cost roughly about £10,000, depending on the type and degree of customisation required.

Henley, the Management College

Like Cranfield. Henley has used existing faculty expertise to produce distance education courses. Unlike Cranfield, Henley develops new material not presently used at the College. With titles such as Information Management, Marketing for Managers, The Effective Manager, and Accounting for Managers, each pack contains materials sufficient for a complete training resource, using text (plus workbooks and case studies), audio, and video. The average cost is around £375 plus VAT for an individual package, although bulk purchase schemes are available for those requiring more than five copies of a course. The marketing course is approved by the Institute of Marketing for entry to their diploma. In addition, Henley has produced a CBT course with Control Data Ltd. It is noteworthy that Information Management was produced in collaboration with the MSC Open Tech project.

A Henley "hotline" is available to students who need help and counsellors around the country are available for advice and guidance. In certain cases, where the company has opted to buy a number of packs for in-house distribution, it can pay for a number of company staff to be sent to Henley for a seminar on tutoring. Other courses under development include Production Management, Employee Relations, The Business Environment, and Investment Decision-Making and Corporate Finance.

The modules can be used to build towards a Henley diploma. Alternatively, using an extra "academic top-up" pack plus a residential requirement, it is possible to obtain a masters degree in management awarded by Henley and Brunel University.

Henley has invested heavily in distance education venture, which was something of a risk, given that distance education on such a scale was relatively unchartered territory. Henley reports that the market response has been favourable to date. Of all the distance management education materials currently available, the Effective Manager is undoubtedly one of the most successful.

Business Education Council (BEC)

The BEC, which was set up in 1974, was given the role of planning, administering, and reviewing the establishment of a unified national system of non-degree courses for people whose occupations fall within the broad area of business and public administration.

BEC fulfils this role on devising or giving approval to suitable courses for which it establishes, and assesses standards of performance. These courses then lead to BEC Certificate or Diploma awards at General, National, or Higher National levels.

In its first policy statement in March 1976, BEC acknowledged its concern for these potential students by stating that directed private study and correspondence course routes should be available in addition to the college-based routes to BEC awards.

The directed private study (DPS) and correspondence course (CC) routes are essentially distance education schemes. Students are recruited on a national basis and study at home using structured learning materials. Tutorial contact is maintained by letter or telephone in response to regularly set assignments, student requests, or tutor initiatives. The essential difference between the two routes is one of compulsory face-to-face tuition. DPS students are required to attend centres for short periods to be taught certain skills difficult to teach at a distance, to be given additional tutorial guidance, and to share learning experiences with their fellow students.

BEC began to encourage development of these routes in 1976. Colleges who had expressed an interest in becoming either a DPS or CC centre were asked to submit proposals. By 1979 a limited number of DPS and CC centres had been approved, and work began on producing the courses. Each of the centres has had, or is experiencing, its own particular set of problems in adapting an existing curriculum into distance education form. For example, most centres have found it difficult to provide students with interactive, interpersonal learning experiences that reflect "real-life" business situations. Face-to-face sessions are useful for practical training, but centres have found carefully written materials, backed up with assignments that require the student to get out into the "real" world or leisure, can also do much to foster these elusive skills. These course design difficulties reinforce the importance of determining which educational goals can be served by distance education techniques, and which demand a more conventional approach.

Future developments in opening up BEC courses to students who would not otherwise be able to take advantage of them are likely to come from within the area of BEC post-experience courses. For example, the BEC Post-Experience Learning Methods Study Group is currently considering ways of providing relevant and flexible learning experience for students on these courses, and is seeking opportunities to "open" the courses further (e.g. providing distance education materials, promoting use of learning centres at colleges and elsewhere, and so forth).

The Open University

Perhaps the most famous name in distance education in the UK, the Open University currently has 300,000 students throughout the UK working towards its degrees and short courses. The Open University launched its Open Business School in 1983 in order to provide some management education for those individuals and companies lacking the time or the resources for conventional study. Each course is self-standing, but can interlock with others if a broader range is required. It is intended that a qualification be offered in keeping with the normal requirements for an Open University diploma (840 hours study) or degree (1260 hours).

The first five courses are:

The Effective Manager
Accounting and Finance for Managers
International Marketing
Personnel Selection and Interviewing
Start Up Your Own Business

Each course is short and practical, requiring about 5 hours of study per week for a period which varies from 3 to 6 months. Price ranges from £245 to £395. A residential requirement is included and personal tutors are assigned. Any UK resident over 21 can apply. Course development continues, and eventually over 20 3-month courses will be offered on various topics.

Conclusion

Few firms have comprehensive experience of distance learning, and there is a danger that some will go this route in a belief that it is cost-saving rather than from any clear demonstration of its effectiveness. A package course is still a package course, whether delivered personally or by distance learning methods.

Tailored distance learning is possible, but care is needed to ensure that the vehicle is appropriate for the task that has to be fulfilled. It is more likely to be an adjunct to the more normal types of training than to be a sweeping replacement.

References

1. M. Peel (1984): *Management Development and Training,* British Institute of Management
2. T. van Wijk (1985): Unisa – a different university with different needs, *Unisa Alumnus,* December.
3. F. Airey and M. N. Goodman (1986): *A Survey of Distance Education in Industry Training,* Harbridge Consulting Group Ltd
4. A. Keith (1986): CBT for management development, *Training Officer,* January

14
Evaluation

A little used tool

We know from the various surveys by Harbridge House and others[1] that evaluation of training is a minority activity in British industry. Harbridge House findings were that few companies were able to indicate the criteria by which programme success is measured in their organisations, and that many respondents appeared embarrassed at the question. Other researchers suggest that few organisations do more than apply a "reactions" – level questionnaire at the end of a course. As we shall see, this is only a little better than no evaluation at all.

In my opinion there is a direct connection between failure to evaluate, the low standing of the training function in many organisations, and the inadequate support training is given in many firms. Every managing director should insist that his training staff demonstrate that the budget allocated to training is spent in the most effective way and has achieved beneficial results for the company. Failure to demonstrate the economic value of training turns it into an act of faith, dependent on the beliefs of the chief executive, or the evangelical zeal of the trainer. It is very hard to be a successful evangelist when the system keeps you out of that inner circle which has easy access to top management. My belief in the connection between the status of training managers and lack of evaluation is based on research and first-hand observation. My examination of published materials for this book shows that I am not the first person to have made the connection. "In many cases, the recognition of the training department, and the extent to which it is given a prominent position in the organisation, is dependent upon how well the results of the services are demonstrated and explained".[2] This statment was published in 1958, and the evidence suggests that few have heeded it.

No evaluation method is perfect, and all require the commitment of resources, but it is possible to take rational judgements when there is some basis of fact, and to develop cost/benefit arguments to justify the basis of a decision. Sometimes a decision may still have to be judgemental, but this is likely to be more acceptable when top management can see a proven record of benefits from other training decisions.

In an earlier chapter I have already argued that the way training is controlled in most organisations leads to decisions being taken on a comparison of out-of-pocket costs without comparison of either benefits or the true costs of various options. Minimum cost does not always equate with maximum benefit, and without a history of evaluation in the past it is difficult to judge benefits.

Harbridge House surveys (Ascher[1]) show that many training initiatives continue unchanged for years, and that when outside academic or consultancy help is obtained this too develops into a long-term relationship. If this continuation is based on evaluation evidence it may well be evidence of strength. In most organisations it is evidence of inertia. One directory of training organisations[3] lists some 330 organisations providing management training. It is impossible that they should all be equally effective. Yet the research evidence is that most training functions will stay with a vendor once the first choice has been made. In some cases this may be a wise decision, but I suspect that failure to evaluate is a major contributor to the lethargy.

Evaluation is not just a question of proving the benefits of a particular course of action. It may also help in improving training that is already beneficial. One area mentioned in Chapter 8, where more effort could be directed, is in taking individual differences of, for example, preferred learning style into account when designing training initiatives. The results of an evaluation may demonstrate the benefits of an initiative beyond doubt, but may also indicate that certain individuals have not responded as expected. This, in turn, may lead to other initiatives addressing the needs of this minority.

Clement[4] showed that evaluation is also a neglected art in the USA:

A 1970 review of the management training criteria found that evaluation studies of management training course tended to be inadequate . . . . First of all, less than a third of the studies had measured the effects of training on individual job performance or on results for the organisation such as sales, profits or productivity. Most had focused on training outcome typically assessed during or just after a course, such as trainees' reactions to the course or improvement in knowledge. Second, very few studies had compared the relative effectiveness of two or more technique of training in reaching a desired objective. For example, no one had attempted to determine which training technique worked best for improving intepersonal skills. Third, no studies had measured the influence of individual differences to the outcome of training. For example, none had investigated how the success of training might vary with the level of a trainee's prior experience or education. Finally, few studies had investigated the effect that organisational environment has on the transfer of learning to the job setting. For example, more had examined the influence that a trainee's superior or subordinates might have on the success of the trainee in applying the new knowledge or skill on the job.

A repeat of this study 10 years later was reported in the same article as showing little difference. The author discussed another survey finding that training functions were growing in the USA, but even less time was being spent on evaluation: "The danger is the potential of growth without accountability in a proportion of ineffective programmes."

One contributory factor to the lack of evaluation is resource constraint.

Many traineers argue that they would prefer to devote all resources to training, rather than divert some of them to measuring the results of that training. This creates a vicious circle: inadequate resources for training means no evaluation; no evaluation means that benefits cannot be proved leading to even less adequate resources for training. In fact, for reasons discussed earlier, I believe that much of the training in many organisations would fail the test of evaluation, because it is not directed at assisting achievement of company objections or implementation of company strategies.

Some objectives of evaluation

Evaluation may have at least three objectives:

1. Is the training initiative fulfilling the objective for which it was established? Ideally this objective should be linked to a corporate rather than an individual benefit, although an intermediate step measuring individual changes may be desirable.
2. Is one method of training more effective than another? This is not the same as asking which is the cheapest. Such questions are becoming more important as companies experiment with computer-based learning, interactive video or other modern distance learning approaches. Frequently these decisions are based on hunch or cost alone.
3. Is the training the most effective method for every participant? This ties to the concept of individual differences discussed in Chapter 8. Often practicability means that only one training method will be offered, rather than a choice to fit a variety of individual learning styles, but this method at least should be appropriate for the majority (and too much weight should not be given to adverse views of the minority for whom the initiative is not the best learning vehicle).

We need some form of evaluation on at least a sample basis to answer questions such as these. But evaluation methods may also be designed to be a continuation of the training initiative: if they force managers to review and apply what they have been taught this may act as reinforcement of the training. One company I know makes the manager who authorises someone's attendance on a course responsible for ensuring that the participant applies that knowledge. This has the result of using management to ensure that the training has an effect. It does not, of course, measure whether the course was the most cost-effective approach, only that some use is made of the things learnt. That same company also frequently uses case studies in a less usual way. Their case studies are of unsolved problems the company is facing, and part of the course output is a solution which can be implemented. Thus the case studies become a form of action learning.

An objective for a course must be defined before progress against that objective can be evaluated. There may be multiple objectives that need evaluation in several ways, but unless these are defined and consideration given before the event to how evaluation will take place, it may be impossible to identify any clear result. The nature of the objective will affect the main method of evaluation used. If the key purpose of a training programme is to increase retention of staff by a defined period, and to make it easier to recruit new personnel, it becomes possible to measure whether the desired result is obtained. These particular objectives are real, and are among the organisational objectives of a development programme designed by Harbridge House for one of its clients, a firm of accountants. The fact that business knowledge training of high quality is given becomes an incentive to join or to stay a few months longer after qualifying, even for people who have not yet attended the course. It is possible to make reasonable assessments of the process of the programmes in achieving these objectives independently of any evaluation of the programme itself. And if the result is that any programme does not achieve the key organisational objectives, it may well be regarded as a failure regardless of it effectiveness in imparting knowledge.

The question of why a course is really wanted is too rarely addressed because, as I have suggested elsewhere, few companies make a direct connection between training and what the company is trying to do.

One of the aims of evaluation must be to ensure that the most important course objectives are achieved. In the example I gave it would be appropriate to evaluate to test the effectiveness of the course in meeting the educational objective, but this only becomes relevant information if the other objectives are also met.

Ultimate outcome level

Whitelaw[5] provides a useful view of the levels of evaluation, which he derived from work by Hamblin.[6] Reversing these, so that they are in the order of importance which I place on them, we start with the ultimate outcome level, which is where the course impacts on the organisational objectives through the changed job behaviour of the trainee. This behaviour may be the result of new skills or knowledge acquired through training, or in the case of initiatives designed primarily with corporate results in mind, may be the result of the building of a common culture, or sense of involvement, or some other dimension of attitude change or enhanced awareness. In most training initiatives this ultimate outcome level becomes impossible to evaluate because it is never defined, and because the time lag between training and ultimate outcome is too long. This is inevitable if the philosophy is that "all training benefits the company because the company must be better off with better-trained people".

In my view every training initiative should be related to a corporate level objective of some sort. This may, of course, be at the level of a business unit or cost centre. The shorter the time lag between initiative and results, the more effective this objective is likely to be as a realistic basis for evaluation. If the aim is to help overcome a problem or implement a strategy, or something similar, it should be possible to define very clear objectives for the training initiative. Much more of the training activity in the UK should be directed this way, which would immediately make training a more useful activity.

There is another category of training initiatives where objectives may be less apparent, but could be defined if thought were given to it. One recommendation I would make is that the discipline of thinking through measurable corporate-level objective should be gone through for every training initiative, any training that cannot be related to a clear outcome at this level should be looked on with suspicion. Every company should include a proportion of training of less obvious corporate value, but this proportion should be lower than the 100 per cent that applies in most companies. Just the discipline of questioning the value of each initiative as part of its justification should lead to more focus, and more training that really does contribute to the bottom line.

The simplest way to evaluate success at this level is to see whether the objective is achieved. This is a little crude, in that it does not isolate all the variables to measure only the results of training, and a degree of judgement is required in interpretation. It is considerably better than having no idea at all of what the training is trying to achieve.

In some circumstances it is possible to be more scientific in measuring results. For example, a programme designed to teach selling methods to increase sales could measure the sales increases gained by each participant against his or her past record and against a matched pair who did not receive the training. A negotiation skills course could set clear objectives for performance and use similar methods of measurement.

The Harbridge House research found a company in the catering industry that tied all management training to business objectives. For example, a *negotiating skills* course was taken by people negotiating for airport contracts. The goal of the course was set at doubling the success rate of these individuals. After completion of the course the results were monitored to see if the goal was achieved.

Evaluation at the ultimate outcome level will probably always remain something of an art, but practice of that art will improve the value of training and help ensure that it is worth doing.

Intermediate outcome level

Evaluation at the job behaviour level also is more appropriate if it is made in the context of clearly defined objectives. All training, whether in skills for immediate application, or education for future development, has an intention to change job behaviour in some way. The only difference is one of time. Some training is also concerned with changing attitudes. Although the two aspects are related, it is possible to change an attitude without altering behaviour (a smoker may now accept that smoking is bad for health, but still continue to smoke) and it is possible to bring about some behavioural changes without affecting attitudes. Very occasionally training may be directed at a fundamental value. Evaluation at the intermediate level only becomes possible when the objectives for the change required are thought out, and an attempt made to measure performance before and after training.

The Harbridge House research found one company who asked managers as part of their training exercise to identify the results of each completed course. The requirement is for these results to be quantified, usually focusing on cost or time. Another approach is to have participants prepare action lists at the end of a course, and for these to be monitored either through the management structure or by the trainer. This does not by itself evaluate a programme, but provides a structure within which evaluation is possible.

Monitoring job behaviour changes is easy when the objectives are simple and short-term. For example, a course in letter-writing can be measured through an analysis of samples of letters written by participants before and after attendance at the course. It is thus possible to measure whether the training has had the required effect. (Whether it is *economically* beneficial depends on the link that can be established by better letters and corporate objectives: clearly there should be such a link which can be defined, even if not quantified.) Teaching a manager in one function an understanding of another function may be more important than a basic skill, but the results in changed behaviour are unlikely to occur for some time after the course. This makes them much difficult to evaluate because:

- changed behaviour will occur in a random sequence as a response to trigger situations, if it occurs at all;
- other events are more likely to "contaminate" the training benefit if the period is long (that is, change may be due to other causes);
- the participant's boss may change, causing different standards to be used to judge job behaviour.

In this sort of situation it is worth considering a detailed study of results of the training on the lines of that used by BP in Chapter 10. Such evaluation is more likely to be useful if the whole training project had been designed with evaluation in mind, so that "before" and "after" assessments are taken and the objectives are clear. It will be more valuable if it includes a control group.

Immediate outcome: measuring what is learnt

The immediate requirement from any course is that something is learnt. It is possible to devise means of measuring learning, and thus measuring the effectiveness of the training initiative. This does not in any way prove that the initiative will be worthwhile. What is learnt may not be applied, and thus behaviour does not necessarily change. If the course is inappropriate it can be very efficient as a learning vehicle, and ineffective as a means of benefiting company results.

Even measuring learning is not without problems, as there has to be some way of measuring the change that has taken place. An examination at the end of a course might measure what participants now know, but would not separate the knowledge brought to the course from that learned on it.

Some skills are relatively easy. Short tests could be given on something like keyboard skills before and after a course, and the differences compared. A technique such as discounted cash flow may begin with participants who have never met the technique, and end with exercises where they apply it and their results can be scored. Knowledge and concepts are much more difficult. Few participants come to a course in complete ignorance of a conceptual subject, and the training course may well be designed to help them re-call and re-evaluate this knowledge as well as adding to it.

One approach I have used is to give a forced-choice questionnaire at the start and at the end of a course. This provides a way of measuring the improvement in score of each person. The practical problems are choosing questions about the important things in the course, and assessing the meaning of results. The first problem can be resolved with care. The second needs many applications and a data bank of results before we know whether a 20 per cent improvement in score, for example, is good or bad. It is possible to use the absolute movements in score to contrast different teaching approaches: for example a case study with one group contrasted with a lecture in another. Even here it is possible to get into difficulties, for to be truly objective we should repeat the experiment many times, and identify factors such as the different preferred learning styles of participants. It is possible to infer that lectures are best simply because the one particular event measured happened to contain people who preferred this learning method, and who were not typical of the organisation as a whole.

A real problem is that in a typical company situation the number of participants taking a training course may be small. On a unique event it is little value to prove that another approach to course design would have been better, unless that knowledge can be used on a different course in the future.

There is a more pragmatic approach which I find useful, because it provides a bridge between the three levels of results discussed so far. This is to include projects either on the course or as a follow-up activity. If observed by the trainer, the project provides a means by which it is possible to see how the knowledge taught on the course is applied. It does more than this in that it is also a way of fixing knowledge by providing a real opportunity for it to be used. If the project is related to (a) the participants' jobs and (b) some corporate objective, this method also increases the likelihood of the initiative's being successful at the intermediate and ultimate outcome levels. Projects take a great deal of organisation, require management support, and need creative thought if they are not to become repetitive or trivial. They add to the total cost of a training initiative.

When appropriate for the situation they can be a very valuable way of ensuring that training is effective on all three of the dimensions discussed so far, and provide some evidence through the results of the project to help evaluate the initiative.

Reactions level

Almost every organisation takes a "happiness" rating at the end of a course, and some set great store by these. The typical questionnaire requires each participant to rate the course: often by session, lecturer, and teaching method. The form will sometimes require an assessment of the hotel as well. It frequently invites participants to suggest change to the course.

The value of this approach can be improved if care is given to the design of the questionnaire, but however good or bad this is, the approach measures what people feel about the course, not whether the course is effective in meeting its objectives.

The results are notoriously subject to manipulation by the trainer. If the last event of the course ends on a high note the probability is that the whole course will score well. If a strong rapport has been built up between trainer and participants they will be reluctant to give ratings that appear to criticise. If the trainer stimulates a discussion on the course immediately before the questionnaire is completed, he is able to bias the rating upwards or downwards, depending on the questions he gets discussed and the participants he asked to start the debate.

My main concern over the questionnaires is the lack of correlation between enjoyment and the effectiveness of the course. It is a reasonable proposition that people will learn more if they are not bored. It is probably not true that a witty, entertaining speaker, whose performance is very pleasurable, causes people to learn more than they would through a case study, role-playing, or syndicate exercise. There are also occasions where learning a truth can be uncomfortable and not very pleasant, but may nevertheless be very important; these disappear from courses if too much credence is given to "happiness" ratings.

Slightly more valuable is to obtain a report from participants, either written or by interview, a few weeks after the course. This removes some of the problems mentioned above but still does not evaluate the course. Unresolved questions are:

- Did participants learn what they were expected to learn?
- Is that knowledge being applied back in the job situation?

- Does this change in behaviour in any way contribute to company results?

Those companies who "sell" training places on an internal market place may well become more concerned over the happiness rating than the effectiveness of the course. Happiness means that colleagues of participants will sign up, and the course will be full and therefore believed to be useful. Unhappiness means fewer participants and perhaps the abandonment of the course. Neither result has much to do with the effectiveness of the course.

Some conclusions

Figure 14.1 shows some of the factors which may impact on the effectiveness of training:-

Aims of the initiative

Do trainers, participants and the rest of the organisation perceive this in the same way? In practice, perception is impaired because no attempt is made to define the aims of many initiatives, or if aims are defined they are often on the basis of what will be taught rather than why the course is needed.

Trainers

Effectiveness of training can be changed through the design of the course, nature of course materials and teaching methods, skills of the trainers, personalities of the trainers, and the physical facilities in which the course takes place. However, what the trainers do is only one part of the equation. Effectiveness may also be influenced by participants and the organisation. This is not a passive relationship, and the design of an initiative should take account of these other actors in the drama.

Participants

Most of the factors are fairly obvious, such as motivation, intelligence, levels of expertise, a concern about whether the initiative is the right level, and his or her perception of the relevance of the initiative. This last factor may be exacerbated by other pressures and claims on time which may be organisational (the work is piling up) or personal (I do not want to stay away from home this week). Learning styles were discussed in Chapter 8. Some of these factors can be addressed through the nature of the initiative, and others through the provision of information. However, the ability of the participant to learn and apply knowledge is in turn influenced by the organisation.

Evaluation 173

```
                    ┌─────────────────────┐
                    │ AIMS OF INITIATIVE: │
                    │ HOW PERCEIVED BY:-  │
                    └─────────────────────┘
```

Trainers	Participants	Organisation
- Design of initiative	- Motivation	- Culture
- Quality of course materials and teaching method	- Intelligence	- Attitude of managing director
- Trainer skills	- Expertise	- Attitudes of participants' superiors
- Trainer personality	- Perception of level of the initiative	- Attitudes of participants subordinates
- Physical facilities for course	- Perceived relevance of initiative	- Knowledge of subject of superior/ subordinates
	- Learning style	
	- Other claims on time	

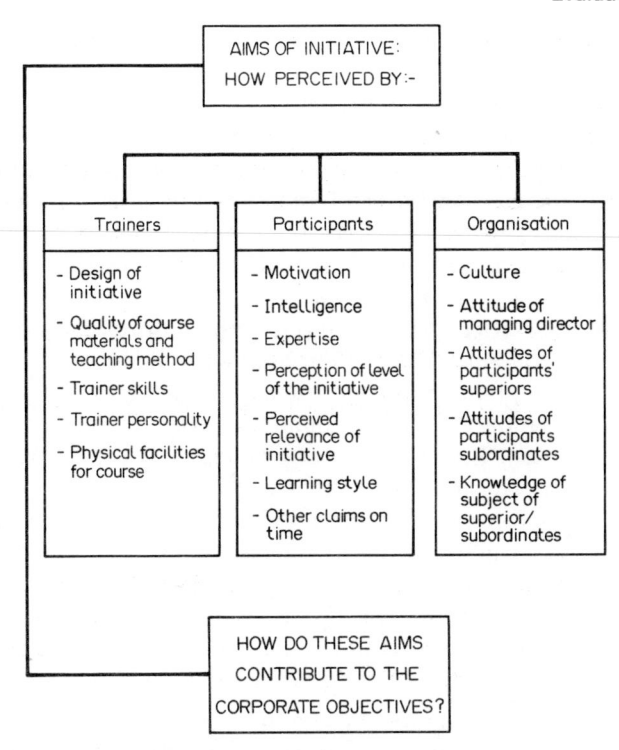

```
          ┌─────────────────────────┐
          │ HOW DO THESE AIMS       │
          │ CONTRIBUTE TO THE       │
          │ CORPORATE OBJECTIVES?   │
          └─────────────────────────┘
```

FIGURE 14.1. Some factors affecting the effectiveness of training

Organisation

Company culture, which to a large degree is affected by the attitudes of the managing director, is one of the major influences. It is not difficult to visualise how some of the cultural issues discussed in the first chapters of this book could cause all training to be ineffective in particular companies. The attitudes of superiors to training have a profound impact on effectiveness, as does the knowledge of a superior. Blockages to implementation are often imposed by the ignorance of the superior manager, who refuses to allow change. Similarly, implementation may be affected by subordinates for similar reasons.

Evaluation may be an important aid to identifying blockages, and ensuring that the more appropriate initiative is designed. Used this way it does not demonstrate the value of training, only that training that is done is appropriate to meet the aims of the course. It may make training efficient, but not necessarily economically effective.

In order to truly evaluate training, one has to address the last point on Figure 14.1. This is the relationship between the aim of a training initiative and corporate objectives. This cannot be explicitly defined in all cases, but this can be done more often than is normal practice. There should also be a bias for more training initiatives to be directed at areas where the link is explicit, and less to areas where it is remote and unknown. This will call for a change in thinking about courses, with many more designed explicity around a company problem or issue and embracing all disciplines needed to deal with it, rather than the more common division of training into single-discipline initiatives.

The argument is that top management should both demand and make it possible for training to grow in stature by allowing it to change focus to the things that really matter. Top management should then insist on evidence that training is economically effective. Training managers need to re-think the way in which training is approached and build in economic evaluation as a criterion as a matter of rule. The other dimensions of training evaluation may follow when needed. In my opinion if training does not do that which is economically effective, and demonstrate the value of what it has done, it has no claim to exist. However, if it does work in the way described it may bring an enormous change in the fortunes of British industry.

References

1. (a) K. Ascher (1983): *Management Training in Large U.K. Business Organisations: A Survey,* Harbridge House.
    (b) M. Peel (1984): *Management Development and Training,* British Institute of Management
    (c) Cooper and Lybrand Associates (1985): *A Challenge to Complacency: Changing Attitudes in Training,* Manpower Services Commission/National Economic Development Office
2. H. S. Belman and H. H. Remners (1958): Evaluating the results of training, *Journal of the American Society of Training Directors,* XX11, 5, pages 28-32.
3. B. Williamson (1986): *Directory of Trainer Support Services,* Kogan Page
4. R. W. Clement (1981): Evaluating the effectiveness of management training: progress during the 1970s and prospects for the 1980s, *Human Resource Management,* Winter 1981
5. M. Whitelaw (1972): *The Evaluation of Management Training - A Review,* Institute of Personnel Management, page 8
6. A. C. Hamblin (1968): Training in evaluation: a discussion of some problems, *Organisational Necessities and Individual Needs* (A.J.M. Occasional Paper No. 5 R. J. Halcon, editor), Blackwell

15
IPM and ABCD

The rather cryptic title of this chapter will soon become clear for those who are not already aware of the Institute of Personnel Management (IPM) and their campaign *A Boost for Continuous Development* (ABCD), the concept being promoted by IPM, in a campaign launched in April 1984.

There are some differences of viewpoint between ABCD and the rest of this book, but there are also complementary areas. The IPM concept is founded on a belief in the need for continuous self-development, to achieve which both the companies have responsibilities. An important element is the belief that there should be an integration of learning with work.

Perhaps the best way of explaining the concept is to reproduce the IPM code[1] on the subject.

The IPM Code: Continuous development; people and work

Introduction and Aims

The IPM code on continuous development has been drawn up to give guidance on elements of any work system which will promote:

(a) the integration of learning with work
(b) continuous self development
(c) improved operational performance.

Within such a work system all employees will have two objectives, one to maintain and improve those things which stimulate learning, the other continuously to practise self-development, both leading to enhanced performance.

The Code has been developed by the Institute of Personnel Management's National Committee for Training and Development (NCTD) which is responsible for the formulation and continuous review of IPM policy on education and training matters. For some time, the NCTD has been concerned to establish a new balance in society between formal, directed, *teaching* methods, experience-based *learning* methods and self-directed development. It wishes to encourage a recognition that learning is a normal part of work (and indeed of all activities), but that, to be effective, the individual must consciously work at the process of learning.

To be successful, continuous development requires that responsibilities are understood consistently by everyone; that priority operational needs are communicated quickly and effectively; that each learner can feel that he/she shares ownership of any collective learning plans; that he/she can feel confident of his/her ability to create some personal learning plans; and that appropriate facilities and resources are available as a normal part of working life.

These issues are covered in greater detail in the Code under six key headings:

Policies
Responsibilities and roles
The identification of learning opportunities and needs
Learner involvement
The provision of learning resources
Results.

Policies

Most organizations find written statements of policy useful.
Any statement of general policy relating to the management of people should make reference to:

1. a corporate commitment to continuous development
2. the inter-dependence of technical and social systems, strategies and objectives
3. self-development as a responsibility of every individual within the organization
4. the need for all to undersatnd as much as possible about learning processes
5. the organization's commitment to acknowledge improved performance, and to provide appropriate rewards
6. the organization's intention to use enhanced skills operationally as work opportunities permit
7. 'who carries responsibility for what' in the identification of learning aims and the promotion of learning activity
8. ways in which operational aims and objectives are communicated to those employed
9. appraisal and assessment methods
10. procedures for career planning
11. any facilities provided for learning during work time, including any policy on paid or unpaid leave for this purpose

12. the organization's policy on employee involvement, especially that relating to involvement in reviewing education and training facilities and resources.

Responsibilities and Roles

All members in the organization should be able to view the operational life of the organization as a continuous learning process – and one in which they all carry responsibilities.

Senior executives: have the responsibility to ensure that policy statements and practices promote continuous development (as set out elsewhere in this Code) and that forward plans incorporate future management needs, particularly to improve performance, taking into account the impact of key changes in legal requirements, technology, work patterns and (not least) ideas. They must encourage managers to plan learning activities to facilitate the process of change.

Managers: have the responsibility to spend a substantial proportion of their time promoting continuous development, that is, discussing needs, creating plans, coaching subordinates, introducing changes which make learning easier and/or more effective. Managers must promote their own 'learning about learning'.

Personnel professionals: have various responsibilities. They should provide an on-going information service on resources and continuously monitor the extent and quality of learning activity in the organization. If they feel the learning activity is inadequate to support the operational needs of the business, they should take the initiative in generating strategic and/or tactical discussions, recommending appropriate action as necessary. They should ensure that review discussions happen at least once a year within the senior executive group and within any consultative groups.

Internal personnel department review discussions should take place more frequently.

All learners: (including the three groups above) should appreciate that they are responsible for clarifying their own learning goals within the framework established by forward plans and discussions with management. They should raise their problems with management; seek new information without waiting for it to be delivered; propose ways of learning which minimize operational disruption; and demonstrate new learning whenever possible. The ultimate aim is for continuous development to become fully integrated into work, with learners managing most of the activity for themselves and everyone contributing to the identification of learning opportunities.

Identification of Learning opportunities and Needs

It is worth repeating that *everyone needs to contribute to the identification of learning opportunities.* But some sources are stronger than others, for example:

Operational plans: every proposal for a new operational element or instrument, that is, a new product, a new item of plant, a new procedure, a new department, a new member of staff, a new accounting convention, a new *anything*, should be accompanied by an estimate of (a) which employees need to learn something, (b) what needs to be learned, (c) how the learning can happen. If these things cannot be defined with confidence the proposal should include a plan which allows this to be completed later. Some needs are indirectly related: new technical systems, for example, may demand not merely instruction in the system *per se,* but also new levels and types of maintenance. Removing existing resources (machines, materials, or perhaps people) may also demand a learning plan.

Job descriptions and specifications: documents outlining *management* responsibilities should normally include references to (a) the roles of appraiser, counsellor, tutor, (b) the responsibility to develop understanding of learning processes, (c) the manager's inclusion of learning elements in operational plans. Separately, all job descriptions and specifications (regardless of level or type) should emphasize the job holder's responsibilities for self-development on a continuous basis.

Appraisal: appraisal forms and guidance notes should explicitly demand reports on improved performance goals and hence learning needs. Appraisal interviews should normally include joint appraiser/appraisee discussions on the extent to which self-development takes place, and again on the frequency of management-inspired learning plans. Ideally, informal appraisal discussions will happen continuously; a standard question on these occasions should be "how long is it since we/you/I learned something new at work?"

Special reviews/audits: parts of the learning system should be specially reviewed from time to time. Diagonal-slice (i.e. varied levels of employee from various departments) working parties, joint consultative committees, trainee groups, and not least, particular individuals, can be charged with collecting data, analysing it and reporting to senior executives or to personnel management. These reviews are particularly useful in those parts of the learning system where knowledge or awareness needs to be renewed from time to time, as, for example, in health and safety.

Learner Involvement

Learners need to be motivated to want to learn. This motivation may be lacking if they feel their learning activities are 'imposed', especially if they seem unrelated to personal aspirations. It is necessary therefore to encourage learners' involvement in the creation of any training plans that will involve them.

To that end

1. *joint appraisor/appraisee decisions* should aim at *joint* definition of objectives and the means to achieve them
2. *standing committees* should include in their agendas, at regular periodic intervals, an item demanding review of their achievements and future aims
3. *special organizational groupings* (e.g. quality circles, briefing groups) should explicitly contain 'improved performance' and 'management of change' aims, and should consciously devote time to discussing the learning aspects of any proposals for future activity
4. when new plant or equipment is introduced, contracts with *suppliers* should explicitly contain reference to the early involvement of staff during the commissioning process. It is normally desirable that suppliers should provide more than written manuals; active dialogue between them and those who are to operate and maintain the new equipment (including *contract* maintenance staff where appropriate) is needed
5. *work teams* should encourage a 'multi-skills' approach to their future operations, minimizing divisions between jobs and maximizing the flexibility that goes with increased versatility
6. where unionized and/or joint consultative arrangements exist, policies relating to training should regularly be discussed with *employee representatives* at all levels. Reference should be made to these policies, and to any current learning priorities, in progress reports, house magazines and through other available communication channels. Incentives towards self-development are as useful in this area as in others.

The Provision of Learning Resources

Self-development, team learning, and continuous operational development, all require resource material and facilities. The organization should clarify its policies and practices on the following:

1. training/learning budgets
2. authorities to approve training/learning plans and expenditure
3. facilities for study during standard working hours, including paid/unpaid leave
4. financial assistance with travel, books, tapes, and other facilities
5. awards and/or scholarships
6. coaching and tutorial resources

7. management's responsibility to create an environment in which continuous development can prosper.

All employees, and especially management, should have access to documents detailing these policies.

Results

How do you spot the 'continuous development' team? Its characteristics are many and varied, but here is a list of the key ones:

- all members, management and non/management, appear to understand and share ownership of operational goals
- immediate objectives exist and are generally understood by all
- new developments are promoted; change is constructive and welcomed and enjoyed, not forced and resisted
- managers are frequently to be heard discussing learning methods with their subordinates and colleagues
- managers frequently ask subordinates what they have learned recently
- time is found by all the team to work on individual problems
- reference documents (dictionaries, manuals, specifications sheets and the like) are available to all without difficulty, and are *used*
- members use other members as resources
- members don't just swap information they tackle problems and create opportunities
- all members share responsibility for success or failure: they are *not* dependent upon one or more leaders
- members appear to learn while they work, and to enjoy both.

The AB was added to the CD when the Institute set out to promote "the evolution of continuous learning system throughout UK society".

The prime objectives of the campaign are:

- to create a ready acceptance of the idea that change offers new learning opportunities to increase an organisation's effectiveness and to stimulate its flexibility;
- to encourage a recognition of the fact that learning is an integral part of work but that, to be effective, it requires the individual to work consciously at the process;
- to promote new techniques and attitudes, with a sensible balance between formal teaching and self-directed learning.

One of the stimuli for ABCD came from an awareness which is explained in the words of Bob Ransey, IPM President: "too much management dedication to short term expediency . . . dooms us to imprisonment within our present inefficient and unacceptable environment".[2] The IPM also recognised the point which I deduced from our own research that money spent on training is not always spent wisely.[3] "The IPM does not consider that the considerable sums spent on education and training are spent sufficiently productively" (page 5).

I like several of the emphases of ABCD; for example, that individuals have responsibility for self-development, that work is a place of continuous learning, that new "learning" is needed when something changes, and that top management needs to think harder about training.

My concerns are that to work effectively it needs the more aggressive relationship of training and company strategy which are described in this book. Without this, I believe the system can easily become corrupted (as so many good ideas are by British management) into something which IPM does not intend. This is the perpetuation of the situation described by Bob Ramsey above, or what I have described earlier in this book as distortion of the perceptual boundaries. I fear that unless top management takes the deliberate choice of turning its management training and development into a competitive weapon, little will be achieved.

References

1. Institute of Personnel Management (1984): *Continuous Development: People and Work*, the IPM Code
2. IMP (1983): Quoted in *IPM: A Positive Policy for Training and Development*, Institute of Personnel Management, September.

Further information on ABCD can be obtained from:

Mrs Susan Wood, Manager, Training and Development, IPM House, Camp Road, Wimbledon, London SW19 4UW (telephone: 01-946-9100).

16

Recent Changes in the USA

In Chapter 1 brief reference was made to the "American disease", which seemed to have similar symptoms to the "British disease", but a fundamentally different and much more recent cause. George Cabot Lodge's[1] diagnosis of the American disease was referred to. Although published in 1984, this book was completed in May 1983.

The American culture is very different from the British, despite numerous elements of a common heritage. Certain elements of the American culture lead one to expect that even while the disease was being diagnosed, progressive managements would have been changing their behaviour to solve the problem themselves. The purpose of this chapter is to look at some of the recent trends, and the extent to which they support the actions recommended in the book.

What is the American culture? It is obviously highly dangerous to attempt to summarise national characteristics in a few words. Rather than take the responsibility, I have drawn on the findings of a NEDO/MSC study.[2] There is a belief in entrepreneurial activity, with America seen as a land of opportunity, and also the country that should be world leader in all its endeavours. People are individualistic, and there is a widespread belief that the person is responsible for his or her own future. There is no expectation of being looked after by the State. Perhaps because of this, people are mobile and flexible, willing to change occupation or state. The rewards are for achievement, rather than effort, and money is the measure of success: scant sympathy is given to the unsuccessful. On the other hand, there is a high energy level and an optimistic view of life, and failure is not seen as a permanent stigma which prevents people trying again. Overall there is "a wide consensus about certain fundamentals of American life". Taking this last part further, it is possible to argue that although an individualistic society, America is not a deeply divided society.

The reader can make his or her own contrasts with this view of American culture, and over our own position in the UK.

Changes have undoubtedly taken place over the past few years. This chapter will look at some of the outside evidence of changes in approach to management training and education, and follow this with some more detailed information based on observation and research by Harbridge House Inc.

Recent Changes in the USA

The Conference Board in a 1985 survey[3] found that these had been significant changes in all aspects of company training since 1980. This was caused by the need to respond to new company strategies, rapid technological change, heightened competition, and other changes in the business environment. A further reason was a drive to achieve greater competitive strength by improving the performance of employees.

This survey found that the proportion of employees participating in company training had increased over the 5-year period, with particularly high increases for managers, professional and sales/marketing personnel. Accompanying this trend was an increase in the resources devoted to training, and in the use of outside resources. More than half had increased their use of external instructors and consultants on in-house programmes, while 40 per cent made more use of outside programmes. (Note that these two headings overlap: some of the 40 per cent may also be in the 53 per cent.)

Quotations from respondents in the survey[3] give some of the flavour of the changed view of training.

- "Management has become convinced that education drives the business."
- "A stepchild until recently, the training function is now seen as essential to the company's strategic goals."
- "Developing our people is now at the heart of our business strategy."
- "Our human resources function was given a new charter three years ago – to contribute to the company's competitive edge by recruiting talented people, training them, and not letting them stagnate."
- "Training departments used to be wiped out by recession, but few were in the recent one" (page 2).

The survey found many examples of how management education and training programmes were being used in the implementation of new strategies. This is exactly one of the points of this book, and it is a management trend which has not so far transferred to the majority of British companies.

Bolt[4] provides case examples of this trend in the USA, quoting Motorola, Xerox, Federated Department Stores and General Foods as examples of companies which had undergone this significant revolution in their use of management training. Bolt maintains that senior management is now playing a much greater role in training in US companies, and that this is caused by "the demand for greater productivity, the threat of worldwide competition, and , recognition of the change many corporate cultures need", and has led to a demand for training at the highest levels of companies.

All the examples quoted by Bolt have implementation as the focus with measurable changes in business results as the desired outcome.

Harbridge House Inc. of Boston USA are in an excellent position to observe some of the changes that have taken place, and indeed were involved in a very large number of the case examples included in the articles and survey already referenced in this chapter. In addition, the firm has recently completed a research project which identified the 10 qualities of management that were judged to be essential by a diverse sample of employees in American industry. These qualities have led to changes in many of the tailored courses designed by Harbridge House for clients, and which form part of the training revolution in the USA.

Harbridge House Inc. believes that a number of factors are now considered important in US businesses, and go so far as to say that a number of executives and middle managers have lost their jobs because they have not kept up with them. The following extract is taken from an internal company paper. *Trends in management.*[5]

November 1986

HARBRIDGE HOUSE
TRENDS IN MANAGEMENT

Executive and middle managers are losing their jobs because they are not keeping up with:

- Understanding and implementing their company's strategy.
- Effectively motivating their direct reports.
- Understanding global business opportunities and competition. Most American business people view the world and their business as US/North America only or as just exporters.
- Utilizing office automation and information technology; for example, one company purchased PCs for its 1,000 top managers, had them go through a three-day program, and found that 60 percent of them would never use the PC.
- Innovative new ways to do business versus traditional ways.
- Understanding and responding to general management and cross-functional implications. Managers continue to be only functional experts; for example, a manufacturing person operates only in terms of what is best for manufacturing without looking at what is best for the total business.

The most successful companies in American industry, defined as producing excellent financial results and having productive, highly-motivated work forces, are able to overcome the above six problems by taking action. Companies such as General Electric, Rockwell, Sears, Colgate-Palmolive, Northern Telecom, are all examples of successful companies. One of the things that they have in common is that they are *using executive and management training to overcome the potential obsolescence of their managers*. They are doing the following:

- They have put in place tailored executive and management training that focuses on understanding where the company is going and utilizing training as a means of implementing the company's strategy.
  For example, defense contractors are utilizing Harbridge House's services in terms of how to most effectively comply with the government's fraud, waste, and abuse standards. The focus is on how to effectively work with the government in a changing business environment.
- They are using confidential management practices and climate feedback reports from the direct reports of the participants attending the program in order for them to know how their direct reports see them. Listed below are the five management practices that have received the highest scores. Also, training is built around how to improve in the areas where the participants score the lowest:
  - Understanding the financial implications of your decisions.
  - Following up on important issues and actions.
  - Demonstrating personal commitment to achieving goals.
  - Using your time effectively.
  - Getting to the heart of problems, rather than dealing with less important issues.
- They focus on how to become a global business as a topic in their management training

programs. Expertise is drawn from outside the company as well as the internal resources who are responsible for non-US business who have been successful in gaining world-wide market share.
- They focus on office automation/information technology as a topic in their management training programs in the context of gaining competitive advantage through the use of information. Also, computer simulations are used, where the PC has a role and people can see the value of automation.
- They are getting their people to think creatively by having new programs on innovation. The innovation model is based on how to more effectively do one's job, by getting executives and managers to think in new ways and bring about greater results.
- Management training programs focus on the general manager's perspective as well as the implications of cross-functional teamwork. An individual who has worked in one area learns the implications of his or her decisions on the general manager, the other functions, and the business overall. Having participants from different functions attend the program is very valuable, as well as having people all from the same function attend where the discussions focus on their impact on other areas.

Beyond having executive and management training programs address these issues, these companies are also having their training programs conducted in Europe and the Pacific basin so that their foreign nationals can be brought up to date on the company strategy and the latest management concepts and skills.

The ten universal qualities of management identified from the research project by Harbridge House came from studies of American managers. It is reasonable to assume that they are equally important to British managers, and indeed would seem to be completely in sympathy with the requirements for the successful implementation of the IPM code of practice for continuous development described in the previous chapter.

This chapter concludes with a description of the research and its findings, which is included with the permission of Harbridge House Inc.[6]

TEN UNIVERSAL QUALITIES OF EFFECTIVE MANAGERS
Background and methodology of the study
Harbridge House Inc. is a Boston-based international management consulting, training, and research firm. The Diagnostic and Feedback Division specializes in executive education and makes extensive use of survey-feedback methods in its training programs. A pioneer in feedback-based training, the division now has a database that captures the managerial habits of over 5,000 managers. Information from this database was combined and analyzed to obtain the "universal qualities" of effective managers.

Prior to attending a Harbridge House Inc. training program, managers in a given company distribute questionnaires to three or more of their subordinates and/or associates. The questionnaire measures subordinates'/associates' perceptions of the management practices used by their bosses/colleagues. (The questionnaire contains items that may measure as many as 50 different management practices.) Each questionnaire item is rated on a scale of 1 to 5 in terms of the extent to which a manager engages in a particular management practice. Responses are combined, averaged, and returned to each manager in a computer-generated report that shows a percentile score for each management practice surveyed. The percentile score is derived by comparing the manager's average score for each practice to the average scores of all other managers in the database. Data presented in the feedback report helps each manager to focus on the specific area that he/she needs to improve upon, and Harbridge House Inc.'s training programs are designed to teach the skills needed for improvement in these areas.

In another part of the survey – feedback process, subordinates/associates are asked to rate (on a scale of 1 to 4) each management practice in terms of how *important* it is to them that their manager engage in that practice. Responses are combined and averaged, and each manager's feedback report lists the 10 practices subordinates/associates thought were most important. The manager can use this list to focus further on key areas for improvement.

186 Management Training and Corporate Strategy

It was this "importance data" that was analyzed to determine the 10 universal qualities of effective managers. By combining the data on every manager in a given company, a list of the 10 practices that subordinates thought were most important was obtained for that organization.

The Research sample
Such company reports were generated for over a dozen business organizations and two major government agencies. These organizations represented a diverse cross-section of American enterprise and included:

- A US government agency with over 13,500 employees and offices located throughout the country.
- One of America's leading money-center banks.
- Several small, regional financial services companies.
- One of the largest insurance companies in America.
- A Fortune-100 computer manufacturing firm.
- An international packaged goods company with over 100,000 employees.
- One of the world's largest and most successful plastics manufacturing companies.
- A multinational, vertically integrated energy company.
- A worldwide food service and restaurant organization.
- A major facility for the US armed services.
- One of America's largest and best known high-tech corporations.
- A midWestern heavy manufacturing company with over 15,000 employees.

Research findings
Analysis of the feedback reports generated from this sample of organizations yielded some surprising results. Although companies surveyed measured anywhere from 25 to 50 different management practices, employees consistently rated the same 10 qualities as being the most important. These 10 qualities that are universally required if a manager is to do his/her job well are:

1. The ability to provide clear direction. This finding is consistent with many earlier studies of effective leadership. Four separate aspects of this quality were identified by the research:
   - Establishing clear goals and standards for people.
   - Communicating group goals (not just individual goals).
   - Involving people in setting goals (not just dictating them).
   - Being clear and thorough in delegating responsibility to others.
2. Encouraging open, two-way communication. Three aspects of this quality were identified:
   - Being open and candid in dealing with people (sometimes described as "leveling").
   - Being honest, direct, and to the point.
   - Establishing a climate of openness and trust.

   Employee expectations regarding the openness of communications have increased significantly in recent years. Harbridge House is often asked to work with managers and executives to improve their communication skills because of its importance to employees. People want straight information from their boss.
3. A willingness to coach and support people. The Harbridge House research again confirmed recent studies of excutives' competence. The three different aspects of this quality that were identified illustrate that the kind of coaching that is required is not necessarily "soft" or "lenient", and therefore entails no lowering of performance standards:
   - Being supportive and helpful in dealing with people.
   - Working constructively to correct performance problems.
   - Going to bat for subordinates with "higher-ups".

   This last practice was consistently rated as one of the most important aspects of effective leadership.
4. Providing "objective" recognition. This quality was divided into two parts:
   - Recognizing people for good performance more often than criticizing them for performance problems.
   - Relating rewards to the excellence of job performance (not to such things as seniority or personal relationships).

As these two practices illustrate, objective recognition involves increasing the *quantity* of positive feedback and assuring that the company's reward systems are perceived as being *fair*. Effective managers see that "the cream rises to the top". Harbridge House has found that most managers don't realize how much criticism they give. They do it to be helpful, but it is the positive recognition that really motivates people.

5. Establishing ongoing controls. This quality was described by two separate practices:
   - Following up on important issues and actions.
   - Giving subordinates feedback on how they are doing.

   Employees want a boss who not only communicates clear expectations but also stays *involved* in important aspects of the work.
6. Selecting the right people to staff the organization. This quality is taken for granted in many organizations. Selection decisions are often delegated to staff specialists. The Harbridge House study highlighted the needed for the line managers to improve their "people judgment" and sensitivity skills.
7. Understanding the financial implications of decisions. This quality was viewed as being critical even for functional managers who don't have bottom-line responsibilities. More and more companies are asking Harbridge House to train their functional specialists in the basic economics of the business, thus allowing them to be more active partners in making decisions.
8. Encouraging innovation and new ideas. This quality was rated as being important even in the most conservative or traditional organizations. Most employees believe that they can contribute new ideas. The best managers reinforce this belief and, thus, stimulate a larger repertoire of innovative thoughts and actions.
9. Giving subordinates clear-cut decisions when they are needed. Harbridge House has seen that decisiveness is a virtue at all managerial levels. Employees want to have a say in things. They want to participate, but they don't want endless debate. There is a time to get on with things – and the best managers know when that time comes.
10. Consistently demonstrating high levels of integrity. The Harbridge House research confirmed that most employees want to work for a manager they respect.

References

1. G. C. Lodge (1984): *The American Disease,* A. A. Knopf.
2. Institute of Manpower Studies (1984): *Competence and Competition: Training and Education in the Federal Republic of Germany, the United States and Japan,* National Economic Development Office/Manpower Services Commission, page 26
3. S. Lusterman (1985): *Trends in Corporate Education and Training,* Conference Board, page v
4. J. F. Bolt (1985): Tailor executive development to strategy, *Harvard Business Review,* November/December
5. Harbridge House Inc. (1986): *Trends in Management,* Boston USA (internal paper)
6. Harbridge House Inc. (1986): *Ten Universal Qualities of Effective Managers,* Boston (internal paper)
7. Stogdill, Ralph M. *Handbook of Leadership: A Survey of Theory and Research,* Free Press, 1974
8. Boyatzis, Richard E. *The Competent Manager: A Model for Effective Performance,* Wiley-Interscience, 1982

17

Towards a Solution

In this exploration of management education and training we have examined a wide span of evidence, varying from research studies to practical examples, and have looked at a number of ideas for improvement. We have ranged from a study of the underlying cultural issues affecting our national competitiveness, to ways in which management training must be improved in the nation as a whole. What is proposed represents something of a revolution for most organisations, but a revolution which is manageable and which has already had a successful outcome in many progressive companies in the USA, and in at least a few companies in the UK.

There are many issues which have been discussed in great detail, with practical suggestions for change throughout. The word "change" was chosen in preference to "improvement", because many organisations need to completely rethink their philosophies for management training. Just making a few "improvements" is not enough. Although many might argue that this is the responsibility of the personnel/training functions, I put the matter on the shoulders of top management. Because scant attention has been given to managerial training by the chief executives of most British companies, despite brave words in many annual reports and public speeches, most of those responsible for training have been prevented from doing a good job. Lack of interest from the top has led to lack of support, inadequate budgets and wrong priorities. Other companies have so downgraded the status of training that they have appointed people of the wrong calibre.

Recent Research from Bath University[1] could find no correlation between expenditure on training and corporate success. Indeed, one correspondent to *The Financial Times*, commenting on this, referred to some research he was aware of which showed a negative correlation. It would be easy to hide behind the difficulties in researching such findings. How does one separate the other critical variables from the one being studied? Or how does one decide how much of this year's training spend relates to this year's results, and how much is an investment in the future?

In fact I should have been surprised if there had been a correlation at national level. This is not because management education and training is a useless cost, but because most British companies do it so badly that it is unlikely to do much for their profits.

We have explored more than training. Overall the issue is about making British business competitive in a way that is sustainable into the future. This, at the level of the firm, is about knowing how to think strategically, making good strategic decisions, implementing those decisions effectively, and ensuring that the quality of people in the organisation can sustain those strategies and adapt to new ones as they become necessary. In the words of Chapter 2, we are talking about mechanisms which give top management the ability to escape the imprisonment of their perceptual boundaries.

A new philosophy for management training

I believe that almost all the responsibility for improving the competitive success of British companies belongs to management. The underlying causes may, as Chapter 1 argued, have roots in our cultural heritage, and managers cannot be held accountable for this. Nor can they change the entire value system of a country. What they can do is to bring about changes in behaviour (including ways of thinking about business) and in the attitudes of employees. Over time this would also change the deeply held values of our society. Management neither can, nor should try, to define a new society, but they can be the catalyst that enables new cultural values to emerge.

One of my colleagues, Dr John Nicholls, in work resulting from studies of company turnaround such as that at Jaguar, has argued the employees need three things. Firstly, they must have a sense of pride and achievement in their own work. Secondly they need a sense of belonging to the organisation. Thirdly, they need to feel that management is leading. Something of these three can be seen in the Otis case study in an earlier chapter.

In my opinion a new training philosophy is required in most companies. Initially this may not always involve spending more on training, and most companies should start by spending their current training budget more wisely. To do this will mean upgrading the status of the training function in many organisations, and in some the present incumbents will be found to be inadequate. The three main planks in my suggested new philosophy are:

- a means of ensuring that top management is trained to challenge the perceptual boundaries;
- the close linking of company training initiatives to company objectives and strategies;
- individuals should take responsibility for their own development on a continuous basis.

None of these suggest that the company should opt out of training, and it is particularly important that the company retains responsibility for causing the last item to happen.

1. Top management

Managing directors and senior executive directors are busy people. In most organisations they have reached their present positions by being good at their jobs. There is thus a tendency to assume that they no longer need training. Now this may well be true if we are thinking of knowledge of their basic functional or professional discipline, such as marketing, accountancy, etc. It is only rarely true when we are thinking about the ability to relate the firm to changes in its business environment, to ensure that the perceptual boundaries are reality not fantasy, or to bring about a major cultural change in a company. In these last situations they need to combine the things being taught *today* in the world's best business schools with the *experience* they have (which of course cannot be taught in business schools). There are several ways of doing this. One is to take a short business school course periodically: another is to make more use of consultants: it is possible to use outsiders as personal coaches and counsellors: or in-company courses and workshops, designed and delivered by outsiders can be arranged.

Yet another way is to ensure that top management takes a *real* interest in the management training plan. A close interest will often bring familiarity with new approaches without the pain of being formally instructed in them.

2. Linking training to company needs.

A plea has already been made, particularly in Chapter 7, for starting with the corporate need when determining training initiatives. Six situations were identified in Chapter 7 when this was essential:

- challenging the perceptual boundaries (not only a top management issue);
- implementing a new policy;
- implementation of strategy;
- changing (or reinforcing) the culture of an organisation;
- meeting a major environmental change;
- solving specific problems.

In my opinion almost all company-run formal training should be related to the corporate need first, with individual need being incidental. This implies that the annual training assessment of individuals, or the results of the residential assessment centre, have to be related to an understanding of the company aims, strategy, the business environment, and the desired company culture.

This change of emphasis requires a fundamental revolution in the way most companies plan, organise and implement management training. Few British companies currently think in this new way. Although there are some who do genuinely, there are many more who would claim that they do and will rationalise their current activities to fit the new model without going through the process of analysis, thought and decision that is really needed.

In an ideal situation I would urge companies only to run an internal training course if it fitted the two categories described so far. What is a relevant course will vary between companies, and in the same company over time. It may be the need for a business school-type programme to help make people more responsive in a rapidly changing world, such as that described in the BP case study. It may be basic, almost remedial training in key functional skills, as given by Otis in the focused workshop case. It may be the tools to undertake competititor analysis in a real workshop situation, or even the undertaking of commitment to a strategy and training in methods of implementation as described in the L'Oreal case study. It may be the training of people in skills outside their own function, such as a finance and accounting taught to marketing and production managers.

The next point of philosophy is that such training initiatives, once decided, should be compulsory. If the training is to achieve an organisational end, all personnel for whom it was intended must receive that training. We saw in Chapter 14 that the organisation can block the implementation of things learned on a course. To make a course work in the six crucial areas it is necessary to have a critical mass of people who have been through that training. Chapter 5 showed that trainers by and large are unable to implement such strategies as they do have, in that they cannot force attendance on courses, however essential those courses may be. "Practical man" of Chapter 1 will ensure that the fruits of training are never harvested by his subordinates, unless he too is trained, and through this changes his attitudes and behaviour.

Training initiatives to satisfy this category of need are likely to be very different from much of the training that currently takes place. These differences have already been demonstrated. Common features of much of this different style of training include the design of the initiative to suit the real situation in the company, a considerable element of real work in the initiatives, such as teaching material based on the company situation and real projects, frequent updating and revision of those courses which are expected to have a long life, and a greater number of multi-discipline courses designed to deal with real problems.

The implementation of this element of the ideal strategy requires a training plan that examines the needs, initiatives, costs and benefits in the context of the strategy. The outcome will vary by company. In one graduate training programme or remedial training in management might be fundamental. In another the emphasis might be entirely on courses related to the solving of problems or implementation of strategy.

If we may expect the type of training needed to vary between firms, we should also expect the need to vary within the firm over time. This implies a requirement to review all training on a regular basis. I would suggest an annual examination, supplemented by a full-scale review at least once every 3 years.

3. Individuals taking responsibility for their own training.

The last category of training initiatives puts on to individual managers the responsibility of reaching standards of excellence in their craft. Much of the training that is currently undertaken by companies falls under this category and in my ideal organisation would be handled in a different way. Instead of internal courses, there would be different initiatives that would lay more emphasis on the individual and the workplace.

Accompanying this acceptance of individual responsibility must come an acceptance by each manager that he has a duty to coach and develop those under him.

At first sight this may sound like a way of saving costs by cancelling most training and leaving it all to the individual: in other words, creating a situation where the company does nothing.

This interpretation would be totally wrong. I offer no expense relief, but instead urge a completely different approach to how such individual training is approached. There are several things which the company has to do:

- A climate must be created in the company where the commitment of the individual to self-development, and of the company to making this happen, is seen as the norm. This requires a value system which sees continuous development as essential and a normal part of work, with excellence as the only acceptable level for the way all jobs are performed.
- There must be a support mechanism available which provides counselling to managers on how to encourage self-development among their subordinates. This is a form of consultancy which in most organisations I would expect to be provided by the training function: another reason why this has to be staffed by persons of an appropriate calibre.
- The manager, with the professional help of the training function, must also be able to work with each of his subordinates to design an individual annual training plan for them. This would specify the training needed, the role of the company and individual in providing it, an acceptance of the time and costs needed to be provided by both parties, the means of training, and a progress review procedure.
- The company must take appropriate action to ensure that training becomes possible. Although the approach puts responsibility on the individual, it is the company's task to facilitate such training. At its lowest level this might be a financial contribution to the cost of an Open University course or evening classes. A more imaginative approach might be for the company to provide a library of distance learning courses, and facilities to run them. In this way the individual's contribution is motivation and time, while most costs are met by the company. A part-time MBA, although not suitable for all managers, is an ideal example of the approach I am recommending: the

individual commits much of his or her spare time to the course; the company provides the costs of the course, a certain amount of time, and facilities for any projects which form part of the course. Included in this view of the company's role would be the provision of action learning opportunities in the job environment; to make this work requires professional help from the training function, the active co-operation of the individual, and a training role by the individual's manager.
- Support groups, such as the Company X Management Association should be established. These might, for example, provide a periodic early evening lecture or discussion, an internal management training journal, and regular abstracts of new books and articles. This move would assist learning by the provision of new inputs. It would also be a major force in developing the internal climate needed to ensure that this approach to individual training really works.

Make management training on economic decisions

The concept outlined above shows how managerial training may be organised so that training decisions can be taken on a rational economic basis. Almost all training initiatives under the first two categories suggested above can be linked to some aspect of company performance. These categories provide a weapon through the use of which the business can improve its competitive performance, and in most cases sustain that improvement in the future because of the training given to participants.

The spearheading of training with action to achieve measurable and self-evident economic advantages to the firm provides a means by which the less easily measurable results of individual training, the third category, can be justified. This represents the need for continuous attention to individual improvement with the aim of achieving excellence. Although it is unlikely to be possible to relate the training given to an individual under this third category to company results, the framework provided gives a context which increases both the probability of the individual's training having a relationship with corporate needs, and the opportunity to take rational decisions in this area.

In addition, this framework provides a way of choosing appropriate training initiatives for each category of training. Although we should not be too dogmatic, we can expect that the tailored course described in Chapter 8 will be the most appropriate tool for all training related to the corporate need. Distance learning, described in Chapter 13, is much more likely to be aligned to the meeting of individual needs. The research shows that many senior managers and training functions are unaware of the immense variety of training options open to them: an improvement in the level of knowledge is needed before the right choice can be made for each situation.

If training is to become an economic decision, it follows that most companies must put more effort into evaluation. This, as has been argued elsewhere, becomes easier when the training is directed at some clear corporate result. It is harder in the case of training to meet an individual need. However, the framework suggested above for continuous individual training would create a culture which facilitates the evaluation and review process, and a closeness of training to the work situation that makes the association of individual training with individual results a possibility. Certainly there is no excuse for the complete failure to evaluate, which is the norm in most companies.

The government and education

Most of my conclusions put the responsibility for change squarely on the shoulders of British management. It is tempting to argue that the government should do more, but I find it hard to accept that management training within companies is a government responsibility. The work of the Manpower Services Commission and the National Economic Development Office in raising the management awareness of the management training failure in the UK is entirely commendable. I feel less easy about some of the seed money which has been spent by the MSC on grants for the development of distance learning courses, or training initiatives within firms and certainly would not demand an across the board increase in this activity. The Audit Commission's report [2] is very scathing about the relevance of much of the direct training provided by the MSC, as it is unrelated to any knowledge of the needs of local industry.

There is one area where Manpower Services Commission intervention is justified, and this is the extension of company-related training to the smaller firm. A tailored course costs the same to develop regardless of the number of participants who will eventually take it. This puts the smaller company at a distinct disadvantage compared with the larger ones: the cost per participant is higher for those companies which probably can also afford training. One answer is for grants to be available for the smaller firms. Another is for the MSC to organise collaboration between a number of small firms in similar industries. In this way it would be possible to develop an industry-related element which would be common to several companies with similar problems, reducing the amount of material that has to be uniquely prepared. Such a scheme would require the MSC to act as facilitators, to develop collaborative effort between companies, and underwriters to pick up elements of development cost should the initiative fail.

Where government does need to do more is in the field of education. British industry, although it may not realise it, needs more MBAs. This is an ideal qualification to convert someone with a non-vocational first degree to someone with employable skills. My strongly held belief, argued more fully in Chapter 4, is that the number of MBAs should be increased to around 10,000 per year, but that the number of institutions giving an MBA degree should be reduced to a few centres of excellence. This influx of MBAs would, through the normal forces of supply and demand, cause a reduction in the level of extremely high salaries earned by new MBAs, thus making it possible for more MBAs to find their way into industry.

The business schools need to ensure that their courses are in tune with the needs of business, which requires many of them to become less arrogant in their dealings with industry. Business school salaries should be competitive with those paid in industry, so that there can be a reduction in the part-time consultancy activity of the faculty, and an increase in the exchange and interchange of faculty with people from industry. It may well be that these aims cannot be achieved while the business schools are in public ownership. If this is so, there is a good argument for privatisation.

In higher education generally we need more opportunities for people to take degree courses. Current structures mean that many youngsters who are capable of benefiting from a university or polytechnic course are unable to gain places. Although the birthrate might have fallen, social change which leads more women to want to move on to higher education means that we need more rather than less places. We should be doing more to ensure that both sexes get the best possible education commensurate with their abilities before they move on to the world of work.

Universities and polytechnics do need constant prodding to ensure that their courses remain relevant, and that qualities of teaching are high. While I can approve of the move to make more courses vocationally relevant, I should be sad if we lost the meaning of education in its broadest sense. There should be room for people to study subjects which are culturally rewarding as well as for those which focus on an employable skill. The UK would be a poorer place if we were denied the opportunity of a broad education.

At the secondary school part of the spectrum there is room to provide a greater awareness of work and business. Recently there have been some excellent ideas about teaching integrated skills around a simulated environment, but these have usually been implemented without regard for the training of teachers or the extra teaching time needed for such a course. The main issue that government should take up is that of the children of lower academic ability, who tend to spend a bored last two years until they are legally allowed to leave. This is a complete waste of time, which could be spent preparing such people for work and providing employable skills.

The future

My belief is that Britain can improve its competitive position in the world, and through this reduce the level of unemployment. Success is not providing jobs that have no economic justification, but in creating jobs because the world wants our products and services.

We can only succeed in world competitiveness through the quality of our people. This book has dealt particularly with issues of managers, and I perhaps should add a reminder that the need for training extends to all employees. However, it is managers who have the job of making strategic decisions, of assessing competitors, of innovating new products and of ensuring that products are profitably marketed. It is managers who have the task of ensuring that their perception of the business world in which they operate matches the realities of the competitive situation. It is managers who must lead in a way that enables others to feel pride in the company and in their own jobs.

Chapter 1 drew on the evidence that showed that many of our failings were a matter of our cultural heritage. It also showed that America had experienced symptoms of loss of competitiveness because their culture was out of tune with the realities of the world business situation. However, Chapter 16 showed that business was changing in the USA as managements came to terms with the new situation, and spearheading their endeavours was a complete change in the way in which they were using management training education.

We can draw a lesson from the Americans. Or we can turn to the examples of that small (but thankfully increasing) number of companies that are making sense of their management training.

In our hands, through a sensible use of management training, we have the power to change the world. We can use training to restore our competitive edge, and gradually to change those elements in our national culture which prevent us from achieving greatness.

The view of training taken in this book is entirely pragmatic. The only things which stand between British business and the use of training as a competitive weapon are ignorance and complacency. I hope the book will have removed much of the ignorance about how to move forward. As for the complacency .... well, that is a matter for you, the reader.

The remedy is in the hands of managers. It does not need governments to help apply it. All it requires is energy, determination, a willingness to take a new view of an old topic, and the courage to challenge the existing state of affairs in our own companies.

Let us start doing something about it.

References

1. I. L. Mangham and M. S. Silver (1986): *Management Training: Context and practice*. ESRC/DTI.
2. National Audit Office. *Department of Employment & Manpower Services Commission: Adult Training Strategy*. HMSO.

Appendix:
The Harbridge House Research into Management Training and Education

At the time of writing the Harbridge House research into management training and education consisted of four reports published over the period 1983–1986, an internal unpublished study, and a survey for a client which is confidential, although elements of it have been released in article form.[1]

This research base has been drawn on heavily in the text, and was the source of inspiration for much of the book. The scope of each survey and details of the authors are collected here for ease of reference.

1. Management training in large UK business organisations (1983)

1.1. Scope

This survey describes what is going on in management training in some of the bigger companies. It covers the organisation and management of the training function, the nature of internal and external training in respondent companies, criteria used for training decisions, and the ways in which the effectiveness of training is measured. In addition at the request of the Cabinet Office (Management and Personnel Department) a number of questions were asked about qualifications in management. It was the disturbing findings about the lack of interest by industry in the MBA qualifications which led to the subsequent more detailed study of the subject.

1.2 Sample and method

1.2.1 Interviews

Most of the interviews were conducted over the telephone. A dozen respondents were interviewed on their company's premises, and another three individuals expressed a preference for a written questionnaire. Transcripts of six interviews conducted by the Management and Personnel Office were made available to us, and information from these has been included in the report.

1.2.2. Sample group

We chose as possible respondents the top 150 companies, half a dozen banks, and a dozen public corporations in the UK. From this group we eliminated holding companies and a number of other decentralised groups of companies. An initial round of telephone calls allowed us also to disqualify firms that have no real management training programme and those that refused to comment on company practices.

We emerged with a sample population of 80 companies, including nine public sector concerns and seven banks. Private sector companies included those involved in manufacturing, construction, oil, and retail operations.

The limitations of our survey should be noted at the outset. Although each respondent was affiliated with a large company, he or she was not necessarily familiar with management training practices throughout the entire organisation. In many of our sample firms, training authority was decentralised. Where we encountered what might be termed "local" training, as we did with ICI, we generally contacted a training manager in one of the larger divisions. Where we found that training was done both centrally and locally, as we did with Shell, we contacted trainers at both levels. (We also interviewed a few smaller firms that are part of a large group of companies. Responses from these firms were not taken as indicative of group behaviour.)

1.2.3. Respondents

The positions occupied by our respondents within their respective companies varied, although all were directly involved in some aspect of management training. Their duties ranged from the purchase of external "prepackaged" courses to oversight of the annual assessment process. A number of our interviewees operated the training function from a company training college or centre.

Harbridge House found that it was very difficult to isolate one individual who has control over all development programmes. At least four separate areas of the company may be involved in training activity simultaneously:

1. *Personnel departments* play an important role in recruitment and usually have ultimate responsibility for all training activity.
2. *Company trainers*, often operating from a training centre, may set up in-house courses, teach them, evaluate participants' work, or select external courses.
3. *Training advisors* can act as link persons between those who do the formal training, senior managers, and line management. They identify company needs and suggest programme changes.
4. *Line management* is often called upon to select candidates for in-house or

external training courses, and plays an important role in annual performance assessments.

Because many levels participate in management training, any one respondent's perceptions of the company picture were somewhat incomplete. We found that only those trainers who had held a number of posts within the organisation felt competent to give us complete answers to all of our questions. (We compensated for this fact by increasing the size of the original sample group.)

1.3. Author

Kate Ascher.

2. Masters of business: the MBA and British industry (1984)

1.1. Scope

The survey examined the present relationship between the MBA programmes and the market for MBAs. This required an examination of the behaviour and attitudes of students, business schools and employing organisations. The result is a comprehensive study which has become what is probably the standard reference book on the topic.

2.2. Approach methodology

The approach to this study was somewhat different from that of previous research in this field. We felt that a comprehensive survey of this subject should involve feedback from MBA students, the major UK companies, and the business schools. A large sampling in each of these sectors gave a reasonably complete and objective picture of the current situation.

The sample group included about 125 MBA students from four business schools, 50 major UK corporations, and 20 business schools in Europe and the US. Students received a comprehensive questionnaire; schools and representative companies were contacted over the phone or in person. Details of sample groups and survey methods can be found at the beginning of Chapters 3 and 4.

A large part of the information we received was qualitative in nature. Emotions run high in the field of postgraduate business education; very much of what is said is heartfelt or instinctive and very little is statistically proven. One company's view of a particular business school will be very different from that of the school's administrators which, in turn, will be different from the general view of that school's student population.

We attempted to minimise the effects of personal and organisational biases in a number of ways. First, we increased the size of each of our sample groups (students, schools and companies) beyond that which was originally intended. Secondly, we contacted more than one person in organisations whose original spokesperson appeared obviously biased. Finally, we collected information from selected American and European business schools to serve as points of reference for our British data.

2.3. Author

Kate Ascher (with research assistance from Julia Davis).

3.

3.1. Scope

The survey was to provide an overview, illustrated by specific examples of the role of distance learning in industry training. The slightly broader term "industry" was used, as "management" was too narrow to describe the uses to which distance learning is put.

The result was the first comprehensive report to be published on the subject.

3.2. Sample and methodology

The research began with a survey of the literature.

In the second part are the results of an examination of what is currently available in distance learning, based on interviews with the organisations, visits to the firms and examination of some of the packages. Twenty-eight suppliers were researched.

The third part consisted of telephone interviews with known users of distance learning material, supplemented by a few firms believed to be non-users. The sample amounted to 55 firms. This structure gives a good understanding of the experience of users, but was not designed to estimate the penetration of distance learning.

3.3. The authors

Frances Airey and Mary Nolan Goodman.

4. Tailored management education (1986)

4.1. Scope

The report examines trends in tailored management education, and the extent to which this form of training is used by the bigger companies. It explores how the various suppliers were responding to changes in the market.

4.2. Sample and method

Telephone interviews were conducted with 42 larger companies, and in several cases were supplemented by a personal interview. In addition ten suppliers were interviewed and their services contrasted with those of Harbridge House.

4.3. Author

Fiona Bateson.

5. The tailored education market in the UK (1985)

An unpublished study for internal use which formed the basis of 4 above. Contains competitor details and a comparative assessment of strengths and weakness which could not be published for commercial reasons.

The Authors

Kate Ascher Until recently was a senior consultant with Harbridge House and specialises in market analysis and strategy. She has conducted numerous market research studies for clients in the UK and USA. She has recently been awarded a doctorate by the LSE for her thesis on privatisation. She is currently working in the USA.

Frances Airey Was formerly a research consultant with Harbridge House, specialising in market studies and research for teaching material. Her degree is in Russian.

Mary Nolan Goodman Is a senior consultant with Harbridge House, working on tailored management education and market studies. She is an expert in business communications, and is in the process of completing her doctorate in English.

Fiona Bateson Is a senior consultant with Harbridge House, mainly working on marketing studies. She has an MBA and an economics degree.

Reference

1. K. Ascher (1986): Mastering the Business Graduate: *Personnel Management,* January